NUMBER FOUR

n+1

SPRING 2006

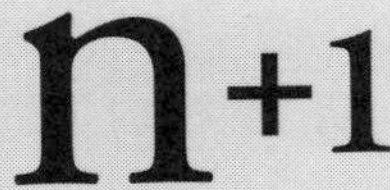

RECONSTRUCTION

THE INTELLECTUAL SITUATION

POLITICS

AMERICAN WRITING TODAY

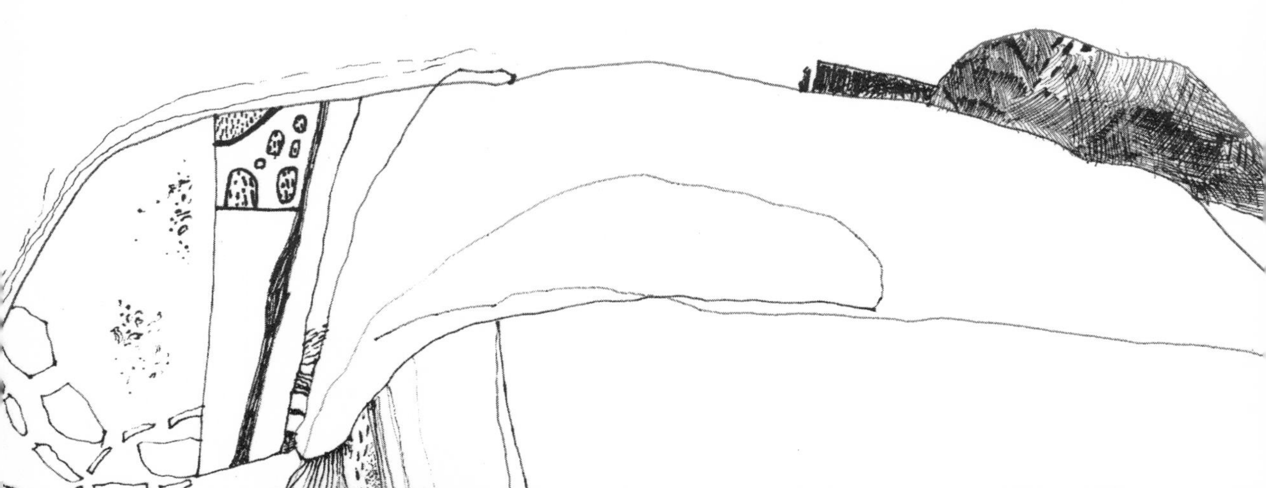

NUMBER FOUR
SPRING 2006

LOST WORLDS

LOST ILLUSIONS

FICTION PORTFOLIO

REVIEWS

LETTERS

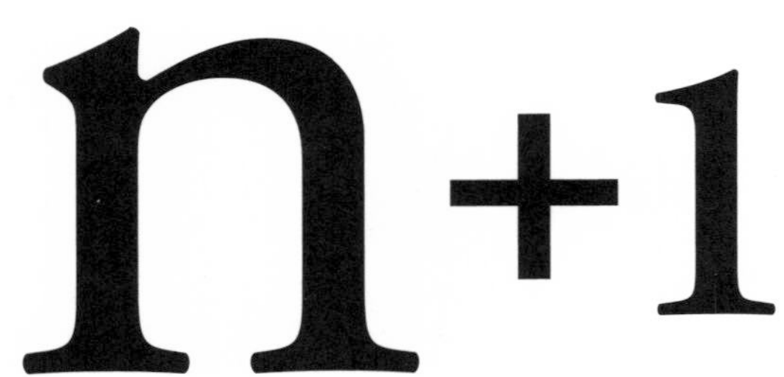

n+1 is published twice a year by n+1 Research, 195 Chrystie Street #200, NY, NY 10002. Single issues are available for $11.95. Subscriptions for $20 (two issues); in Canada, $25; other international, $30 (surface), $40 (airmail). Subscriptions and correspondence to the Editors, Park West Station, P. O. Box 20688, NY, NY 10025. Manuscripts will not be returned. Please correspond before submitting. *n+1* is distributed by Ingram, Deboer, Ubiquity, and DoorMouse in Canada. To place an ad in *n+1* contact editors@nplusonemag.com. *n+1*, Number Four
 ISSN 1549-0033. ISBN 0-9760503-3-1.

Editors
KEITH GESSEN
MARK GREIF
BENJAMIN KUNKEL
MARCO ROTH

Web Editor
CHAD HARBACH

Managing Editor
ALLISON LORENTZEN

Design
DAN O. WILLIAMS

Photo Editor
SABINE ROGERS

Circulation Manager
ISAAC SCARBOROUGH

Editorial Assistant
CARLA BLUMENKRANZ

Copy Editors
SAM FRANK
EMILY VOTRUBA

Correspondent
CHRISTIAN LORENTZEN

Website
SUZANNE SCALA AND PANIX

WWW.NPLUSONEMAG.COM

THE INTELLECTUAL SITUATION

An Interruption

This section usually scrutinizes the products of our culture and the problems of everyday life. It's become apparent, though, that our culture and everyday life may not exist in their current form much longer. Unless things improve, our Intellectual Scene diarist may not come back from Prudhoe Bay, where he's chained himself to an oil rig. But he'd like to return for Number Five.

OVER THE COURSE OF THE PAST CENTURY, mean global temperatures increased by 0.6°C. This change seems slight but isn't: in the winter of 1905 my great-grandfather, a coppersmith, installed the roof on a new reef-point lighthouse two miles from Lake Michigan's shore. Each morning he drove out across the open ice in a horse and buggy laden with his copperworking tools; today the water that far from shore never freezes, much less to a depth that could support a horse's weight.

Well into the 1990s, such changes had happened gradually enough to seem salubrious, at least in the Upper Midwest—a karmic or godly reward, perhaps, for hard work and good behavior. No snow in October! Another fifty-degree day in February! It was as if the weather, too, partook of the national feeling of post-WWII progress: the economy would expand, technology would advance, the fusty mores of a black-and-white era would relax, and the climate, like some index or celebration of all this, would slowly become more mild. This was America. Our children would not only have bigger cars, smaller stereos, a few extra years to find themselves—they'd have better weather, too.

Now we know what we've done. Or we should. The fuel-burning binge (and the beef-eating binge, and the forest-clearing binge) we've been on for the past 150 years, and especially the last 60, and increasingly and accelerantly, has brought into view the most dangerous threat in the brief history of our civilization. It's become possible to glimpse the disappearance of so many things, not just glaciers and species but ideas and institutions too. Things may never be so easy or orderly again. Our way of life that used to seem so durable takes on a sad, valedictory aspect, the way life does for any 19th-century protagonist on his way to a duel that began as a petty misunderstanding. The sunrise looks like fire, the flowers bloom, the morning air dances against his cheeks. It's so incongruous, so unfair! He's healthy, he's young, he's alive—but he's passing from the world. And so are we, healthy and alive—but our world is passing from us.

FOR A LONG TIME, we feared that we would destroy ourselves by a sudden spasm of bomb-dropping. We still fear this, and should: the bombs are everywhere, attached to missiles that are meant for us, for our cities and our skins, though they point toward the empty sky. Despite our fear, we've learned to rest almost easily in the idea that for nuclear catastrophe to happen buttons must be pushed; that though it's easy to push buttons the imaginative connection between the buttons and their consequences will not be lost; that no human being would willingly push those buttons and accept those consequences again. We may well be wrong about this, but it is possible we are right; each day that passes without nuclear disaster implies the hope of decades, centuries, eons of the same.

Global warming—and the other environmental disasters that will exacerbate and be exacerbated by global warming—doesn't permit this hope. It takes forty years or more for the climate to react to the carbon dioxide and methane we emit. This means that the disasters that have already happened during the warmest decade in civilized history (severe droughts in the Sahel region of Africa, Western Australia, and Iberia; deadly flooding in Mumbai; hurricane seasons of unprecedented length, strength, and damage; extinction of many species; runaway glacial melt; deadly heat waves; hundreds of thousands of deaths all told) are not due to our current rates of consumption, but rather the delayed consequences of fuels burned and forests clear-cut decades ago, long before the invention of the Hummer. If we ceased all emissions immediately, global temperatures would continue to rise until around 2050.

This long lag is the feature that makes global warming so dangerous. Yes, this is how we *would* destroy ourselves—not by punching red buttons in an apocalyptic fit, but by appropriating to ourselves just a little too much comfort, a little too much warmth, a little too much time. Like Oedipus, we've been warned. Like Oedipus, we flout the warning, and we'll act surprised, even outraged, when we find out what we've done.

WARMING OF 3°C—five times as much as has occurred since 1900—is a standard projection for the century just begun. Though such a change would cause unimaginable destruction, it doesn't constitute a worst-case scenario by any means; in fact, it's the amount of warming assumed by the US Climate Action Report of 2002, a carefully combed and vetted State Department document that begins with a heartening quote from President Bush ("My Administration is committed to a leadership role on the issue of climate change"). Three degrees Celsius is a conservative composite of the numbers produced by our best supercomputer climate models, and it doesn't presuppose any of the dramatic events—the shutdown of the Gulf Stream, the disintegration of a major ice shelf, the collapse of the Amazon rainforest—that have climate scientists increasingly worried.

These computer models grow continually more sophisticated and detailed—but to truly understand *how it's going to be*, to know what life will be like with a warming of 3°C, we would need a Borgesian computer model that stretched from the height of the thermosphere to the ocean floor; a computer model to account for the possible extinction, migration, or adaptation of every living species; a computer model to assess the reactions of cowed, calamity-shaken governments to widespread flooding, food and freshwater shortages, storm-wrecked shorelines, aggressively rising seas. In a few short decades, nothing will be as it is now, everything will have to be recalculated, and the task of laying out even one of the many possible scenarios is akin to imagining in full a science-fiction planet sort of like our own: no matter how many dozens upon dozens of novels you wrote, there would always be details and consequences that escaped your consideration, and, once recognized, forced you to reconsider the whole.

CERTAIN CONSEQUENCES, however, are obvious and inarguable, because they're already underway. Increased rainfall and evaporation will intensify cycles of drought and flooding worldwide. The Climate Action Report describes an America where, within our lifetimes, "Drought is an important concern virtually everywhere. Floods and water quality are concerns in many regions." Equatorial countries—which depend on the decreasingly reliable summer monsoons for life-sustaining rains, and which tend to be hardest hit by El Niño's storms and droughts—will suffer even more.

Sea levels will continue to rise, partly due to glacial melt, but mainly because water expands as it warms. Higher seas, combined with increasingly powerful overwater storms, will devastate, destroy, or simply consume low-lying areas. The Dutch have begun making plans to abandon large tracts of their hard-won, dike-drained nation to the advancing sea. Tuvalu and other low-lying islands are reluctantly plotting the relocation of their entire citizenries. Some studies estimate that there will be 150 million environmental refugees by midcentury, largely as a result of flooding in poor countries like Bangladesh, where 13 million people live within three feet of sea level. The billions of dollars needed to rebuild New Orleans will be needed again and again and again, mostly by countries that don't have them.

Extirpation of other species has long been a human specialty, but global warming, combined with continued habitat destruction, will accelerate the process by orders of magnitude. Our coral reefs and alpine meadows will be destroyed. Tropical diseases like malaria and dengue fever will spread to ever higher altitudes and latitudes. Food production will be hampered or crippled in many regions, and some people, perhaps many people, will starve.

And so on. Only one feature of our otherwise forgotten 20th-century world seems likely to remain and be reinforced—the supreme importance of wealth. Rich countries will do better than poor countries, rich households will do better than poor households, rich species (Homo sapiens and their pets) will do better than poor species (all the rest). Global warming will deepen the divide between haves and have-nots—Hurricane Katrina offers a one-off example of how this can occur even in the US, but the sharper distinction will be international. As poor countries are hammered by sudden disasters and longer-term droughts, shortages, and epidemics, wealthier countries will paradoxically and perversely provide less aid, as they struggle with their own resource problems and future uncertainties.

In a world of relative stability, governments can make decisions with relative leisure and even magnanimity. They think twice about bombing one another; they sometimes indulge ideals of generosity, equity, humanitarianism. This cannot remain true of a world where the most fundamental stability of all—the sameness of climate on which agrarian civilization was founded—has been casually discarded. Exiled from a more or less predictable world, we will become desperate and confused, and no computer program can model that desperation. Our President has declared a perpetual borderless war as a consequence of a single unforeseen attack; even a much saner administration may become unhinged when nothing, least of all the weather from one year to the next, can be relied on. Skirmishes or worse will flare as resources dwindle. Our isolation will grow as millions of fellow species become extinct. The suppressed nightmare of nuclear war will recur during daylight hours.

These are not worst-case scenarios. The worst-case scenarios are much worse.

OF ALL THE CRIMES committed by our current administration—institutionalized torture, pursuit of war under false pretenses, et cetera—its ecological crimes are the most damaging and regrettable. George W. Bush has dismantled decades' worth of environmental legislation, but his worst offense has been to take the oil companies' despicable campaign of disinformation about global warming and make it national policy. Even in the not-so-likely event that our next administration fully understands the scope of the danger, the costs of these eight years of paralysis will prove incalculable.

In 1988, NASA's top climate scientist, James Hansen, testified before Congress that he was "99 percent sure" that human-induced global warming was underway. His words made the front page of the *Times* and marked the entrance of global warming into mainstream public discussion. The following year, Al Gore called Hansen to testify again; this time, the first Bush Administration forced him to alter his prepared statement. A furious Gore called the incident "science fraud" perpetrated by the "Science Politburo of the Bush Administration."

But Bush Sr., who oversaw the Montreal Protocol that reversed the destruction of the ozone layer, was a staunch ecologist compared to his son. (In between, Clinton and Gore were crucial to the forging of the Kyoto Protocol, and generally much sounder on environmental matters, but also presided over a 14 percent increase in US greenhouse emissions.) The second Bush has shown a Bolshevik flair for asserting ideological control over scientific inquiry. Hansen, who still heads NASA's climate program, was recently warned of "dire consequences" if he persisted in speaking out about the need for immediate reductions in carbon emissions. Scientists at the National Oceanic and Atmospheric Administration have been muzzled too. The White House has altered or excised passages on climate change in several EPA reports; the former head exciser, Philip A. Cooney, took a job at ExxonMobil after resigning.

After his first Congressional appearance, Hansen was criticized by many scientists for drawing premature conclusions. He alone understood the difference between science, which demands constant skepticism in a search for total certainty, and politics, which demands reasonable assessments of probabilities and costs. The rigors of science look like weakness and temporizing when viewed through the lens of politics. This is the same blurred distinction on which the second Bush has based his devious insistence on "sound science"—i.e., perfect foreknowledge of future events as a prerequisite for action.

Meanwhile the Pentagon has begun scenario-planning for abrupt climate change. A DoD-commissioned report from 2003 begins by noting that "there is substantial evidence to indicate that significant global warming will occur during the 21st century" and goes on to envision the consequences of one abrupt-change scenario that has increasingly captured the attention of scientists—the shutdown of the Gulf Stream, which could plunge most of Europe into a deep chill while the rest of the world continues warming. The report isn't terribly imaginative or grammatical, but it is based on sound fundamentals: "With at least eight abrupt climate change events documented in the geological record, it seems that the questions to ask are: *When will this happen? What will the impacts be?* And, *how can we best prepare for it?* Rather than: *Will this really happen?*"

The authors go on to conclude that, while superior wealth and resources would allow the US to adapt moderately well to such a scenario, we would find ourselves in a world "where Europe will be struggling internally, large numbers of refugees are washing up on [US] shores, and Asia is in serious crisis over food and water. Disruption and conflict will be endemic features of life." Such conclusions force us to consider the most cynical of all possible interpretations of our indifference to global warming: on some level, we believe not only that we'll be fine, but that our relative advantage over other countries will actually increase. Instead of yielding aspects of our dominance to bigger nations like China and India, we'll maintain our hold over a troubled world—an idea as unethical as it is dubious.

THE US, WITH 5 PERCENT of the world's population, produces 25 percent of the world's greenhouse gases, and thus is disproportionately responsible for the warming that has occurred so far and will occur in coming decades. The Climate Action Report maintains—and the White House continues to insist—that US "strategies are expected to achieve emission reductions comparable to the average reductions prescribed by the Kyoto agreement, but without the threats to economic growth." Two paragraphs later, it's made clear that our emissions are scheduled to increase by 43 percent between 2000 and 2020—a "comparable" amount, somehow, to the 7 percent reduction prescribed by Kyoto.

It's often said that Kyoto doesn't matter, because the cuts prescribed are so small as to be wholly inadequate—but our refusal to go even this far has brought the international political effort to address global warming to a dead halt. Kyoto expires in 2012, and governments should now be creating far more ambitious post-Kyoto plans, but such plans are unthinkable in the absence of US economic leadership. EU countries can act as responsibly as they like, but China and India, the slowly waking behemoths of US-style fossil-fuel use, will do nothing until the United States demonstrates that a grand-scale transition to renewable energy can be achieved by big industrial countries.

This is the responsibility incumbent on us, and its fulfillment could easily be couched in the familiar, voter-friendly language of American leadership, talent, and heroism. But it has not been. Instead we are welcoming the prospect of running shipping routes over the thawed North Pole, and scheming to drill for fresh oil beneath what used to be tundra. Instead of enacting a Manhattan Project for renewable fuels, we continue building technologically fossilized infrastructure at massive cost. After a profit-minded turn away from coal-fired power in the '80s and '90s, scores of new coal plants are scheduled to be built in this country by 2025. China and India are following suit, adding coal-fired capacity as fast as they can. A slow, self-congratulatory creep toward sustainability—a small investment in solar power, a fleet of "green" SUVs that get thirty miles a gallon—is no match for billions of dollars of deathly infrastructure. Once built, these plants will remain online for decades, pouring gigatons of carbon into the air, unless some humanitarian-minded nation sends its fighter planes to bomb them.

HARD, BUT NOT IMPOSSIBLE, for a free democratic people to circumvent their government. In the past year, there's been a definite uptick in public attentiveness to global warming, spurred by Elizabeth Kolbert's quietly harrowing three-part piece in the *New Yorker* and then by the horrors of Katrina. New books abound and are selling well. A full-length documentary debuted at Sundance. *ABC News* and *60 Minutes* have run prime-time specials. *Rolling Stone* publishes pieces by Al Gore and Bill McKibben. And yet the impression on our consciousness remains a dangerously shallow one. An accumulation of editorials has not amounted to a political movement, much less a transformation in our thinking. There remains an eerie discrepancy between the scope of the problem and our attention to it.

This is true not just of the pollsters' America, that amorphous TV-watching body that extracts convenient messages—Drive that SUV! Build a five-bedroom house when the kids leave home!—from their administration's silence. It's true of the mainstream press and the left as well. The *Times* continues to give column inches to global-warming skeptics, as if such skeptics existed outside the protected biosphere of petroleum-company funding. The *Nation* devotes as much space to the dangers of warming as anyone, but it also publishes "A 'Top Ten' List of Bold Ideas," which aims at "positive, aggressive post-Bush (and post–New Democrat) near- and long-term change." So what do progressives boldly wish for? A thirty-hour workweek and universal daycare—but the words *global warming* are nowhere to be found, and the weakly worded "investing in conservation and renewable energy" rates only an honorable mention. This is as perverse as it is typical. Imagine a historian in the year 2080, reading such lists as she researches the vexing question of how even educated, "progressive" people could have refused to face what was happening.

If such a thing as a literary/political/intellectual left exists, it is defined by its capacity for imaginative and sympathetic reach—by its willingness to surmount barriers of difference (class, distance, nationality) and agitate for a more equitable distribution of the goods and goodnesses that make up our idea of human (and nonhuman) well-being. To be able to imagine what it might be like to be tortured, or to live in abject poverty, or under the watchful eyes of US Predator drones—this capacity is crucial to the project of any political left in a wealthy country. But in the case of global warming, our collective imagination has failed us utterly.

There seems to be a persistent if unstated resistance on the part of the left to the precepts of ecology. Environmental causes haven't captured the attention of our subtlest thinkers and writers, but remain cordoned off to be pursued by nature lovers and nonprofiteers. In fact, global warming represents the third great crisis of technological civilization. The first two have not been resolved—they stay with us, in the form of third-world sweatshops and slums (the brutal conditions and wealth discrepancy that first spurred Marx and Engels) and stockpiled hydrogen bombs (the application of each new technology to the art of killing humans). The third promises to overwhelm them both, even while it exacerbates them.

The most powerful and cogent critique that can currently be leveled against our mode of capitalism is that markets fail to account for ecological costs. In a crowded world of finite size, our political economy values only acceleration and expansion. Scarce natural resources like clean air and water, not to mention more complex systems like rainforests or coral reefs, are either held at nothing or seriously undervalued. Corporations could clear-cut all our forests, reduce croplands to swirling dust, turn rivers to conveyors of toxic sludge, deplete supplies of minerals and metals, double and redouble carbon emissions—and all our economic indicators would show nothing but robust growth until the very moment the pyramid scheme collapsed. Indeed, most of these things are happening, with only scattered opposition. When our math improves, when the costs of our products fully reflect the resources used and the wastes produced—especially CO_2: then and only then can capitalism begin to become a viable and humane economic system.

MEANWHILE IT FEELS STRANGE to be alive and well, strange to keep riding the wave of our wild prosperity, strange to feel the warmth of the February sun on our necks. Do we know what's happening or don't we? It seems like we know, it seems like everyone knows—the news is out, the science corroborates our senses, until it seems impossible *not* to know—but we refuse to believe it. We've been taught to imagine ever longer and happier and healthier lives for ourselves—we can't help half-consciously numbering the walks we'll take, the books we'll read and write, the grandchildren we'll hoist in the year 2060. And maybe these dreams will come true. Maybe, as the Pentagon report suggests, the same privileged caste of people who engineered the coming disasters will live in fifty years much as they do now, buffered from harm by money and medicine and force of arms. The weather will be an erratic and dangerous spectacle, economies and ecosystems will collapse, millions will die elsewhere in the world, but we'll seal our borders, abandon our ideas of nature, buy Canada ("the Saudi Arabia of freshwater"), and adapt.

Fifty years after that? We won't be around. Those who will be can fend for themselves, and call us what they like.

—Chad Harbach

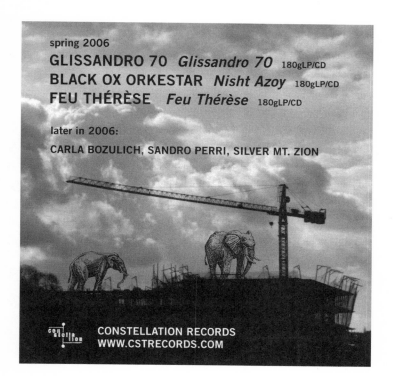

POLITICS

Memoranda

NOTE FROM LA PAZ

I ARRIVED IN LA PAZ, BOLIVIA, TOO LATE TO get a press pass, so I watched Evo Morales's inauguration on television with my aunt and some friends. There were nearly a dozen of us—my aunt is a political exile from Peru, and many of her old friends had made a special trip. We reserved a long table on the second floor of a Peruvian restaurant called Machu Picchu. It was a celebration, with drinking, laughter, applause. There was a brightly colored swing-set in the room, and periodically the cook's daughter would climb on. The noise was just awful, but no one seemed to notice.

Among the guests in from Peru to witness the event was a white-maned wolf of a man named Hugo Blanco. It took me most of the speech to realize it was him—mostly because it had never occurred to me that a man like that could still be alive. Blanco is a celebrity in certain circles, a myth even, a man who began making his considerable reputation leading land takeovers in Cuzco in the early 1960s. He was eventually captured, jailed for six years, sentenced to death, then pardoned and deported in 1970. He returned in 1978 to participate in the elections for the Peruvian Constituent Assembly, and, despite the fact that he was again deported, this time in mid-campaign, Blanco was elected with the most votes of any candidate nationwide. He made a run for the presidency in 1980, failed, and then, naturally, the Peruvian left splintered and weakened, the coup de grâce coming in three parts over the next twelve years: the homicidal war of Shining Path, the disastrous populist experiment of President Alan García, and the mafia bribery-state of President Alberto Fujimori. My aunt and others like her—union leaders and activists, many now labeled terrorists—were forced into exile. Others were jailed. Hugo Blanco briefly returned to the political scene in 1989, when he was arrested and accused of terrorism, but the charges were eventually dropped, and he was released. After five years in Mexico, he has lived for the last ten in the kind of monastic austerity one would expect from a man with his résumé: a simple room in Cuzco, with a cement floor and a cot to sleep on.

He sat across the table from me, eating *papa a la huancaína* and hardly pausing to breathe, with a cone-shaped wool hat pulled low over his eyes. He didn't take off his blue windbreaker, which was adorned with a Peasant Confederation of Peru logo on the left breast—and a Nike swoosh on the right. Every now and then he looked up to ask what Evo was saying, since at his seventy-two years of age, Hugo Blanco is nearly deaf. And still Blanco was joyous. Evo made his speech before the Congress—one of the best political speeches I've ever heard: combative, funny, hopeful, charming—and Hugo Blanco laughed when we laughed, clapped when we clapped, as if the words, no matter how well delivered, were beside the point. He never took off his hat; periodically he would scratch his white beard, look up at the television, and offer me a grin. He said almost nothing. When it was over, we shook hands, and he left.

Later, one of my aunt's friends told me that Blanco always wears a hat because he feels it protects his brain. It turns out that four years ago he suffered an aneurysm and almost died. Fate had done him a tremendous favor in granting him these four extra years. What if he had passed away then? This old socialist, this lion of the left, wouldn't have seen Lula in Brazil or the election of Bachelet in Chile. He wouldn't have seen Tabaré in Uruguay or Argentina under Kirchner or Chávez in Venezuela, and most importantly, he wouldn't have seen Evo.

LA PAZ IS A BEAUTIFUL CITY, a knot of high-rises dropped in a sharp valley, a colonial center in miniature on steep narrow streets. In January, a day that dawns rainy and cold can become sunny and bright almost without warning, and so one never knows what to expect. The night of Evo's inauguration, in the Plaza San Francisco, the physical space yielded completely to the needs of the people, and tens of thousands of Bolivians made of the city a festival. It was impossible not to feel hopeful, and I'll admit that hope—at least as regards politics—is an altogether foreign sensation for me. On another day, the scene would have struck me as irredeemably optimistic, but that day I kind of enjoyed it. The rain threatened, but did not come, and one suspected that if it had, it hardly would have mattered. Bolivians and their guests from all over the world danced in the streets, offered toasts to the new president, and nothing could have quelled that optimism.

Of course, there is hope, and there is reality. The following day I went to the Hotel Sucre in downtown La Paz for a conference of the so-called new Latin American left. The first speaker, Zacarías Flores, a representative of Evo's own MAS party, was far and away the most lucid exponent of a nonideological, nondogmatic, and practical approach to dealing with the pressing issues of poverty and the marginalization of the indigenous majority in the nation-state. He offered real ideas, and perhaps most comforting was that he seemed to have a real respect for the immense challenge of governing. It began so well, I began to think that perhaps all of the previous day's optimism had not been unfounded. But then it unraveled: speaker after speaker rose to the dais, spouting jargon that we all know by heart. It was a toss-up between the triumphalist and the conspiratorial schools of sloganeering. Every time one of these men (they are almost always men) won an election in his country: THE PEOPLE CANNOT BE FOOLED! Every time one lost (and they lose quite often): THE IMPERIALISTS HAVE MANIPULATED THE PEOPLE'S WILL!

It was an altogether dispiriting day: there was Schafik Handal, a representative from the FMLN, presenting a preposterous apology for Stalinism and mourning the fall of the Berlin Wall. (Tragically, though perhaps not surprisingly, Handal returned to El Salvador and promptly died of a heart attack.) There was Mohammed Lashpar, representing Qaddafi's Libya, urging us all to read the Great Leader's Green Book, and saying that electoral democracy wasn't really that important, what mattered most was unity (behind a demagogue, Mr. Lashpar? behind a dictator?)—dismissing, in other words, the most significant lesson of Evo Morales's long political struggle. More surprising and therefore more disappointing was the legendary Bolivian mining leader Domitila Chúngara revealing a frightening authoritarian streak, calling for nationalizing the media and chastising those who didn't vote a straight MAS party line. But most nauseating was Tomás Borge of Nicaragua, whose self-aggrandizing speech was demagoguery of a fine vintage, enough to make me grind my teeth. He name-dropped for fifteen minutes—I was talking to Fidel, Torrijos and I were saying, et cetera—stopping only to lead the crowd in a few vivas: *Que viva Bolivia! Que viva Fidel!* He is married to a Peruvian, and many Peruvians, including some of my aunt's friends, fought in the war against the Contras. Everyone I spoke to said the same about Borge: There is no man more corrupt in all of Latin America. It was something I could sense intuitively—his was perhaps the exact opposite of Evo's speech the previous day.

HUGO CHÁVEZ AND HIS PEOPLE were expected but did not make an appearance. They were across town, where the *Comandante* was receiving an honorary degree from the local university. I came across the crowds walking home: the main avenue leading to El Prado was closed, and hundreds of people were listening to Chávez's speech on loudspeakers, waving tiny Venezuelan flags. I listened for a moment, long enough to hear him declare that machismo is a by-product of capitalism, just after he insulted Lourdes Flores, Peru's first serious woman contender for the presidency. He rambled: My mother wanted me to be a priest, he said, be patient with Evo, and his rhetorical meandering made me dizzy. Later I read that he spoke for three hours.

It's easier to like Hugo Chávez from afar. Up close, the spectacle of his ego is grotesque. When people propose Venezuela as a political-economic model for Latin America, I'm reminded of high school physics classes, where each problem assumes an infinite plane and zero friction. Every country has resources, but not every country sits on the world's fourth-largest reserves of oil. This is the kind of wealth that allows a leader to behave in pretty much any way he wants. Whatever social and wealth redistribution programs Chávez may be pursuing in his country, many of which are certainly producing admirable results, he is self-evidently a man in love with the spotlight, an egocentric *milico*, and Latin American history is full of these types. If you can take your social programs with a strong dose of authoritarianism and cult of personality, then Chávez is your man. He spent the first week of the new year provoking a diplomatic spat with Peru by taking sides in Peru's upcoming elections. Then he showed up in La Paz, perhaps Latin America's safest capital, with two planes, one just for his security detail. There was something unseemly about Chávez throwing his weight around, his caravan (two SUVs, a bus full of soldiers, a limousine, and an ambulance) speeding through the crowded streets with horns bleating. His security guards kept busy harassing reporters, checking credentials, patting down local journalists, and acting as if they owned the place.

Immediately after the inauguration, Evo and his vice president, Alvaro García Linera, stood on the balcony of the Palacio Quemado to preside over a military display, soldiers marching and whatnot. They were soon joined by Chávez, who placed himself slightly behind but between the president and vice president of Bolivia before eventually throwing his arms around both, as if he were a proud father presenting his children at a society cotillion. *Oh look, they're all grown up.* Every now and then he took Evo by the hand, and they raised their arms together. It was awkward. The Peruvians I was with all groaned. García Linera was visibly uncomfortable, and finally left, so the aforementioned Tomás Borge took his place next to Chávez, the two of them chatting like they were at the racetrack, as if this were not the inauguration of a popularly elected president in a foreign country, neither paying Evo any mind.

THE FESTIVAL OF ALASITAS fell on the Tuesday after the inauguration. Change had already begun: the Ministry of Sustainable Development was renamed the Ministry of Coca. The new cabinet was sworn in, including miners and domestic workers and the kinds of people Bolivians have never before seen in government. On the streets, the festival was under way. Ordinary people engaged in the serious task of buying scaled-down versions of their dreams: tiny houses to hold in the palm of your hand, cars, miniature cell phones, little plastic baskets of food, stacks of fake dollar bills and euros, computers, building materials, passports. You could buy almost anything in miniature: it was reported that Evo Morales bought a marriage certificate—he is single—committing him to the nation of Bolivia. Vendors lined the avenues and filled the plazas, and everyone rushed to get their items blessed. For a day, it's a frenzy, the local obsession. The entire city smelled of incense. Even office workers were released from work for a half-hour at noon to buy their *alasitas*. There's a similar holiday in Puno, Peru, but I'd only read about it, never seen it myself.

Apart from being good fun, Alasitas is also an X-ray of the needs of Bolivia, and therefore an indicator of the sorts of challenges Evo Morales now faces. He has earned the presidency through two decades of organizing and dogged persistence; he has been jailed, threatened, bullied, elected to the congress and then expelled, been called a terrorist and a narco-trafficker, declared an enemy of the United States and Bolivia—and still he won. Evo was able to carry his core constituency—*cocaleros*, Aymara Indians and peasants, the militant neighborhood associations of El Alto—along with an important segment of the middle class, without whose support he never would have passed the 50 percent threshold necessary to win. And suddenly Evo Morales is not the opposition anymore. It's unlikely we will ever again hear him say *Wañachun Yanquis*, death to the Yankees in Quechua. Governing requires different language and different skills. Who would have thought that Evo Morales could become the consensus builder in Bolivia, a country that has had five presidents since 2000?

But because he is, Evo Morales cannot be ignored. What to do with the natural gas? How to deal with the tense issue of coca? What about land reform? On a very basic level, one wonders whether the symbolic gestures of former miners and domestic servants with little formal education being installed as ministers will translate into good governance. Evo's opponents will look for corruption, and when they find it, or even a hint of it, they will pounce. But Bolivia has strong neighborhood and community organizations, perhaps the most vital in all of Latin America, and with the right leadership, these can be a positive force in the complex work of reducing poverty. By celebrating the indigenous core of Bolivian identity, the ceremony itself set a tone which cannot be easily dismissed.

Evo Morales spent his transition traveling, paying his respects in Venezuela and Cuba before hitting Europe and South Africa and the Far East, and in so doing, managed to raise his domestic approval rating another 10 percent. The inauguration made Bolivia briefly feel like the center of the world, and it seemed like everyone understood the singular opportunity that Evo Morales represented. The very next day the new president went to work at four in the morning and cut his own salary in half. This was a good start: there is always a future for a politician who understands the power of symbolism.

—*Daniel Alarcón*

FIRST, DO NO HARM

I SAT RECENTLY IN THE CONFERENCE ROOM attached to my hospital's intensive care unit, thinking about ethics and the end of life. Our ICU was remodeled last year, and the conference room has a clean, corporate feel; the wood intentionally unfinished, the chairs black nylon with hinges optimized for back support. My fellow medical residents—many of whom, having worked the night shift, were intermittently falling asleep—flanked me at the table. We wore blue scrubs.

With our help, the physician in charge compiled a list of the ethical precepts that guide end-of-life decision-making (in the US, in 2006) on the white erase board. There were four:

1. Autonomy
2. Non-malfeasance
3. Beneficence
4. Social justice

The order of the terms implied hierarchy. Autonomy, in fact, was written larger. Extra white space separated it from the other precepts. Ironically—since end-of-life decisions are often made by distraught relatives via a slippery concept called substituted judgment, whereby they divine what their loved one "would have wanted" were he or she of sound mind—self-determination rules the ICU.

Non-malfeasance, a fancy term for the promise we made in the Hippocratic oath to do no harm, came in a distant second. As with autonomy, which instructs us to defer to a patient's wishes even when the patient couldn't possibly have any, non-malfeasance, from the perspective of the physician as moral actor, is passive, avoidant—a cynic might have sniffed fear of litigation. It wasn't until number three that we actually got to try to do some good.

I was paying close attention, and not only because I'd been able to sleep in my own bed the night before. This was a welcome departure from our usual stay-on-point talks about drugs, intravenous lines, and breathing machines. ICU doctors often find themselves delivering fantastically expensive and brutally invasive care to patients with little chance of survival. Such practices are based on complex assumptions about our society and what it values—but for doctors, the time to step back and think about those assumptions is a rare luxury.

"Is social justice ever invoked in ICU decisions?" I asked. "And if it is, could you give an example?"

"Um, not really," replied my superior indifferently. He equivocated a bit, and the discussion was over.

While we learned, twenty patients under our care lay in solitary, glass-doored rooms, hooked up to breathing tubes, feeding tubes, hydrating tubes, urinating and defecating tubes, and virtually every antibiotic on God's green earth. Yet many of them, inexorably, would succumb within days or weeks.

THE PROBLEM WITH AUTONOMY and end-of-life decisions is largely a problem of information—its transmission and, more fundamentally, its adequacy.

There is information asymmetry: doctors train for years to prepare to make decisions in the ICU, and the knowledge they acquire is scientifically complicated and shrouded in jargon. It takes a talented communicator to keep anxious, suffering patients up to speed, especially while alarms blare unremitting warnings of high or low vital signs. With notable exceptions, though, physicians are not known for their interpersonal skills. And while the emphasis placed on autonomy seems to demand that doctors play the role of disinterested newsbearers, in practice they more often attempt, consciously or otherwise, to nudge patients toward the decisions that they believe are correct—this is termed "framing bias" in decision-science literature.

More troublingly, many patients are incapacitated and unable to make decisions at all. One of the hardest things to get used to as a new ICU doctor is examining people who, at best, are sedated beyond a hint of purposeful movement. (At worst, patients are moaning in pain, unable to communicate but for barely distinguishable lip or eye movements that, no matter what the patient intends, always seem to mean *help me.*)

In an effort to obviate the problem of incapacity, we obtain "advanced directives," whereby we ask patients well before an emergency what they want done should one arise. These directives are a major component of federal end-of-life policy—the Patient Self-Determination Act of 1990 requires hospitals and other medical institutions to inform patients about their state's options for advanced directives and living wills. Unfortunately, as argued in a 2004 Hastings Center Report, the 100 million–plus dollars spent to comply with the PSDA have had little effect. Many patients balk at filling out a menu of hypothetical options for artificial resuscitation: If your heart were to stop, would you want chest compressions? With shocks or without? Even when patients do file directives, relatives and physicians find it very difficult to interpret them, and there is rarely meaningful influence on the care received. Every medical resident can tell stories of patients who were DNR/DNI—do not resuscitate or intubate—but wound up receiving full, aggressive care.

When a patient is incapable of deciding—because she is unconscious, because she has a breathing tube in, because she's oblivious to person, place, and time—then a family member (provided one can be found) is called to stand in. But relatives are often no better than doctors at knowing what the patient would have wanted. And their decisions are tied inextricably to their own interests, whether an understandable wish to avoid the burden of "giving up on" their loved one, or messier concerns related to finances or family dynamics.

So the concept of autonomous, informed, rational decisions at the end of life is porous at best. Beyond this relative information gap, furthermore, lies a vast and growing information deficit. Our technologic capabilities—glorious as they are—have far outstripped our understanding of how and when they will work. Well-conducted studies of medical interventions test a medically homogeneous population by manipulating one aspect of their care. ICU patients are so sick, in such diverse and unique combinations of ways, that there is shockingly little sound information on whether or how much the interventions we can offer will help. And so a day seldom passes on rounds without us standing around scratching our heads about what to do next. Dialysis? Could work. Twelve-thousand-dollar-a-day drug that is "effective," at least temporarily, in 10 percent of cases? Let's give it a shot.

Put yourself in the position of an ICU doctor. You cannot tell a patient and his family with 100 percent certainty that all hope is gone—yet you're damn sure that even the best-case scenario does not involve a comfortable, independent existence. You have an irrational fear of litigation and a more rational fear of withholding care in one of the rare cases when last-ditch efforts grant a patient extra months or years of quality life. You have little incentive to limit the interventions that you offer (scarce resources? whatever). In many settings, you are actually paid more money for performing more procedures. So what do you do?

In the name of preserving autonomy and choice, our system leads to little choice at all. Technology takes over. We simply do everything.

THERE IS A REAL TOLL TAKEN—on health-care workers, families, and patients alike—by persisting with highly aggressive medical care when meaningful recovery is impossible. The procedures that make up the daily ICU routine are exceedingly invasive and uncomfortable. Tubes are inserted through noses into stomachs and down throats into airways. Big needles are stuck into necks, chests, or thighs so that large IVs can be placed. The slang term we use for performing these procedures on people unlikely to benefit from them, "flogging," is actually rather precise. Patients require continuous, heavy sedation to tolerate their ICU stays. They often become delirious and hysterical as a consequence.

Nurses describe taking hour-long showers to cleanse themselves of the metaphysical dirt that accumulates from providing invasive care in hopeless situations. But their hands will not come clean. I know the feeling.

My own most damning experience involved caring for a man in his sixties who was mentally disabled from a congenital disorder. The usual life expectancy for someone with this disorder is roughly forty years. This fellow, having experienced unusual longevity, had become both blind and deaf. Unfortunately, he grew critically ill after an arthritis-related surgery—his heart, like his eyes and ears, had ceased to function optimally, and he just didn't tolerate the procedure. With no family around to allow him to pass naturally, as his body so clearly indicated he was ready to do, we aggressively resuscitated him. This meant, among other things, that he needed a feeding tube.

A feeding tube, even for a person who knows why he needs it, is one of the more unpleasant procedures people undergo in the name of a healthful recovery. I have grown accustomed to a particular look of betrayal in my patients' eyes while I am placing a tube, having warned them beforehand that it might be "a little uncomfortable." In this case, though, there was no way to communicate why the tube would help. It wasn't even possible to give him fair warning before we began.

And so with the help of a colleague, I shoved the tube through his nose, down the back of his throat, and into his stomach while he thrashed wildly. It was terrible the first time we did it. Then, and amazingly, considering that his arms were tied to the bed and an attendant was constantly in the room, he managed to get the tube back out, requiring its replacement. This happened on three consecutive days. It felt as though I was torturing him. The dreams I had reflected this. So did the news, with reports of feeding tubes used as torture tools coming from Guantánamo Bay.

Despite all our efforts, and the pain we inflicted, the patient died a few weeks later. I felt angry and at fault. What could have been done differently? We might have worked harder to find a family member who might have allowed us to adjust the goals of his care—but when, amid the constant chaos of the ICU? And what if, long-distance from New Hampshire or California or wherever—far from the feeding tubes and needles—the indifferent relative we spent hours tracking down told us to forge ahead anyway?

And when no family exists? Who decides then? There's no sound protocol to cover these cases in real time. Without patients' wishes or certain prognoses to serve as guides, doctors are frequently trapped in a messy middle ground, where the path of least resistance for us is the path of most resistance for the patient. Keeping people alive at all costs becomes the protocol.

WHILE OUR FAILURE TO MAKE difficult choices on an individual level has painful consequences, on a collective level it amounts to a crisis.

The many failings of our health system have become cliché. We spend much more on health care than any other country—15 percent of our GDP in 2003, compared with an average of just under 9 percent for all developed countries. Yet our population is neither particularly healthy nor happy with its health care by comparison. Our major employers increasingly cut into the health-care coverage offered to employees because of cost, and the number of us who lack basic health insurance grows each year.

The reason that we are not as healthy as people in other countries, despite our excessive spending, is that overall population health is largely determined by factors other than health care. Modern medical interventions do prolong lives, but at such a high marginal cost that this expenditure does not affect average life expectancy nearly as much as the physical environment in which we live and work (clear air, clean water, safe streets, low stress); personal behaviors (Whoppers, Marlboros, trips to the gym); and genes.

So what do our extra dollars buy us? The short answer is: more. More tests, more procedures, more administrative costs, more technology. A few more machine-dependent days, months, or sometimes years at the end of life.

Prominent US health economists have argued that we have more because we want more. Who's to say how much a country should be spending on its health care, anyway? Americans demand higher technology and more aggressive care, and are willing to bear the extra costs.

But economic theory itself predicts the endgame played out in our ICUs. While insurance in this country for cheap, effective preventative services is patchy at best, the coverage for high-cost, acute medical care is pretty close to a blanket. Hospitals are ethically and legally obliged to provide for patients who are acutely ill, regardless of insurance—care for the uninsured is paid out of a pool of funds from the insured, reimbursed at a higher rate and often bolstered by state funds. By the time a person is sick enough to wind up in the ICU, someone else is always footing the bill.

Our dependence on a poorly defined notion of autonomy leads us to treat patients as consumers; but in health care there is no functioning market to regulate their choices. Modern medical innovations have created an environment in which even seconds of life can have a considerable financial cost, but the cost at the end of life is always borne by others, and so frightened patients and rattled families have little incentive not to forge ahead, trying treatment after hopeless treatment. At present, these costly, compromised seconds are considered the right of every American. Meanwhile the modestly priced interventions that could add productive, pain-free years to millions of lives—for instance, better management of a chronic, epidemic disease like diabetes—are not.

The best study on the kinds of deaths people want, conducted by researchers from Duke and the University of Chicago, suggests that aggressive ICU care does not play a major role. In a large survey of patients living with chronic illnesses, families of the recently deceased, doctors, and other health-care workers, more than 90 percent of respondents agreed on the importance of such attributes as being kept clean, maintaining their dignity, trusting their physician, and being free of pain. Eighty-eight percent valued being able to help others, and 81 percent not being a burden to society. But only 48 percent of patients felt it was important to "use all available treatments, no matter what the chance of recovery." Physicians and health-care workers were much more emphatic; only 7 percent and 5 percent, respectively, wanted all available treatments for themselves—testimony, perhaps, to the information asymmetry that exists between doctors and patients.

And so many patients end up dying deaths they do not want, deaths their caretakers certainly would not want for themselves. When families are involved, they agonize over decisions that often merely drag out the dying process by excruciating days or weeks. The information failures that plague health-care transactions throughout life only increase in magnitude and intensity as we approach the end.

A WEEK OUT FROM MY ROTATION in the ICU, I received an e-mail urging me to complete a dictation on another patient who had died during my tenure. He was a man with a painful terminal cancer whose death had been forestalled by "palliative" chemotherapy and aggressive ICU care.

The palliation was anything but successful, however; no amount of narcotics could dull his constant pain, while his life was artificially prolonged by a breathing tube, a feeding tube, kidney dialysis, three powerful antibiotics (vancomycin, meropenem, flagyl) and an antifungal (voriconazole), all delivered through a large IV that had been placed, at the risk of puncturing a lung, just under his collarbone. Each day, the extensive battery of blood tests, radiology tests, and scopes inserted into his airways and stomach documented his steady decline. The dictation needed to be done immediately, I was informed, so that the hospital could be paid the more than $250,000 it was owed.

I suppose it is only fitting that we should die as we live—surrounded by technology, consuming vast amounts of resources, too often alone—but that makes it no less distressing. There is such a thing as too much. But how will we say: "Enough"?

—Andrew Ellner

THE TROUBLE WITH BEING GERMAN

IN GEORGE MIKES'S SERIES OF BOOKS, carrying titles like *How to Be a Brit* or *How to Be an Alien*, a book on *How to Be a German* is missing. I admit there might be practical reasons for this negligence. But there may also be metaphysical reasons: it is not possible to *be* a German.* If it were, hardly anyone would like to be one. The Germans

* In fact, when among his 44 books Mikes wrote one on Germany, *Über Alles: Germany Explored* (1969), he dropped the "How to Be" format that had worked so well for him elsewhere.

themselves would like it even less. Just imagine a German meeting one of his compatriots on a foreign beach: he would be glad to continue speaking English and be taken for a foreigner. If recognized by his countryman, what he would probably feel is shame. Most Germans are glad to be in any place where there are no other Germans. That is what accounts for their fame as the world's traveling champions. In his lectures on the World War II bombings, W. G. Sebald saw a continuity between the traumatic flight of our mothers and grandmothers from the burning cities Dresden and Hamburg, carrying their dead babies in suitcases, and today's tourism. I would add to this the contribution of a community in which neither the perpetration of atrocities nor victimization has ever been discussed and experienced outside of severe political constraints. If it is impossible to *be* German, this may be because the link between individual experience and political collectivity has been severed. There is no experience of being German, even if German-language college textbooks say there is.

Nowhere does this radical ontological break that occurred in Germany become more visible than in our emotional culture. The image that typifies it is a photograph that appeared in one of Berlin's major newspapers after Angela Merkel won the recent national elections. It shows her and five of her supporters carrying signs saying "Angie." All six have bitter and tired faces, and only her nickname on the signs—borrowed by strategists of the conservative party from a Rolling Stones song—signals enthusiasm for a conservative party that has never been more devoid of substance. A lack of vision is understood as authenticity. There is no display of emotion, be it political or private, but the borrowed glitter of an old and all-too-popular tune. Familiarity and fatigue validate the lack of ideas in the face of major problems: slow economic growth despite a booming export economy, high unemployment rates, an aging population whose pension plans and social security benefits may be forcing the state into debt, and immigrants whom Germany needs but can't integrate into its social fabric.

Of course, a second place where the same deep rupture in the country's traditions shows is its academic culture. Whereas up to the 1920s students from all over the world came to Germany, searching for knowledge and education in one of the world's most distinguished university systems, today the German academy, especially in the humanities, has developed into a feudal bureaucracy mostly devoid of courageous thought and pedagogical vision. The break in confidence is manifest in what was once the highest discipline: philosophy. After WWII, the school of Joachim Ritter came to dominate the scene, and, with its historic and philological orientation, a decay was confirmed that had begun with the brain drain of Germany's most brilliant scholars during the war, from Erich Auerbach to Hannah Arendt. Thinking equaled specializing in the history of thought. Ritter's achievement was to edit one of the best encyclopedias of the history of philosophical notions.

The return to Germany of Adorno's Frankfurt School only contributed to the inertia, as it did not provide new theses but faded into the gray of an inflexible social theory kept upright by its moral prestige. And even recent developments like Niklas Luhmann's sociological constructivism and Friedrich Kittler's and Bernhard Siegert's media analysis show clear traces of bureaucratic language and an unequaled fetishism of technology. Is it really technology that makes the world run? Is it courage to leave thinking up to the machines and system because we are afraid of making things happen as men and women?

Lyotard may have been right with his thesis that after the Jewish genocide during WWII, the dialectic of history that forms the basis of experience has been frozen. The period had no positive result—nothing one could point to for redemption—and results are what progress relies on. The consequence in Germany has been the eradication of rich personal experience. Against this backdrop of the ultimate evil, nothing else has real weight. Imagine you come from a country known to many people only through the Holocaust Museum: this country is "Germany." Is it possible to be German?

THE FIRST TIME I WAS almost reconciled with being German was at an American university, where I learned to appreciate thinkers of my own tradition. Whereas until recently hardly any but a far-right-wing German intellectual would admit Martin Heidegger to be one of the most original and influential thinkers of the last century, I became aware that generations of Americans (and Argentines!) had never stopped reading Georg Simmel, Max Weber, Heidegger, and even Carl Schmitt—not just Walter Benjamin and Theodor Adorno. Intellectually, the real heirs to the German tradition live in Buenos Aires today, where the Argentines debate the question of whether socialism is national or international, informed by the controversy at the beginning of the last century between the Austrians Karl Kautsky and Otto Bauer.

The second time that I was glad to be German was at the start of the Iraq war, when I discovered antiwar demonstrators in New York wearing T-shirts saying "Thank you Schröder" to acknowledge an act of genuine political courage. This courage characterized the generation of politicians that had governed the country since 1998. They were a generation that had confronted its parents with their involvement in the Nazi period; the foreign minister, Joschka Fischer, especially carried this confrontational attitude into office, much to the dismay of the diplomatic corps. Although the final perception of their era was one of stagnation, the Schröder government introduced more reforms than any of its recent predecessors. And it was mostly the resistance of the conservative federal states, blocking important decisions in the second chamber, the Bundesrat, that led to claims of failure. Schröder's was in fact a generation that came to power after Helmut Kohl's conservative revolution had immobilized German society for almost two decades. Kohl had been a quite unpopular politician, doomed until the wall came down in 1989 and rescued him from oblivion. In his fourth cabinet, Angela Merkel managed to be a family minister who left no trace.

The Schröder government introduced major changes in German society: the first proper immigration law, for instance. Germany used to understand itself as a nation where blood determined citizenship. Naturalization was not really a legal possibility unless you had German ancestors; that changed. For the first time in its history, Germany also had a kind of culture minister, though he was called a secretary of state; in a structurally conservative state that is not friendly toward intellectuals, this was a big step. Schröder's government chose to abandon atomic power altogether and invest in wind power. A tax on gas was introduced to protect the environment. His government changed and simplified taxation despite the conservative majority in the Bundesrat.

Yet it was always clear that what made Germany struggle was the reunification. No one says it out loud, but the western part is still doing much better economically than the East, even though the West took over the burden of eastern health, social, and retirement insurance. A lot of money was pumped into the East without leading to any real recovery. Most of those who were able to left the East; those who stayed are not really attractive workers to business (with exceptions, of course); the same businesses, anyway, use the perception of stagnation to justify laying off workers (to stay "globally competitive") while making record gains in exports.

I REMEMBER WALKING down the boulevard Saint-Michel in Paris the day after the elections of 1998, feeling that finally I could be German without having to be ashamed. When I read the papers a few months ago, the key word was *interpretation*—because a left majority had to be reinterpreted as a conservative victory. The elections produced an absolute majority of the left parties SPD, the Greens, and Die Linke, but the strongest "single" party—which usually selects a chancellor to form the government—was a compound of CDU and CSU, traditionally accepted as a unified entity at the federal level. Yet the CDU and CSU had suffered one of their worst electoral showings in postwar German history. Following constitutional confusion, a weeklong power vacuum, and a retreat by Schröder followed by his ineffectual protest, a conservative-led coalition government emerged under Merkel—and I was ready to be ashamed again. Of course it was the splitting of the left that led to this situation, and the founding of a new left party by former finance minister Oskar Lafontaine, with which no other party wanted to enter into a coalition. By February, the German media were engaged in a massive TV and print campaign: "Du Bist Deutschland" ("You Are Germany"). You see prominent living Germans, then Albert Einstein; and because not everyone can be an Einstein, also a baker and some "ordinary people." It's meant to boost everyone's positive feeling for being German, since there are certainly no political developments to cling to. It feels as if we are on a sinking ship.

I am ashamed at how little debate has been stirred by the fact that a generation of politicians has disappeared from the political scene, and that without them Germany faces the gray zone of an impoverished political imagination. The one breakthrough has ended; the generation of '68 ascended to power and was sent back to its room like an unruly child—while the victors play its songs. The surest sign of our loss is the patronizing way the German media greet every minor success of the new chancellor, as if they were afraid of a complete disaster. And this is precisely what characterizes Germany: it lives waiting for disaster.

—Johannes Türk

GUT-LEVEL LEGISLATION, OR, REDISTRIBUTION

ONE OF THE LESSONS OF STARTING A MAGAZINE today is that if you pay any attention to politics you will collect a class of detractors, who demand immediately to know What and Wherefore and Whether and How. Are you to be filed next to *Mother Jones* and *Z* and *American Spectator* in the back row, or with the *Nation* and *Weekly Standard* and the *American Prospect* up front? Is it possible you have not endorsed a candidate, or adopted a party? Within the party, a position? If not a position, an issue? The notion that politics could be served by thinking about problems and principles, rather than rehearsing strategy, leaves them not so much bemused as furious.

The furious political detractors need "responsibility," which in their hands is a fiction of power. If you question the world from an armchair, it offends them deeply. If you believe you run the world from it, it exalts them—because you have bought into the fiction that justifies their elitism. These commentators who have no access to a legislative agenda and really no more exalted basis for political action than that of their ordinary citizenship (but they do not believe they are ordinary citizens) bleat and growl and put themselves on record for various initiatives of Congress over which they have no influence and upon which they will have no effect. To be on record is to be "politically responsible" in that false sense. No rebuke is made to the process of opinionating itself—this ritual of fomenting an opinion on everything, and so justifying the excited self-stimulation of a class of unelected arbiters who don't respect the citizens within themselves.

"What do you stand for! What will you do!" Legislatively? Are you kidding? Well, there is something one can do, without succumbing to the pundits: for the day when the Congress rolls up to our doorsteps and asks for our legislative initiatives, maybe it is up to every citizen to know what is in his heart and have his true bills and resolutions ready. Call it "political surrealism"—the practice of asking for what is at present impossible, in order to get at last, by indirection or implausible directness, the principles that would underlie the world we'd want rather than the one we have.

§ *Principle:* The purpose of government is to share out money so that there are no poor citizens—therefore no one for whom we must feel guilty because of the arbitrariness of fate. The purpose of life is to free individuals for *individualism*. Individualism is the project of making your own life as appealing as you can, as remarkable as you like, without the encumbrances of an unequal society, which renders your successes undeserved. Government is the outside corrective that leaves us free for life.

§ *Legislative Initiative No.1:* Add a tax bracket of 100 percent to cut off individual income at a fixed ceiling, allowing any individual to bring home a maximum of $100,000 a year from all sources and no more.

§ *Legislative Initiative No.2:* Give every citizen a total of $10,000 a year from the government revenues, paid as a monthly award, in recognition of being an adult in the United States.

THE REDISTRIBUTION OF WEALTH can be unnerving whenever it comes up, and most unnerving to those who have least wealth, because they have worked hardest for every dollar and can't afford to lose it.

But redistribution comes in two steps, and when you look at the steps it's not so unnerving. The first step was already accomplished last century. It was the permanent establishment of a graduated income tax, one of the greatest triumphs of civilization. A consensus was built to grade taxation to equalize the relative pain of taxation for each income earner. A little money is as useful to a person with little money overall as a larger sum is useful to a person with lots of money—and so, for equal citizenship, they carry an equal burden. Tax them proportionately the same, and everyone pays the same stake for government with the same degree of sacrifice.

The second step is our task in *this* century. It is an active redistribution to help dissolve the two portions of society whose existence is antithetical to democracy and civilization, and which harm the members of each of these classes: the obscenely poor and the absurdly rich. Each group must be helped. That means not only ending poverty, but ending absurd wealth. Obscene poverty doesn't motivate the poor or please the rest of us; it makes the poor desperate, criminal, and unhappy. Absurd wealth doesn't help the rich or motivate the rest of us, it makes the rich (for the most part good, decent, hardworking and talented people) into selfish guilty parties, responsible for social evil. It is cruel to rig our system to create these extremes, and cast fellow citizens into the two sewers that border the national road. For all of us, both superwealth and superpoverty make achievement trivial and unreal, and finally destroy the American principles of hard work and just deserts. Luckily, eradicating one (individual superwealth) might help eradicate the other (superpoverty).

TRUE PROPERTY IS THAT which is proper to you: what you mix your hands into (Locke), what is characteristic of you and no one else, and would change state in anyone else's possession. It is your clothes, your domicile, the things you touch and use, the land you personally walk. Property is the proprium, a possession which becomes like a characteristic; it starts as if it could belong to anyone, and comes to be what differentiates you. If it wears the mark of your feet and the smudge of your fingertips, your scent and your private atmosphere, then there is indeed something special and inviolable about property, even where it has come into your hands inequitably, by inheritance or a surfeit of income. The diamond worn at the throat every evening must share a certain protection, under the law, with the torn cloak that keeps some shivering person warm.

This is distinct, however, from all wealth which is not capable of being used in the ordinary necessities of a life or even the ordinary luxuries. From any wealth that cannot be touched or worn or walked every day by its possessor, which neither comes from nor enables the mixing-in of hands but always and inevitably exists as a kind of notional accumulation of numbers, the protection of the proprium withdraws. When you have more houses than you or loved ones can live in, more cars than you can drive; more income in a year than can be spent on what you or your family can actually use, even uselessly use; then we are not speaking of property anymore, not the proprium, but of the inappropriate and alien—that which one gathers to oneself through the accident of social arrangements, exploiting them willfully or accidentally, and not through the private and the personal.

THUS THE RATIONALE for restricting *income.* Inequality will always exist, but in itself it is something different. One has to recognize that while the proprium may be passed down in nonmonetary forms, too—in the peculiarities of your genetics from your parents; in the heirloom, dwelling, tool, or decoration which wears the traces of hands and breath—income always comes as a consequence of arrangements of the community, via the shared space of trade, the discussion and rules, the systems of investment, and all the voluntary associations of society, of which the largest association is government.

A rich person—continuing to draw $100,000 a year in income—stays rich, but puts part of it into his own home and bank account and part into the needs and luxuries he may actually use. This sum will be converted reasonably into the *proper,* the personal, without any absurdity. A superrich person, however, who takes in $1 million, $10 million, or $100 million, will not and can never spend it on any sane vision of the necessities of life, at least not without a parasitic order in which normal goods (a home, a dinner) are overpriced (by the existence of those who will compete to pay for them) and other goods are made to be abnormal and bloated (like the multiacre mansion). The social system allocates the extra $9,900,000 mistakenly. Reallocated, it would do much more benefit in a guaranteed citizens' income for many individuals in households with total incomes both above and below the median (now about $45,000 per household). But this is without—and this is very important—doing any harm to the formerly superrich person; if anything, it may do him a great benefit.

(And it should also be without any person or office to decide to whom money should be allocated. The goal is an automatic mechanism and universal good, not a form of control. Everyone must be given an equal sum, the $10,000, to help him be free. And that must include the rich top earner of $100,000—to keep him free, too, with the opportunity, through all the years of his adulthood, to *change* his life.)

THE THREAT FROM THOSE who oppose this line of thought is that, without "incentives," people will stop working. The worst-case scenario is that tens of thousands of people who hold jobs in finance, corporate management, and the professions (not to mention professional sports and acting) will quit their jobs and end their careers because they did not truly want to be bankers, lawyers, CEOs, actors, ballplayers, et cetera. They were only doing it for the money! Actually they wanted to be high school teachers, social workers, general practitioners, stay-at-home parents, or criminals and layabouts.

Far from this being a tragedy, this would be the greatest single triumph of human emancipation in a century. A small portion of the rich and unhappy would be freed at last from the slavery of jobs that aren't their life's work—and all of us would be freed from an insane system.

If there is anyone working a job who would stop doing that job should his income—and all his richest compatriots' incomes—drop to $100,000 a year, *he should not be doing that job*. He should *never* have been doing that job—for his own life's sake. It's just not a life, to do work you don't want to do when you have other choices, and can think of something better (and have a $10,000 cushion to supplement a different choice of life). If no one would choose to do this job for a mere $100,000 a year, if all would pursue something else more humanly valuable; if, say, there would no longer be anyone willing to be a trader, a captain of industry, an actor, or an athlete for that kind of money—then the job should not exist.

The supposed collapse of the economy without unlimited income levels is one of the most suspicious aspects of commonplace economic psychology. Ask yourself, for once, if you believe it. Does the inventor just not bother to invent any more if inventions still benefit larger collectivities—a company, a society—but do not lead to a jump in his or any other inventor's already satisfactory personal income? Do the professions really collapse if doctors and lawyers work for life and justice and $100,000, rather than $1 million? Will the arts and entertainment collapse if the actors, writers, and producers work for glory and $100,000? Do ballplayers go into some other line and stop playing? If you're panicking because you can't imagine a ceiling of $100,000, well, make it $150,000. Our whole system is predicated on the erroneous idea that individuals are likely to hate the work they have chosen, but overwhelmingly love money. Presumably the opposite should be true. Even the really successful trader *must* love his work in some way—he enjoys the competition, temporarily measured in money, and the action and strategy and game of thought and organization, which are his life's calling. And all this glory could be pursued in a society in which he only took home $100,000 from this sport of kings—and he, and all of us, might be better off.

"BUT HOW CAN YOU ASK other people to lower their salaries, without giving your life to charity, first? Isn't it hypocrisy to call for change for everyone without turning over your own income?" Morality is not saved by any individual's efforts to do charity, a pocketful here, a handful there. Charity is the vice of unequal systems. (I'm only repeating Wilde's "The Soul of Man Under Socialism.") We shouldn't have to weigh whether our money would do more good in a destitute person's pocket, or our time do more good if we ladled soup to the hungry, or our study do more good if it taught reading to the illiterate. It always, always would. Because it is hard to give up your money, however, when not everyone else does, and hard to give up your time when not everyone else does—and nearly impossible when you have less time, and less money, than the visibly rich and comfortable—and frankly, because it's not often a good idea to give up your true calling or your life at all, our giving is limited and fitful. It can never make a large-scale difference.

Not only decency, justice, and community but nobility, excellence, and individualism can only come about by redistribution, not charity, in a society organized against drastic monetary inequality in the first place. It would be a good society in the broadest sense, one in which life was worth living, because the good life (as a life of morality, and as a life of justified luxury) could be pursued without contradiction.

THE ESSENCE OF INDIVIDUALISM is *morally relevant* inequality. The misuse of inequality occurs when it comes to be based on wealth rather than ability; on birth rather than talent; on positioning rather than genius; on alienable money (which could belong to anyone) rather than action and works (which can only be done by you). These distortions spell the end of a society of individualists. Money inequality creates a single system which corrals every person and places him above or beneath another, in a single file stretching from hell to the moon. These so-called "individualists" will then be led, by the common standard of the dollar, to common interests, common desires, and little that's *individual* at all.

Some say, the more the rich are rich, the better off will everyone be. But really the Dick Cheneys of this world are obese because they're eating everybody else's dinner. Trickle-down economics is an alimentary philosophy: The more the rich eat, the more crusts they stuff in their maws, the more they create for the benefit of all the rest of us underneath them. Even if it worked, one could not forget that what they pass on to us is predigested, already traveling through their stomachs and fattening them first, giving excess nutriment to the undeserving. Their monuments, too, which we do marvel at, are composed of waste. Why gain the world as excrement? Why should we not take it in its morally original form—if money need not pass through the rich to reach us?

§ *Legislative Initiative No.3.* It makes most sense to have a president and vice president who will forswear wealth permanently. A man who rules for the *demos* need not come from the *demos*. But he ought to enter it; he ought to become one of the people he is responsible most for helping—that means the rest of us.

WORST-CASE SCENARIO TWO, if we prioritize human satisfaction instead of productivity, is de-development. For centuries, it has been at the back of the Western mind that technological development might reach a point at which a democratic community would want to stop, or change direction. So the Erewhonians, in Butler's utopia, broke their machines.

It's finally become possible to take a better view: not unlimited laissez-faire hubris, and not irrational machine-breaking either. In a country where some portions of development have gone further than anybody would like, because of everyone's discrete private actions (as in the liquidation of landscape and the lower atmosphere)—while other portions, as in medical insurance and preventive care, have not gone far enough—then *intentional de-development* might be the best thing that can occur. The eradication of diseases is not something you would like to see end; nor would you want to lose the food supply, transportation, and good order of the law and defense. On the other hand, more cell phones and wireless, an expanded total entertainment environment, more computerization for consumer tracking, greater concentrations of capital and better exploitation of "inefficiencies" in the trading of securities, the final throes of extraction and gas-guzzling and—to hell with it. I'd rather live in a more equal world at a slower pace.

—Mark Greif

MARK SACKMANN, *LOOKOUT TOWER*, 2006, WOODCUT ON RAG PAPER, 6 X 7". COURTESY OF THE ARTIST.

MY LIFE AND TIMES IN AMERICAN JOURNALISM

Philip Connors

MY WHOLE FORAY INTO JOURNALISM arose from a misapprehension. I wanted to be a writer, and I thought the most important thing about being a writer was seeing your work in print. Becoming a newspaper reporter seemed like the quickest way to see my work in print. I was 18 and callow. What can I say.

I spent six years, off and on, and $60,000 at two universities to obtain a bachelor's degree in print journalism, but six years and sixty grand weren't enough, according to my professors. I needed internships—as many and as illustrious as possible. This is how I allowed myself to be talked into a summer job at the *Fargo Forum* by a professor who knew the managing editor there. I would cover the beats of reporters who went on vacation, one by one: cops, courts, agriculture, religion, et cetera.

Eight weeks into it, I knew I didn't have the fortitude to write against deadline, day after day, on subjects I didn't give a damn about—city water-board meetings, the travails of emu farmers. The managing editor kept putting my stories on the front page, but the thrill of seeing my work in print wore off pretty quickly. The only really interesting story I covered was an anti-abortion protest at a women's clinic, during which the protest leader stood and shouted, "Fargo is a nice town full of nice people. But when people hear the word 'Dachau,' they don't think of a nice little Bavarian town. And Fargo, unfortunately, is known as the city in North Dakota where they kill babies." I wrote that down in my notebook and used it to lead my story. It seemed like something the residents of Fargo would be interested to learn about their town over breakfast the next morning.

One of my professors had justified this sort of story by calling it "Swiss-cheese journalism." He said people will often stage events or call press conferences that are plainly acts of demagoguery, and although reporters generally have a duty to report on these events with a straight face, most readers will recognize them for what they are.

It's like Swiss cheese, he said. You hold up a piece of Swiss cheese, and everyone can see what it is. You don't have to point at the holes.

I was beginning to doubt whether I wanted to make a career out of holding up pieces of Swiss cheese. One Monday morning, not long after my feature on the artistry of local pet groomers was splashed across the front of the B section, along with big color photos of poodles and dachshunds undergoing various forms of beautification, I decided I'd had enough. One month remained of my internship—one month more than I could take. I skipped breakfast and went straight to a neighborhood sports-medicine clinic. To a kindly but perplexed nurse, I explained that I was with the drama department at the university. We were putting on a play in the fall, and in the play there was a character who wore a sling on his arm. Our prop room didn't have a sling. I asked whether she might let us borrow one, or, if that wasn't an option, whether she might take cash for it. She seemed to pity me, for some reason; she let me have the thing for free. I told her I'd stop by with a couple of complimentary tickets in the fall, before the play opened, and she looked pleased. I was relieved when she didn't ask the name of the play.

Half an hour later I appeared in the office of the managing editor, empty shirtsleeve dangling pathetically at my side. I explained my history of shoulder trouble, told him in detail how I'd dislocated it over the weekend in a game of pickup basketball, and informed him that I needed to leave immediately to see my doctor back home about the likelihood of major rotator cuff surgery. The old man stabbed out his cigarette and lit another, wheezing as he shifted his enormous girth in his chair.

Listen, kid, he said, peering at me over the top of his half-moon glasses. I can't lose you. I've got people going on vacation. I'm shorthanded.

I'm sorry, I said, but I can't stay. I can't even take notes anymore.

You can use a tape recorder, he said.

I don't have one, I said.

We'll get you one, he said.

I can't type, I said.

Sure you can, he said. You'll just have to use one hand. Hunt and peck. Half the monkeys in this newsroom type that way.

Give him credit for trying, but I didn't budge. By noon I'd packed my car, having worn the sling the entire time in case a colleague from the paper drove past the empty frat house where I'd rented a room for the summer. I was thirty miles down the interstate before I decided I could safely remove the sling.

Newspapers were not for me; clearly I was a magazine guy. Back at school that fall, I heard about an internship program run by the American Society of Magazine Editors. It placed forty interns at forty different magazines, most of them in New York. I applied for the next summer and was accepted. I was ecstatic as I ticked off the glossies on my list of preferences: *Time, Newsweek, Rolling Stone*. I'd worked at North Dakota's Largest Daily Newspaper. I'd written front-page stories. Now I was getting my due. I bought a Manhattan guidebook and reserved a flight to LaGuardia. I should have known the lack of the words Harvard and Yale on my résumé would put me at a disadvantage. When ASME sent the letter informing me of my assignment, I learned I'd be spending the summer in Washington, D.C., at *Kiplinger's Personal Finance* magazine.

I almost backed out, but one of my professors reminded me to consider my résumé—my future résumé. I spent the summer fact-checking lists of mutual funds, money-market funds, and tax-exempt bond funds ranked by risk and return. To relieve the boredom, I drank appalling amounts of Paul Masson wine—you know, the kind with the pop-off plastic caps that used to sell for $2.95 a bottle—late at night on the Mall by the reflecting pool with the intern from *National Geographic*, who became a good friend, despite my envy of his future résumé. Toward the end I even wrote an article for the magazine, a profile of a telemarketing entrepreneur, and although the managing editor told me it was a fine piece of work, it bore almost no resemblance to my original draft when it was finally published. This was an unsettling development: seeing my name in print over a whole page of words I hadn't even written.

I HAD ONE MORE CRACK AT AN INTERNSHIP before I left college, so I placed my hope in the pugilistic world of political magazines. I applied to be an intern at the *Nation*, whose leftist orientation appealed to my underdog sympathies, and despite the fact that I'd worked for the glossy capitalist press, I got the job.

Here was a magazine with substance, a magazine with an exciting history. It was America's Oldest Continuously Published Weekly Magazine, having been founded at the end of the Civil War. Its pages had been graced by the work of Henry James, Willa Cather, Hannah Arendt, James Baldwin, Hunter Thompson, Gore Vidal—a world above the sausage-factory hackery of the *Fargo Forum*, or the service-mag boosterism of *Kiplinger's*. I prepared for a glamorous, amorous season of rubbing elbows with the New York literati, engaging in passionate but casual affairs with my fellow interns, the libertine girls of elite Eastern schooling—my just compensation for having been trumped, on the ASME internship, by the boys of Harvard and Yale.

The condition of the office was the first bad omen. The windowsills were coated in dust so thick it might have been there since the magazine's inception. The air smelled vaguely of unwashed underarm and cigarettes, and moldering paper lay everywhere in piles. Thankfully, the production assistant had the good sense to smoke his daily, fragrant joint in the men's room, where a perpetually leaking pipe kept the humidity high and the fire danger low.

When I showed up the first day wearing a tie, wanting to make a good impression, everyone looked at me nervously, as if I might be a poorly disguised FBI agent. I spent the next four months hunched over a telephone in a windowless room we called the bullpen, fact-checking articles on how to reinvigorate the labor movement, a longtime staple of *Nation* reportage whose frequency and desperation of tone increased as union membership declined. For variety, I did research for a contrarian columnist on "the hoax of global warming," but occasionally I avoided the research by acting as the columnist's courier—dropping off film of him and his girlfriend in racy poses, picking up the prints, and mailing them to him in a plain manila envelope. Those tawdry four-by-sixes were the only element of those months that could be considered vaguely amorous, although they didn't do much for me.

The hundred-dollar-a-week intern stipend matched exactly the cost of my sublet room in Queens. With a six-hundred-dollar cash advance on my very first credit card, I was left with fifty dollars a week for food, coffee, and subway fare. Mostly, I passed my evenings writing long, lugubrious letters to friends about the irony of working as an indentured slave for a magazine founded by abolitionists. The girls of elite Eastern schooling were more interested in guys who could discourse with easy intimacy on the works of Habermas and Derrida; an earnest Midwesterner with firsthand knowledge of techniques in pig castration did not exactly set their loins aquiver, at least not with desire. I missed my one chance to mingle with Kurt Vonnegut and E. L. Doctorow when I called in sick the day the interns were enlisted to serve hors d'oeuvres at a fund-raising dinner for the magazine, which had lost money 132 years running. I very much doubted Vonnegut would want to discuss with me the bombing of Dresden while I held a tray of stuffed dates wrapped in prosciutto. I counted the days till I could return to school in Montana.

I did get one break just before I left. One of my weekly duties involved opening all the packages sent to the literary editors, an unceasing wave of review copies of the latest books, and on one such occasion I came across a book about a cyanide heap-leach gold mine a company had proposed near the headwaters of the Blackfoot River in Montana. I knew the Blackfoot well and agreed with the author that the mine would be a disaster, so I proposed an essay on the book and the mine, and the literary editor accepted it. Back in Missoula that winter, after the piece appeared, I waited for the phone to ring, thinking that now all the important editors in New York would be aware of what a stylish writer I was. When the phone remained mum for several weeks, I let my service lapse. The silence was too depressing, and I was too broke to pay the bill. If they wanted to find me they could write a letter to the *Nation* and have it forwarded, like people did in the old days.

After graduation I stayed on in Missoula, where I paid $180 a month for a studio apartment above a downtown movie theater. On summer days fishermen cast their flies upstream from the Higgins Avenue Bridge, seventy-five yards from my window, and a bagpiper went through his mournful musical paces, using the bridge abutments as acoustic enhancement. Mornings I eked out a living baking bread alongside a failed novelist who'd mastered the texture of the baguette, though not the art of fiction, during two years in Paris in the 1970s. Afternoons I worked on what I hoped would become my own first novel, an imitation of Paul Auster's *New York Trilogy* that stalled forever at forty pages. For a time I felt sort of authentically bohemian pounding on my old Olivetti while the muffled sound track to that week's feature film droned through the floor. The building's manual elevator, one of the few of its kind still in operation west of the Mississippi, was staffed by a woman who'd never abandoned the apartment upstairs where her husband had blown his brains out a decade earlier. More than once I heard a rumor that David Lynch had spent some time around the place during his stay in Missoula, long enough to use it as a model for the apartment building in *Blue Velvet.*

I'd finally given up on journalism. I wanted to devote myself to art, to real writing, to an eccentric vision along the lines of David Lynch. I might have been content to live for years hand-to-mouth in that heady mixture of squalor and beauty, within walking distance of eleven bars, had an old flame not dropped back into my life.

We'd broken up a few years earlier; she'd moved to Paris, and I hadn't seen her since. When she wrote to say she was coming to Montana for a cousin's wedding, we planned to meet for one last bittersweet romantic good-bye.

We drove through the mountains, camped by an alpine lake, and, gripped by sentimentality, agreed to try again: she'd leave Paris, I'd leave Montana. We'd meet in the middle, New York. I guess we had to prove to ourselves, once and for all, that we weren't meant to be. Which of course we did. One gray morning I woke up and found myself alone in a Hell's Kitchen sublet with the owner's four cats, wondering how I was ever going to pay my bills. Journalism beckoned.

I SENT MY RÉSUMÉ TO DOZENS OF MAGAZINES and waited to hear back, but in the end only one of them called me for an interview. I only got the interview because I knew someone who knew someone at the magazine. It was called *Civilization* and was affiliated with the Library of Congress. The magazine was glossy but kind of boring. I didn't care. I'd been in the city for two months and was buying groceries with my credit card.

I showed up in a jacket and tie and tried my best to look like a diligent and respectable young college graduate from the American Middle West. I was shown to the office of the editor, a man named Nelson Aldrich, who asked me about my various internships. I told him about all the intrepid reporting I'd done at the *Fargo Forum*, the article I'd written for the *Nation*, the many things I'd learned about the ways of the world while staring into the abyss of an impending deadline. I tried to make it sound as if I were the prairie incarnation of H. L. Mencken and no doubt went too far, because Nelson Aldrich immediately said I was overqualified for the job. He was looking for an editorial assistant. I told him I really wanted the job. He said I'd probably find it boring and he didn't want a bored assistant moping around the office. I told him I didn't mope. He said the pay was poor and I could find something better. I told him I'd already been looking for two months and didn't share his optimism. We spent most of the interview in this way, me begging in an unseemly manner for the job, him trying to talk me out of wanting it.

I'd done some research about Nelson Aldrich before I arrived for the interview. In addition to helping found the *Paris Review*, he'd written a book called *Old Money*, about growing up in a family that had a lot of it. I wanted to tell him that I'd grown up in a family that had hardly any of it, that I needed a job to begin paying my student loans and my extortionate New York rent, that if he hired me I'd be the most attentive and responsible editorial assistant he'd ever known, and that even if I became bored I'd pretend I wasn't, because I just wanted money—new, old, crisp, soiled, I didn't care. But he was from old money, and I figured he didn't understand such things, so I didn't bring them up, and he didn't hire me, and after I left his office I never spoke to him again.

I may have had to leave the city in disgrace if I hadn't called the former head of the journalism department at the University of Montana, a man named Frank Allen. He'd once worked at the *Wall Street Journal* and knew a lot of people in New York. When I called him, he gave me the name of a woman at the *Wall Street Journal* and told me I should call her and ask her to coffee. The idea was she might know people who knew other people who might want to hire a hungry young journalist from the northern Plains.

The woman was the newspaper's legal editor. I called her, and we met for coffee. She said, in her gravelly Brooklyn accent, that Frank Allen had hired her when he was chief of the Philadelphia bureau of the *Wall Street Journal*, and for that she was eternally grateful. There was no longer a Philadelphia bureau of the *Wall Street Journal*, and about that she was sad.

As luck would have it, she said, I've just been given permission by my boss to hire a news assistant. Would you be interested in the job?

I said, Yes, absolutely.

She told me to send her six samples of my writing by the end of the week.

I told her I would.

When I left the interview, which I hadn't even known was going to be an interview, I was conflicted. All of a sudden, I had a chance to get a job at a place that considered itself the World's Most Important Publication, but I didn't want to work at the world's most important publication. In fact, I'd hardly ever read it; I thought it was a fusty rag for middle-aged bankers, as predictable in its celebration of capitalism as *Pravda* had been in its defense of Communism. My politics at the time were fierce and not always coherent, but if they were given a one-word description I suppose you'd call them socialist. And while socialism taking root in America was about as likely as a manned space flight to Pluto, journalism, I thought, might at least be a means to afflict the comfortable and comfort the afflicted, as one of my professors liked to say. The *Wall Street Journal* seemed about the least likely place in the world where a writer could do that.

Soon I decided my politics mattered less than the anemic balance in my checking account—and then I realized I had an even bigger problem. The legal editor had wanted to see six samples of my writing—six—but I had only four or five really good ones from the *Fargo Forum*. The best thing I'd written was the essay on the Blackfoot River in the *Nation*. As fate would have it, I'd said an unkind thing about the *Wall Street Journal* in that piece. In reference to a logging company whose clear-cuts of healthy forest had fouled the river with silt and killed untold numbers of fish, I'd written: "Even a newspaper as sympathetic to corporate plunder as the *Wall Street Journal* once called Plum Creek the 'Darth Vader of the [timber] industry.'" I doubted that the legal editor thought of her employer as sympathetic to corporate plunder, and I very much doubted that she would hire me if she discovered I'd written such a thing.

You can see my quandary.

Soon, though, I thought of a solution. I still had friends at the *Nation*, and I called one of them, explained my situation, and asked if he'd do me a giant favor. Would he go into the electronic archives of the magazine and touch up the article that said unkind things about the *Wall Street Journal*, and then print for me a copy of the doctored article, which would no longer say unkind things? At first he was reluctant. He didn't want to tinker with the historical record of the magazine. I told him he should of course change back my wording before saving and closing the file.

In the end he capitulated, and I sent a copy of the doctored to the legal editor. She was impressed by it, and I was hired.

When I showed up for work that first day, on Liberty Street in Manhattan, just across the West Side Highway from the World Trade Center towers, in World Financial Center building number one, I had my picture taken and affixed to a little magnetic pass card. When waved in front of a laserlike beam of discerning red light, the pass card unlocked doors for me in the paper's austere corridors. My qualms about working for the bible of American capitalism were in quick retreat. I felt proud, powerful, important: I was going places.

I'd been hired as a news assistant. I thought this meant I'd help with the gathering and writing of news. In practice, this meant I fetched faxes and replenished water coolers. I spent most of each day standing over a squadron of a half-dozen fax machines, manually collating and stapling press releases and court documents, then delivering them to reporters who covered corporate law, telecommunications, and the pharmaceutical industry. I performed this task with actuarial efficiency, the paper a blur in my hand like a magician's trick; I served the reporters their faxes with the cordial discretion of a waiter in a fancy restaurant. My only means of discriminating good days from bad was by noting, at the end of my shift, whether I'd avoided a paper cut.

All day long I inhaled the hot ink fumes wafting from the fax machines. I felt an irrational fear that the fumes might have some secret, insidious effect—hastening the onset of lung cancer, shrinking my testicles. My job was pointless. I'd spent the prime years of my education working menial jobs and borrowing heavily to pay for a college degree that qualified me for a position that was already obsolete. Al Gore had invented the internet. People didn't need to send faxes anymore. They could send e-mail. But they went on sending faxes on paper, laying waste to great swaths of forest, enriching pulp mills and timber companies. I thought about mentioning this to my boss: Why don't we encourage people to rechannel their communications electronically, saving the world lots of trees and me lots of time? But then I wondered whether that would result in me losing my job, whereupon I'd be forced to wait tables at a tapas bar. So I kept my mouth shut and sorted and stapled the faxes, and cashed my check every two weeks, which still came quaintly on paper, despite the invention of direct deposit.

Once in a while I came across an amusing press release, which I tucked in a folder marked "GREATEST HITS OF PUBLIC RELATIONS."

New York University Medical Center: FOR IMMEDIATE RELEASE: NEW YORK, NY (November 29, 1999)—FREQUENT NIGHTTIME BATHROOM VISITS AFFECT SLEEP AND QUALITY OF LIFE. . . .

THE AYN RAND INSTITUTE—October 20, 1999. FOR IMMEDIATE RELEASE: FIFTH ANNIVERSARY OF AMERICORPS = FIVE YEARS OF SACRIFICE. Marina Del Ray, CA—The AmeriCorps should be abolished, said the director of communications for the Ayn Rand Institute. "The AmeriCorps aims to indoctrinate young people into a life of sacrificing to society," said Scott McConnell. "That is a recipe for slavery, not freedom." . . . Since 1997, the Ayn Rand Institute has been the only voice morally opposing volunteerism. Through the Institute's Anti-Servitude Internship Program, students have the opportunity to fulfill their school's volunteer requirements by working to abolish volunteerism.

NEWS: Re: *PEOPLE MAGAZINE*'S TRIBUTE ISSUE RELEASE. July 22, 1999. Please note that there was an error in the press release forwarded to you this morning: JOHN F. KENNEDY JR. WAS *PEOPLE*'S 'SEXIEST MAN ALIVE' IN 1988 (NOT 1998). We regret the error.

March 30, 1999: FOR IMMEDIATE RELEASE: News from State Senator Roy M. Goodman: SENATOR GOODMAN URGES PASSAGE OF LEGISLATION TO REGULATE SPERM RETRIEVAL FROM DEAD MEN.

ONE DAY, ABOUT EIGHT MONTHS AFTER I WAS HIRED, I learned of a job opening on the Leisure & Arts page. It was listed on the company's internal website, a copyediting job, repairing split infinitives and run-on sentences and the like. I figured I could do that. More important, I knew the job would double my salary and probably halve my chances of lung cancer. I had my résumé and cover letter polished by the end of the day.

I was confident of my chances until I learned that, in order to get the job, I would have to sit for an interview with Bob Bartley, the editorial-page editor of the paper, who also oversaw hiring for the Leisure & Arts page, which he otherwise supervised with benign neglect. Bob

Bartley, who has since passed away, was among the most influential American journalists of the second half of the 20th century, although his name was not widely known outside of New York and Washington. He was fairly soft-spoken, and his posture was poor. He rarely smiled, but when he did he looked like a cat who'd just swallowed your canary.

His abiding obsessions were taxes and weapons. He thought taxes should be cut always and everywhere, except for poor people, and he thought America should build as many weapons as possible. The more weapons we had, in his view, the less likely we were to need them. But he believed that occasionally we might need them to bomb other nations that were trying to get them too, because those nations couldn't be trusted not to use them, the way we could. In order to further thwart the nations that, unlike us, couldn't be trusted not to use their weapons, he thought we should spend however many trillions it took to build a missile-defense shield, that sci-fi sort of umbrella that would protect America from the rain of other nations' missiles. (I always admired the childish simplicity of the concept: like one man shooting a bullet at another man, and instead of the second man shooting back at the first man, he shoots a bullet at the first man's bullet. That way, no one dies. Only bullets die.) Bob Bartley believed that with tax cuts, lots of weapons, and a missile-defense shield, Americans would remain safe, happy, and prosperous.

Bob Bartley had been writing editorials about these ideas for more than thirty years.

Someone once made a joke about editorial writers. Why is writing an editorial like pissing yourself in a blue serge suit? Because it gives you a warm feeling, and nobody notices what you've done.

Bob Bartley was no trouser-wetter, though. From what I could discern, he never had warm feelings, and people in power tended to notice what he wrote. The arena in which he'd had his greatest influence was tax policy. He was a ceaseless proponent of trickle-down economics: by cutting taxes for rich people and raising them for poor people, he argued, more money would end up in the hands of not only rich people but, because the rich people would spend it on maids and yachts, in the hands of people who cleaned houses and sanded the decks of yachts. Because everyone would be making more money, the government would generate more money in taxes, even though the top tax rates were lower. Since bloating the government with more taxpayer money was actually a bad thing, an evil outcome of good policy (I know, I know, it all gets very confusing), the government would be obliged to funnel the extra tax revenues to bomb-building projects—in effect throwing the money away, since it created wealth, in the form of weapons, that could only be used once, if at all, and then only to destroy, never to create more wealth, which was supposed to be the essence of capitalism, wealth creating wealth—while at the same time cutting programs for poor people, which would make the poor people angry at the government and entice them to vote for Republicans, just like the rich people did, ensuring Republican rule forever.

Despite the baroque strangeness of some of his ideas, Bob Bartley had once won a Pulitzer Prize.

When I first joined the paper, Bob Bartley was in the late, hysterical stages of his obsession with Bill Clinton. Bob Bartley's editorial page had printed enough editorials about Whitewater to fill 3,000 pages in six thick anthologies (now available on CD-ROM!). Bob Bartley was proud of these books, even though no one read them. He thought Whitewater was comparable to Watergate; he was hoping to bring down a president, like Woodward and Bernstein had, and win another Pulitzer Prize. But despite his 3,000 pages of editorials, Whitewater ultimately degenerated into an ontological squabble about whether fellatio is actually sex, and the president did not resign and was not forced from office, although Bob Bartley was adamant that he should have been, because Bob Bartley did not approve of extramarital fellatio. At least not for Democrats. When a reporter asked him whether he would've attacked Newt Gingrich or another prominent Republican faced with similar charges of sexual misconduct, Bob Bartley admitted that, "We would have defended them. That's the way it is."

I was nervous when I went to Bob Bartley's office for my interview. My internship at the *Nation* featured prominently on my résumé. While the work I did there was utterly harmless to the spread of corporate capitalism—fact-checking articles on a labor movement that was doomed no matter what anyone said; researching articles on "the hoax of global warming," which Bob Bartley agreed was a hoax—the *Nation* was known to say kind things about socialists. Bob Bartley detested socialists.

Bob Bartley held my résumé in his hands. I feared he would ask me about socialism, taxes, trickle-down economics. Then I would face a choice: I could either tell him what I thought about these things, whereupon he would refuse to hire me to work on the Leisure & Arts page, or I could betray my own principles, barter away my soul, and lie. I'd been here before, and I knew which path I'd choose.

He did not ask me about any of these things. We talked about Minnesota and Iowa, where, it turned out, we had both lived as boys. He'd been born in southwestern Minnesota but grew up mostly in Ames, Iowa, while I'd been born in Ames, Iowa, and grew up mostly in southwestern Minnesota. This seemed apt, our moving in opposite directions at the beginning of our lives—me upward and to the left on the map, him downward and to the right.

Bob Bartley asked me only one serious question, with two leading follow-ups: What is your ambition in life? Do you, for instance, want to be a reporter? Or do you want to be editorial-page editor of the *Wall Street Journal*?

I was sure I didn't want to be a reporter, especially not at the *Wall Street Journal*, where most reporters covered a single industry (insurance, airlines) or even a single company (AOL, Microsoft), had very few opportunities to comfort the afflicted, and never detached themselves from their cell phones. And even though a part of me did want to be editorial-page editor of the *Wall Street Journal*, which was the same thing as saying I wanted to be the Most Important Person at the World's Most Important Publication, I knew I never would be, because I didn't believe any of the things Bob Bartley believed. If I said no, he might be insulted. If I said yes, a part of him would always suspect that repairing split infinitives was merely the first step in my devious plan to succeed him, after which I would install a cadre of liberal editorial writers who would call for higher taxes on rich people, the abolition of nuclear weapons, and government-sponsored extramarital fellatio for all American Democrats.

I chose my words carefully. I said, No, I want to write a novel.

My answer pleased him, as I figured it would. When I left Bob Bartley's office, I knew I had the job.

SHORTLY THEREAFTER, I CEASED TO HAND OUT FAXES, and instead wrote headlines and edited copy for the next three years. I was anonymous, efficient, and discreet. Nothing slipped past me. Day after day an unblemished page was shipped electronically to seventeen printing plants across the country, and the following morning nearly two million readers held the fruits of my labor in their hands. At first I resented the lack of attention paid my mastery of English grammar and the intricacies of the house style book. Not once did I receive a letter from an armchair grammarian in Dubuque or Terre Haute, one of those retired English teachers who scour the daily paper with a red pen in hand, searching for evidence of American decline in the form of a split infinitive. Nor did my immediate superior mention, even in passing, that I did my job diligently and well. But over time I began to take delight in this peculiar feature of my job—that my success was measured by how rarely people noticed what I did. In this way I believed myself akin to oil-tanker captains and air-traffic controllers, those anonymous technicians of social stability whose identities become known only through catastrophic failure.

When I moved to the Leisure & Arts page, I assumed I'd have little contact with the editorial writers. I was wrong. My cubicle was situated smack in the midst of theirs. A couple of them came forward to welcome me, but most of them didn't. The ones who welcomed me overlooked the fact that my politics were repugnant. Those who didn't welcome me couldn't overlook that fact. By hanging a campaign poster of Ralph Nader in my cubicle, I made it a hard fact to overlook.

I had almost nothing in the way of social interaction with the editorial writers, although I began to read their writing very closely, sometimes even dipping into the archives to sample their obsessions over the decades. They wrote with the zeal of converts, as if they'd all been Communists in their youth, and each of them clutched, with merciless loins, the flanks of a favorite right-wing hobby horse: not only taxes and weapons but the treachery and moral lassitude of the Palestinians, the creeping fascism of fluoride in the water supply, the heroic necessity of Pinochet's bloody dictatorship in crushing democratic socialism in Chile. In this way the collective voice of the newspaper, the unsigned editorials, was always the furthest to the right of the range of beliefs held by the editorial-page writers, no accident on Bob Bartley's part. He himself held the most extreme position on every issue, and although he couldn't write three editorials a day himself, he took great care in his choice of surrogates. He hired people who could just as well have been Republican speechwriters, as indeed some of them had been (Peggy Noonan) or soon would be (Bill McGurn)—a line of work that seemed to me, if not exactly noble, then at least more intellectually honest than masquerading as a journalist.

I tried once and only once to engage in a reasonable discussion about politics with one of the editorial writers. She was a voluble and attractive young blonde who'd grown up in Oregon and gone to college at Princeton. She worked in the cubicle next to mine. She wrote a lot about environmental issues, and one time I told her I disagreed with something she'd written about federal forest policy. The essence of my argument was simple: I don't think trees should be cut down carelessly. She told me that trees existed to be cut down. Needless to say, I was surprised; I sort of assumed people from Oregon liked trees. She said she preferred clear-cuts—essentially, forests transformed into nonforests. She said that clear-cuts grew back as peaceful meadows, which were aesthetically superior to forests. I disagreed. She said I had an unhealthy, sentimental attitude about trees; she accused me of wanting to hug them. I told her I didn't want to hug them, I just didn't think they should all die. But she said most trees would be better off dead, after which they could be given a more useful second life as chairs, ranch houses, or fax paper.

We didn't talk much after that, although we always said hello when passing in the hallways.

MY BOSS, RAYMOND SOKOLOV, was the one true sophisticate among the bunch. He'd founded, in 1982, the Leisure & Arts page as a daily staple of the paper. Before that he'd been a book and movie critic for *Newsweek*, a food editor at the *New York Times*, and a columnist for *Natural History* magazine. He'd also written several books, among them a biography of A. J. Liebling. With his diminutive stature, his shock of white hair, and his colorful bow ties, he had the appearance of a mischievous, elfin intellectual. He was no ideologue when it came to politics. He seemed, from what I could gather in our occasional, brief conversations, to be a sensible moderate, but he had a streak of iconoclasm, some inherent desire to tweak the sensibilities of the powers that be.

One day he came to me with a proposal. Our regular TV critic was going on vacation. Would I care to try my hand at filling her column? I could pick through the piles of tapes she was sent by the networks and write on anything that struck me, as long as he approved it first.

I was flattered—but I hadn't owned a television in seven years. This, I told him, might rob me of the requisite tone of authority, the breadth of reference, that is the currency of the modern newspaper critic.

He stroked the tips of his mustache with his thumb and forefinger and sagely nodded his head.

Why don't you write about life without television? he said. For one day we can make the TV column an anti-TV column.

He flashed a devilish smile.

The next week, for the first time in anyone's memory, the paper's TV column failed to offer a blurb for the latest darling project of some cable or network exec. Nor did it provide Fortune 500 ad managers with a hint of where to place their commercials. Nothing was hyped or sold. In fact, a half-dozen subscribers wrote letters to the editor and claimed they'd been emboldened to unplug their sets and stow them away in their attics. And while all of this gave me a small but palpable thrill, it may have been that assignment that first helped me move beyond a conception of myself as a hardworking and dedicated foe of split infinitives and run-on sentences, an honest working stiff in the salt mines of American journalism. My little column suddenly helped me see myself through the eyes of the men in the suites upstairs: another peon doing his part to enhance shareholder value at the flagship editorial product in the universe of Dow Jones brands. So this peon doesn't have a TV set. How droll.

Nonetheless, the paper had an audience of millions, and a part of me couldn't quite shake the idea that the point of writing is to have your work read by as many people as possible. So, once a month or so, I'd propose an article for the Leisure & Arts page, and more often than not Ray would go for it. In this manner I smuggled the occasional outré sentiment into the paper.

The assignment I enjoyed most was a profile of a radical black performance artist named William Pope.L. He'd once walked the streets of Harlem with a twelve-foot white phallus strapped to his midsection, a comment on white fears of black sexuality that sent the National Endowment for the Arts—which had once bestowed on Pope.L a grant of taxpayer money—into a tizzy. His most famous work, however, involved eating a copy of the *Wall Street Journal* with the aid of ketchup and milk, then regurgitating the meal, all while sitting on a gleaming porcelain toilet perched atop a ten-foot scaffold. He told me he'd once seen an ad campaign for the paper that made it out to be the modern equivalent of a primitive cultural object imbued with mystical powers. I quoted his explanation at length: "The ads suggested that if you bought a subscription, good things would happen to you. It proposed that the paper could have magical effects. You didn't have to read it. Just having it near you, having it land on your doorstep, would multiply your wealth. So I took the logic to its absurd conclusion. Shouldn't ingesting it increase your wealth ten-fold?"

It was Ray's idea to run the piece on the day the paper, after more than a hundred years in existence, first enlivened its pages with color ink. Thus I could quip that we'd spiced up the product mainly for the sake of its digestibility. Nothing I wrote elicited more comments from my colleagues, and everyone thought it was a gas.

BOB BARTLEY AND I TALKED SO INFREQUENTLY I remember every occasion with total clarity. I even recorded these encounters in my journal, for posterity and biographers. The first time, he asked if I would proofread something he'd written. I didn't want to proofread his editorials. I thought they were wrong; copyediting would only prettify their idiocy. But you don't say no to the Most Important Person at the World's Most Important Publication. The people who usually proofread his editorials were gone for the day, and apparently I was the only one left in the office who knew how to repair dangling participles.

I read the editorial. I disagreed with everything in it, but it was powerfully written. That's the thing about his editorials—even if you thought they were wrong, they left you with no doubt about what he believed. He claimed to craft everything he wrote for optimal "muzzle velocity," as he once put it to another journalist. His style owed a great deal to the old yellow journalism of personal invective, and he didn't just savage his opponents' ideas, he aimed to obliterate his opponents altogether.

I told him I saw only one mistake. It wasn't a split infinitive, it was an unsplit word. He'd made the words "pipe dream" one word, with no space between them. I told him it should be two words, according to *Webster's New World Dictionary*, which was my authoritative source in such matters.

He told me he didn't care what *Webster's New World Dictionary* said. It was his editorial, and he wanted "pipe dream" to be one word. He said I should delete the space I'd inserted between "pipe" and "dream."

I did.

I never edited anything by Bob Bartley again.

We talked a second time a few months later. I was standing in the hallway with some colleagues from the Leisure & Arts page, and Bob Bartley approached us. He said he had two doctors' appointments on the Upper East Side of Manhattan the next day. He had a bit of leisure time to spare between them and wondered if there was any art at the museums on the Upper East Side that he ought to see.

I said, Yes, there's a wonderful show of Walker Evans photos at the Met. Anyone who cares about photography—or America—should see it if he can.

He said, Thanks, I may just go.

A few days later I met him in the hallway. I said hello. He did not say hello.

I said, Bob, did you see the Walker Evans show at the Met?

He stopped and looked at me. I wondered if I should have called him Mr. Bartley instead of Bob.

He said, Yes, I saw it.

What did you think? I asked.

It wasn't for me, he said. I stayed for five minutes and went to the Egyptian galleries.

After I thought about it for a while, his answer made sense. Walker Evans was the great documentarian of Depression-era Southern poverty; Bob Bartley was appalled by the very idea of poor people. In fact, he'd once said he didn't think there were any poor people left in America—"just a few hermits or something like that." (This quote can be found in the *Washington Post Magazine* of July 11, 1982.) On this issue Bob Bartley was the intellectual heir of an old American idea expressed most succinctly by the preacher Henry Ward Beecher: "No man in this land suffers from poverty unless it be more than his fault—unless it be his *sin*." For Bob Bartley, the agrarian pictures of Walker Evans and the homoerotic pictures of Robert Mapplethorpe were morally equivalent. Both depicted human beings in a sinful state of filth and degradation, and such images had no place in an American museum.

Of course I disagreed. Not only did I appreciate the unadorned honesty of Walker Evans's photographs, I'd grown up in a poor family myself. As a child, while living on a rented farm where we struggled to make enough money to feed ourselves, I'd stood in line with my mother for handouts of surplus government cheese. Pictures of people like us from the time of the Great Depression hung in many museums, a testament to certain unappealing aspects of the American experience.

Bob Bartley didn't believe the government should be in the cheese-handout business.

I never recommended a museum to Bob Bartley again.

The last time we spoke was on the day of his retirement. Dow Jones & Company required senior executives to retire at the age of 65. Bob Bartley was now 65, and would be replaced as editorial-page editor by Paul Gigot, who'd won a Pulitzer Prize for commentary and often appeared on the *News Hour with Jim Lehrer* on PBS. Paul Gigot wrote signed columns that made him sound like a reasonable conservative, although some of his unsigned pieces hinted at a fear that the Boy Scouts might soon become a front group for initiating American boys in the fine art of fellatio. As for Bob Bartley, he would still write a weekly column called "Thinking Things Over," in which he would say the same things he'd been thinking for thirty years all over again.

I went to the men's room on my way out of the office. Bob Bartley was in the men's room too. We stood next to each other, pissing contemplatively, not talking. When I was finished, I went to the sink and washed my hands. When Bob Bartley was finished, he looked at himself in the mirror and walked out.

We boarded the elevator together. His hair was mussed, and his shoulders were slumped. He had the doleful look of an injured horse aware it's about to be taken out to pasture and shot.

Big day, I said.

Yes, he said.

I thought a little flattery might cheer him up.

Now Paul gets to see how hard you work, I said.

That's right, he said. And I have to figure out how to disengage. Not sure how to do that. Maybe stop coming into the office every day.

Yes, I said, I can imagine that would be a challenge after thirty years.

He didn't respond.

As we got off the elevator, I tried to think of something else to say to him—something serious and substantive, something intelligent people may have wanted to ask him but were too afraid—since I knew I'd probably never speak to him again. I considered asking him how he felt about an in-depth study of his editorials by the *Columbia Journalism*

Review, which found that his page "rarely offers balance, is often unfair, and is riddled with errors—distortions and outright falsehoods of every kind and stripe." I thought to ask whether he felt in any way responsible for the death of Vincent Foster, the White House counsel to Bill Clinton who'd killed himself shortly after Bob Bartley ran a series of harsh attacks on his integrity. A note found in Foster's briefcase expressed anguish that "the *WSJ* editors lie without consequence." After Foster's death, Bob Bartley's editorials hinted darkly that Foster may have been murdered for knowing too much about Whitewater, and called for a special counsel to investigate. "The American public is entitled to know if Mr. Foster's death was somehow connected to his high office," Bob Bartley wrote. I sort of thought the American public was entitled to know if Bob Bartley thought Vince Foster's death was somehow connected to irresponsible journalism.

In my heart I knew it was the wrong day for such questions, so I didn't ask them. We parted ways in the lobby, him heading for his limousine to Brooklyn, me for the subway to Queens.

Well, I said, enjoy your newfound freedom.

I'll try, he said.

I never talked to Bob Bartley again.

RAY'S MOST PROVOCATIVE MOVE HAD NOTHING to do with my writing for the paper. It was March of 2000 when he hatched a plan to get a poet friend of his the exposure Ray thought he deserved. The poet's name was Frederick Seidel. I'd never heard of him. Ray said he was brilliant but had a devil of a time getting started on a poem; in fact, in a review in the late '80s, Ray had called him "gifted" but "maddeningly unproductive." Ray's plan was to give Seidel a monthly deadline, as if he were a journalist. Seidel would write one poem a month under the title of that month, and not only would the deadline prod him into action, the paper would offer him an audience the size of which most poets could only dream.

Here, Ray said, reaching into his bookshelves. Take these home with you. See what you think.

I spent that evening with three of Seidel's collections. Some of it was profoundly beautiful, like this, from a poem called "The Childhood Sunlight" in his book *The Cosmos Poems*:

The parking lot washed clean smells sweet,
And even has a rainbow that
A little girl tiptoes toward,
Hoping not to frighten it.

The neighbor's dog that won't go home
Is watching her—which she can't see—
With naked eyes of love and awe.
She feels that way herself sometimes.

When you are sure that you're alone,
Tell yourself to not be sure.
This universe is not the first.
The other ones are not the same.

This sort of poem was atypical, though. Generally, reading Seidel was like riding shotgun on a Ducati racer, a machine that appeared on occasion in his poems. It was a ride full of quick, propulsive accelerations and sudden, screeching stops, hairpin turns into spooky alleys. In addition to racing bikes there was a lot of racy sex. Ray could not have picked a poet better suited to offend the sensibilities of wealthy born-again housewives or buttoned-up corporate executives in the great American suburbs.

Seidel began to write his poems, one per month, and it was my job to typeset them, make sure all the italics and em-dashes and capital letters were just so, and then fax him a copy to inspect and approve. When we talked on the phone, I felt like a peasant in the presence of royalty. He always said, Phil, my boy, how are you? in the most sophisticated voice I'd ever heard, very precise, as if his concourse was always with the gods but he'd learned English as a second language, so he could order lunch. He always wanted to know what I thought of his poems. What could I tell him? I was on deadline every time, late in the afternoon, with headlines to write and stories to cut to make them fit on the page. I didn't have time to read his poems the half-dozen times required for me to make sense of them, at least not until the next morning, before the hum of the day began, when I could sit with a cup of coffee and my feet up on my desk, reading the paper. What I really wanted to say was,

Dude, I can't believe you're getting away with this in the *Wall Street Journal*! You're my hero! But that seemed a little lowbrow, so I'd focus on a particular stanza whose music I liked, or a particular image that struck me. I think he believed I wasn't a very bright boy, at least when it came to poetry.

My favorite of his early poems for the paper was this:

DECEMBER

My Christmas is covered
With goosepimples in the cold.
Her arms are raised straight
Above her head.

She turns around slowly in nothing but a
Garter belt and stockings outdoors.
She has the powerful
Buttocks of a Percheron.

My beautiful with goosepimples
Climbs the ladder to the high diving board
In her high heels
And ideals.

The mirror of the swimming pool is looking up at her
Round breasts.
She bounces up and down
As if about to dive.

In her ideals, in her high heels,
The palm trees go up and down.
The mirror of the swimming pool is looking up at her
Bikini trim.

The heated swimming pool mirror is steaming
In the cold.
The Christmas tree is on.
A cigarette speedboat cuts the bay in two.

It rears up on its white wake.
Ay, Miami!
Ninety miles away
Is Mars.

The cigarette smokes fine cigars,
Rolls hundred dollar bills into straws.
My Christmas
Is in his arms.

Around this time, not surprisingly, there began to be heard complaints about the political thrust and aesthetic sensibilities of the Leisure & Arts page. Ray mentioned these complaints to me in elliptical asides to conversations on other matters. He'd apparently been forwarded some scolding letters to the editor about a couple of Seidel poems; he'd also received a memo from the publisher that raised concerns about propriety and sound judgment. But Ray was a cagey fellow, a survivor of twenty years in the shadow of Bob Bartley, and although I never asked him how he responded to questions about his stewardship, I imagined him pointing out that the occasional kerfuffle proved he had his readers' attention, and besides, every single day a big fat ad appeared on his page. For a time he managed to forestall these complaints, in part because the paper was awash in ad money.

We were, after all, in the midst of millennial madness. The paper was both an avid chronicler of and an unashamed participant in that madness, and, as Bob Bartley believed and Ray was aware, a balance sheet deep in the black was the strongest proof of virtue known to man.

One month after I was originally hired, the Dow Jones Industrial Average—comprising thirty companies chosen by the managing editor of the *Wall Street Journal*, and the only company brand more recognizable than the paper itself—closed above 10,000 for the first time. The paper celebrated this triumph with a banner six-column headline, only the third in its history, the others having blared the news of the bombing of Pearl Harbor and the start of the first Gulf War.

Nearly a year to the day after I began at the paper, the NASDAQ index reached an all-time high of 5048.62. The paper was so fat with "New Economy" advertising, the average subscriber—white, fiftyish, male, with a yearly household income of around $200,000—risked a hernia when he lifted it off his doorstep. Management went on a hiring spree to fill an ever greater need for copy to offset the profusion of ads. The paper started whole new daily sections and weekly supplements to cash in on the marketing lucre of companies that would go belly up before the end of their second fiscal year. I knew colleagues who charged every movie, every dinner, every new book and bottle of high-end wine to company credit cards. Ad managers at the paper's sister publication, *Barron's*, were known to keep open tabs at various Manhattan bars and to entertain clients by expensing the cost of strippers. No one in the suites batted an eye. Company executives merely increased their own bonuses.

It was easy to be carried along on this tide of giddy prosperity, writing the occasional mildly subversive piece in order to cling, however tenuously, to what I thought of as possession of my soul. I made a salary in the mid-five figures, more than I'd ever expected. I saw jazz for free in any club I cared to visit, just by calling ahead and telling the doorman where I worked. When I wrote a profile of a writer or a musician—Larry McMurtry, Jacky Terrasson—the subject's latest book or album shot up the Amazon.com sales charts. I was moving units and meeting people.

I built a sweet little home library from the spoils of the weekly book give-away, the constant pile of review copies sent by American publishers to the paper's book editor. Not only did I make off with reissued classics from Penguin and the Modern Library, I surreptitiously swiped the volumes on Tantric sex, slipping them into my bag when no one else was looking. When uttered during the exchange of small talk at parties in Brooklyn tenements—always somewhat sheepishly, and only in response to direct questions about my gainful employment—the words *Wall Street Journal* had the effect of a good narcotic: dilated pupils, flushed face, and what seemed to me a perceptible slackening of sexual inhibition, which, being a shy and socially awkward young man from the American Middle West, I never did take advantage of, despite my collection of books on Tantric sex.

YOU MIGHT THINK AN INSTITUTION WHOSE VERY PURPOSE is to chronicle the ups and downs of American capitalism would be uniquely prepared for a swing in the business cycle. You would be wrong. Dow Jones was notoriously bad at running its own business. In the late 1980s, the company bought an electronic provider of business information called Telerate for $1.6 billion. It was meant to compete with Reuters and Bloomberg. A decade later, Dow Jones sold Telerate at a loss of almost $1 billion. The "New Economy" boom was a chimera that allowed the company to believe it might escape the shackles of Telerate and its other dumb decisions, but the sudden implosion of tech stocks in 2000 hit Dow Jones like a blow to the solar plexus. Ad revenue plummeted. Managers at the flagship editorial product in the universe of Dow Jones brands were instructed to streamline their budgets. In the summer of 2001 we received a memo that said the following:

> Dear Ladies and Gentlemen, We are discontinuing the ownership and maintenance of indoor plants throughout our office space in the World Financial Center. This, combined with a similar move in South Brunswick, will save Dow Jones more than $40,000 per year. The WFC plants will be moved from the floor space to the reception areas for disposal late Friday, July 13, 2001. If you would like to take over the maintenance of any of the plants, please attach a yellow Post-It note with your name to a visible part of the plant container. Or, if you would like to take any of the plants home, please feel free to do so before this Friday, July 13. If you have any questions, please call Bill at ext. 2072.

This was a novel form of outsourcing, I thought.

At the time, Dow Jones CEO Peter Kann made almost $2 million per year in salary and bonuses. In his glory days, he and his wife had been known to fly to the office in a helicopter from their home in New Jersey. I wondered whether the company could just get rid of Peter Kann—it had already jettisoned the helicopter—and save the indoor plants. But I never said anything.

Other ominous things happened. We received a memo from Peter Kann in which he wrote: "As most of you know, over the last two or three weeks we have done a number of layoffs in some parts of the company as part of a cost-reduction program aimed at getting our expense structure aligned with reduced revenues in a tougher business environment."

Peter Kann had once been a journalist. In the 1970s, he'd won a Pulitzer Prize as a foreign correspondent for the *Wall Street Journal*. Moving to the suites had hampered his prose style, but if you read the memo enough times, you could figure out what he was saying. He was saying: Since I'm not giving back my $1 million New Economy bonus, lots of people are getting canned.

He later named his wife to replace him as publisher of the *Wall Street Journal*, a rather brazen bit of nepotism, I thought, but I never said anything.

Things got worse. There were rumors the company would be sold to a competitor—the *New York Times*, the *Washington Post*. In the office cafeteria, reporters and editors had the look of a dwindling tribe being hunted by enemies with superior weaponry.

The atmosphere around the office was clammy with portents of doom.

ON SEPTEMBER 11, 2001, just as I finished my breakfast, I received a call from a friend who knew I lived without a TV. She told me, in a voice wracked with panic, that the World Trade Center towers had been hit by airplanes. I put on my suit jacket, left my apartment, and ran to take a subway to work. I was on journalistic autopilot: there was a big story, I was within reach of the story—it was right across the street from my workplace—and therefore I had a professional obligation to get there, even if I usually copyedited pieces about theater and books.

Partway to the office, my train stalled and didn't move for an hour and a half. Since we were stuck underground, we had no way of knowing the severity of the situation downtown, and when at last we were discharged from the train at Union Square, I continued the journey to the office on foot. In Chinatown, the police had cordoned off the streets. No one was allowed any farther, not even people with press credentials, although as a copy editor I had none. The towers, in the distance, were swathed in a cloud of black smoke; my mind, still stuck in a news vacuum, couldn't comprehend that they no longer stood, though in fact they'd fallen an hour earlier. I did know that if I was truly intent on getting to the office, I had but one choice. I would have to reenter the subway system and walk through the tunnel.

The entrance to the Franklin Street station was blocked with yellow police tape. I looked at the campaign posters for the mayoral primary taped to the railing above the stairs and thought that, if I crossed the police line, there would be no one to rely on thereafter but myself. What else was I going to do? Go back to my apartment and listen to the radio? Sit in a bar and watch TV? I lifted the tape, descended the stairs, and, in a last gesture toward civilized norms, swiped my MetroCard instead of jumping the turnstile.

No trains were running. No clerk was in the token booth. I waited a few moments to see if a train or an MTA worker would appear, but there was only an otherworldly quiet. With no one around to stop me, I lowered myself onto the tracks and began walking through the tunnel, creeping through the dark, careful to avoid touching the third rail. Not even the squeak of a rat marred the silence. It would be the only time I ever heard nothing in New York.

Ten blocks later, when I emerged into the light of the Chambers Street station, the platform was coated in dust, and ahead in the tunnel I heard water rushing with a sound like a waterfall. A couple of cops were in the station, hanging around the token booth. I waited until they wandered off and then I climbed the stairs to the street.

I emerged a couple of blocks north of the towers, or at least where the towers had been. The streets were covered in ash and office paper. A cop stood alone in the middle of the street, watching a burning building, which I later learned was World Trade Center number seven. I walked over and stood next to her, both of us mesmerized. After a couple of minutes she looked at me. That building's probably gonna go, she said, you might wanna get outta here. She didn't order me to leave. She seemed to assume I wouldn't. She merely offered it as a suggestion, one among a series of options, take it or leave it.

I picked up a discarded dust mask, put it on my face, and began to make my way around the smoking rubble, through streets flooded with greenish-yellow water, or ankle-deep in fine gray powder. After crossing the West Side Highway, I entered the World Financial Center complex. The Winter Garden's glass roof was shattered in places, and the palm trees in the courtyard were pallid with ash. All the shops were empty. I climbed the emergency fire stairs in World Financial Center building number one. No one was there. The office had long been evacuated and was now, at least on our floors, coated in a thin gritty film blown in through shattered windows, though the computers still ran on the power of a backup generator. It was one of the most unnerving moments of my life, standing in that empty newsroom, wondering where everyone was, hoping none of my colleagues had been hurt or killed, all those computers humming with no one in front of them.

I went to my cubicle, blew the ash off my keyboard, set a newspaper over the dust on my chair, and logged on to my computer. I sent an e-mail message to the entire editorial-page staff, asking if anyone needed anything, since I'd made it to the office. Those equipped with laptops immediately wrote back and told me I was crazy, that I ought to get the hell out as soon as possible, there was nothing I could do for them there, a gas line might explode, the building might collapse. I logged off and walked around the office, inspecting the damage, hoping I might see another editor or reporter, but I couldn't find a soul. I circled back to my desk. The telephone rang. It sounded a little forlorn, even spooky, amid the unusual silence of the newsroom. I picked it up. It was my mother calling from Texas, where she was on vacation with my father, watching TV with her in-laws. I could tell from her voice that she was frightened witless. I said I was fine, we were just now evacuating the building, all was well, I would call her later in the afternoon. I hung up and checked my voice mail. There were eight frantic messages from friends wondering if I was OK. I got up and went to the men's room. I felt strangely reverent as I stood before the urinal, aware I'd be the last man to piss there that day, that week, perhaps even that month or longer. (Almost a year, as it turned out.) The irony, when I thought about it later, was vertiginous: I had less devotion to the idea of the paper than anyone else I knew there, yet I'd risked my safety to get to the office—and for nothing. I was useless. Little did I know that if I'd wanted to be of help I should have hopped a ferry to New Jersey, where a small group of editors was putting together a paper that would win a Pulitzer Prize for spot news coverage. The *Wall Street Journal* of September 12, 2001 carried the fourth banner headline in the paper's history, in letters nearly as big as the masthead: "TERRORISTS DESTROY WORLD TRADE CENTER, HIT PENTAGON IN RAID WITH HIJACKED JETS."

I suppose I could tell you how the smoke smelled when I went back outside, like every kind of burning you've ever known in your life rolled into a cloud so thick you could almost drink it. I suppose I could tell you how, if you looked up at the bright blue sky a certain way, you could see waves of tiny glass crystals floating and sparkling like iridescent sea anemones. I could also tell you about the firefighters standing around in the smoke and dust, holding their heads in their hands, some of them openly weeping. But I've already gone on too long. Hundreds of people have written about what they saw on September 11, and I have nothing to add to that. I was just another of the spectators at the edge of the rubble, vainly hoping for a call to join a rescue operation, snapping pictures with a digital camera I'd snatched from the office, as if to preserve in some other form, outside of myself, the ghastly images searing themselves on my brain.

PHOTOGRAPH BY PHILIP CONNORS, 2001

FOR A FEW WEEKS WE ALL COMMUTED to the cornfields of New Jersey. We put out the paper in a makeshift newsroom, a windowless bunker in the training wing of Dow Jones corporate headquarters near Princeton. My commute was two hours each way. All the stories in the paper concerned terrorism. It felt, for a time, utterly asinine to have anything to do with leisure and art. After anthrax turned up in the offices of other media companies, all of our mail was heat-steamed. The men in the mail room sorted it with masks on their faces and rubber gloves on their hands. They looked like lab technicians working with a deadly poison. When we opened our mail, the envelopes crackled like dead leaves, and the ink on the letters was often illegible.

When Danny Pearl was abducted in Pakistan, most of us had an inkling how that would end, and we braced ourselves. On the day we learned he'd been beheaded, you could have heard a pin drop in the office. He was entirely the wrong man for such a fate—not to say that there's a right man. But he wasn't a slavering ideologue. He wasn't a rhetorical flamethrower who never left the home office. He was out in the danger zones, seeking to understand radical Islam by talking to the people who were shaping and being shaped by it. He believed in the democratic function of storytelling. The horror of his end was unimaginable.

About the only thing in the paper that made much sense anymore was Fred Seidel's monthly poem. All the news stories tracking terrorist recruiting and finances, all the editorials calling for "total war" and a full-scale invasion of the Middle East in response to September 11—all of it seemed inadequate next to those eight monthly stanzas of Seidel's verse, which, by adopting a voice as twisted and chilling as that of Osama bin Laden, seemed to get much closer to the heart of the matter. Consider this, written two months after the attacks:

I don't believe in anything, I do
Believe in you.
Down here in hell we do don't.
I can't think of anything I won't.

I amputate your feet and I walk.
I excise your tongue and I talk.
You make me fly through the black sky.
I will kill you until I die.

Thank God for you, God.
I do.
My God, it is almost always Christmas Eve this time of year, too.
Then I began to pray.

I don't believe in anything anyway.
I did what I do. I do believe in you.

Down here in hell they do don't.
I can't think of anything we won't.

How beautiful thy feet with shoes.
Struggling barefoot over dunes of snow forever, more falling, forever, Jews
Imagine mounds of breasts stretching to the horizon.
We send them to their breast, mouthful of orison.

I like the color of the smell. I like the odor of spoiled meat.
I like how gangrene transubstantiates warm firm flesh into rotten sleet.
When the blue blackens and they amputate, I fly.
I am flying a Concorde of modern passengers to gangrene in the sky.

I am flying to Area Code 212
To stab a Concorde into you,
To plunge a sword into the gangrene.
This is a poem about a sword of kerosene.

This is my 21st century in hell.
I stab the sword into the smell.
I am the sword of sunrise flying into Area Code 212
To flense the people in the buildings, and the buildings, into dew.

Needless to say, some of the paper's more sensitive readers were not impressed; they wrote letters calling for Seidel to be silenced.

Now when I wrote for the paper the stakes were higher, and with Fred as my, dare I say, moral example—the writer willing to say the unsayable in a climate of fear and self-censorship—I chose my subjects with the utmost care. Still, it was easier as a journalist: I could simply quote the words of others, neither condoning nor condemning. In a profile of jazz trumpeter Dave Douglas, for instance, I quoted him calling the war in Afghanistan "more of a trade show and a laboratory for new weapons than a real pursuit of those who perpetrated that horrible event" already known by the glib shorthand 9/11. But it wasn't as if the paper's readers were looking to the arts pages for an understanding of what would soon be christened "the war on terror."

° ° °

ONCE WE WERE RESETTLED IN MANHATTAN, in temporary quarters above the West Side's Garment District, the men in the suites looked again for places to squeeze. Eventually a quarter of the company's workforce would be cut, and Ray was among the downsized. At the age of 60, after twenty years of service to the company, he was strong-armed to take early retirement and replaced by a guy who'd cut his journalistic teeth at the Moonie-owned *Washington Times.*

Soon it came to pass that I was given a chance to work on pieces of greater world-political import. I was sitting with my feet on my desk, editing a story about a play in Chicago, or an opera in Seattle, or maybe the lovely wines of the Alsace region, when Paul Gigot asked me to follow him into an empty conference room. He invited me to sit. He cut straight to the chase. He said that for the foreseeable future I would continue copyediting for the Leisure & Arts page, but beginning in a few weeks I would do the same for the editorial page of the *Wall Street Journal*'s European edition.

I told him I didn't want to do that.

He seemed surprised.

I told him I didn't agree with the politics of the editorial page.

He said he wasn't asking me to write things I didn't believe. He was asking me to delete serial commas and repair split infinitives.

I told him I didn't want my hands on the editorial page in any way, shape, or form.

He said he would give me a small raise in compensation for my added responsibilities, and I would do whatever he told me to do.

I thanked him for the raise.

I'D BEEN KEEPING ANOTHER FOLDER, much like the one I'd called "GREATEST HITS OF PUBLIC RELATIONS," though the title on this one said "FULL-BLOWN INSANITY ON THE *WSJ* EDITORIAL PAGE," and when I got home that night I opened it and read the clippings again, slowly. I'd known all along there would come a time when I'd need them, and this was it.

On the day after September 11, an editorial stated: "We are entitled to presume that this is the work of the usual suspects—Saddam Hussein," et cetera. Two days later a news article in the paper reported that "U.S. Officials Discount Any Role by Iraq in Terrorist Attacks." The editorial page was unruffled. "Reports are swirling," an unsigned piece announced the next day, "that Saddam Hussein was also behind last week's attacks.... Deposing Saddam has to be considered another war aim."

Immediately the paper called for speeding up the deployment of a missile-defense shield—an effort that seemed to me like that of a man lifting an umbrella over his head while being pelted in the groin by snowballs. An unsigned editorial argued that the first and most important steps in combatting terrorism ought to include capital-gains tax cuts and immediate drilling for oil in the Arctic National Wildlife Refuge. The same editorial stated: "Throughout history the periods of greatest military innovation have been wars." Apparently war was needed, because military innovation was needed, because nineteen men had flown passenger jets into three buildings on American soil. I didn't follow the logic but I could see where this was headed. On and on it went. October 4: "Clinton Didn't Do Enough to Stop Terrorists," under the byline of pain-med addict Rush Limbaugh. October 9: "The Answer to Terrorism? Colonialism."

It was clear they wouldn't stop clamoring until they got themselves an honest-to-God war.

AFTER I'D READ ALL THE CLIPPINGS and put them aside, I was acutely aware that if I removed so much as one serial comma from an editorial calling for "total war," capital-gains tax cuts, or the despoiling of wildlife refuges in response to September 11, I would find myself chin-deep in a malodorous swamp of hypocrisy. Here, finally, was the line I could not cross. After promptly using my allotment of yearly paid vacation, I served notice that I was terminating my employment at the World's Most Important Publication, ostensibly to finish work on a novel which did not, in fact, exist. Instead I arranged to take a seasonal job in New Mexico as a fire lookout with the United States Forest Service, an appropriate form of penance, really, that involved alerting authorities when trees caught on fire, so crews could come and save them. Alone in my little bird's nest, my glass-walled perch, I would add almost nothing to the gross national product, which was gross enough on its own.

I met Paul Gigot in the hallway on my second-to-last day of work, and we had one last brief conversation, which I recorded in my journal for posterity and biographers.

Well, it's been a pleasure, I said.

Yes, good luck, he said.

At least now you'll be able to hire someone who's more enthusiastic about working on the editorial page, I said.

Oh, we decided against that plan, he said. Whoever replaces you is only going to work on Leisure & Arts.

He stepped onto the elevator and threw me a little half-wave, half-salute.

So long, he said.

As a connoisseur of subterfuge and stealth—having earned my original position at the paper by means of manipulating the truth to my advantage—I at first had the thought that I'd been purged by my own hand, by a pure ballsy bluff. This would have been in keeping with the whole mind-set of the editorial page—that their enemies were treasonous, despicable, and deserving of nothing but ruination and contempt. But I didn't want to think like them. I didn't want to share in their paranoia. I wanted, in the end, to believe it had been miscommunication, a mistake. (Oh, it had been a mistake all right, from the very beginning.) And anyway, what was I going to do? Take it back? Beg him to let me stay?

So long, I said, waving. +

PHOTOGRAPH BY PHILIP CONNORS, 2001

PAULINE SHAPIRO, *MODERN* (TOP) AND *CONTEMPORARY* (BOTTOM), 2006, B/W PHOTOGRAPHS, 6 X 4". COURTESY OF THE ARTIST.

AMERICAN WRITING TODAY: A SYMPOSIUM

In Number Three, n+1 *published a long reply from the critic James Wood to our earlier commentary on contemporary fiction and criticism. With all the ardor of critics facing an honored adversary, the Editors sat down to reply to Wood's reply and to clarify the position of a progressive and confrontational literature against his defense of the permanent and humane. Editor 1 wrote an elegant manifesto—which Editor 2 crossed out before writing his own. Editor 3 cut the result in favor of his contrary views. Editor 4 mixed in. This went on for weeks. Once everyone had deleted everyone else's unique position, we were left with a magisterial 250-word thank-you note.*

We concluded that perceptions of contemporary writing and criticism differ so sharply, even among those who think they agree, that the last word should not belong either to Wood or to us. We've asked a number of critics and writers representing different areas of contemporary writing to join the debate.

Contributors were asked about the conditions of production of new work; its character and traits; and the figures and creators who have most influenced each field. In an era of repetition, we need a debate on American writing that begins where academic histories end.

ELIF BATUMAN
SHORT STORY & NOVEL

"NEW AMERICAN FICTION" IS, to my mind, immediately and unhappily equivalent to new American short fiction. And yet I think the American short story is a dead form, unnaturally perpetuated, as Lukács once wrote of the chivalric romance, "by purely formal means, after the transcendental conditions for its existence have already been condemned by the historico-philosophical dialectic." Having exhausted the conditions for its existence, the short story continues to be propagated in America by a purely formal apparatus: by the big magazines, which, if they print fiction at all, sandwich one short story per issue between features and reviews; and by workshop-based creative writing programs and their attendant literary journals. Today's short stories all seem to bear an invisible check mark, the ghastly imprimatur of the fiction factory; the very sentences are animated by some kind of vegetable consciousness: "I worked for Kristin," they seem to say, or "Jeff thought I was fucking hilarious." Meanwhile, the ghosts of deleted paragraphs rattle their chains from the margins.

In the name of science, I recently read from cover to cover the Best American Short Stories anthologies of 2004 and 2005. Many of these stories seemed to have been pared down to a nearly unreadable core of brisk verbs and vivid nouns. An indiscriminate premium has been placed on the particular, the tactile, the "crisp," and the "tart"—as if literary worth should be calibrated by resemblance to an apple (or, in the lingo of hyperspecificity, a McIntosh). Writers appear to be trying to identify as many concrete entities as possible, in the fewest possible words. The result is celebrated as "lean," "tight," "well-honed" prose.

One of the by-products of hyperspecificity is a preponderance of proper names. For maximum specificity and minimum word count, names can't be beat. Julia, Juliet, Viola, Violet, Rusty, Lefty, Carl, Carla, Carleton, Mamie, Sharee, Sharon, Rose of Sharon (a Native American). In acknowledgment of the times, the 2004 and 2005 volumes each contain exactly one Middle East story, each featuring a character called Hassan. I found these names annoying, universally so. I was no less annoyed by John Briggs or John Hillman than by Sybil Mildred Clemm Legrand Pascal, who invites the reader to call her Miss Sibby. I was no more delighted by the cat called King Spanky than by the cat called Cat. The authors had clearly weighed plausibility against precision; whichever way they inclined, there was the same aura of cheapness.

Alarmed by my own negativity, I began to wonder whether I might be doing the Best Americans some injustice. For a point of comparison, I reread a few stories by Chekhov, who is still the ostensible role model for American "short-fiction practitioners." (Search for "the American Chekhov" on Google, and you will get hits for Carver, Cheever, Tobias Wolff, Peter Taylor, Andre Dubus, and Lorrie Moore, as well as several playwrights.) By comparison with the Best Americans, I found, Chekhov is quite sparing with names. In "Lady with Lapdog," Gurov's wife gets a few lines of dialogue, but no name. Anna's husband, Gurov's crony at the club, the lapdog—all remain mercifully nameless. Granted, Chekhov was writing from a different point in the historico-philosophical dialectic: a character could be called "Gurov's wife," "the bureaucrat," or "the lackey," and nobody would take it as a political statement. The Best Americans are more democratic. Every last clerk, child, and goat has a name.

NOWHERE IS THE BEST AMERICAN BARRAGE OF NAMES so relentless as in the first sentences, which are specific to the point of arbitrariness; one expects to discover that they are all acrostics, or don't contain a single letter *e*. They all begin in medias res. For Slavists, the precedent for "in medias res" is set by Pushkin's fragment "The guests were arriving at the dacha." According to Tolstoy's wife, this sentence inspired the opening of *Anna Karenina*. Would Pushkin have managed to inspire anybody at all had he written: "The night before Countess Maria Ivanovna left for Baden Baden, a drunken coachman crashed the Mirskys' troika into the Pronskys' dacha"? He would not.

Pushkin knew that it is neither necessary nor desirable for the first sentence of a literary work to answer the "five w's and one h." Many of the Best Americans assume this perverse burden. The result is not just in medias res, but in-your-face in medias res, a maze of names, subordinate clauses, and minor collisions: "The morning after her granddaughter's frantic phone call, Lorraine skipped her usual coffee session at the Limestone Diner and drove out to the accident scene instead"; "Graves had been sick for three days when, on the long, straight highway between Mazar and Kunduz, a dark blue truck coming toward them shed its rear wheel in a spray of orange-yellow sparks." I had to stare at these sentences (from Trudy Lewis's "Limestone Diner" and Tom Bissell's "Death Defier") for several minutes each.

A first line like "Lorraine skipped her usual coffee session at the Limestone Diner" is supposed to create the illusion that the reader already knows Lorraine, knows about her usual coffee, and, thus, cares why Lorraine has violated her routine. It's like a confidence man who rushes up and claps you on the shoulder, trying to make you think you already know him.

Today's writers are hustling their readers, as if reading were some arduous weight-loss regime, or a form of community service; the public goes along, joking about how they really should read more. Oprah uses identical rhetoric to advocate reading and fitness; Martha Nussbaum touts literature as an exercise regime for compassion. Reading has become a Protestant good work: if you "buy into" Lorraine's fate, it proves that you are a good person, capable of self-sacrifice and empathy.

Another popular technique for waylaying the reader is the use of specificity as a shortcut to nostalgia—as if all a writer has to do is mention Little League or someone called Bucky McGee, and our shared American past will do the rest of the work. Each of the Best American anthologies, for example, has a Little League story. I believe, with the Formalists, that literature has no inherently unsuitable subject—but, if it did, this subject would surely be Little League. Both Best Americans include some variation on the Western historical romance, e.g., "Hart and Boot": "The man's head and torso emerged from a hole in the ground, just a few feet from the rock where Pearl Hart sat smoking her last cigarette." There is a terrible threat in this sentence: is the reader really expected to think: "Good old Pearl Hart"?

THE BEST OF THE BEST AMERICANS are still the old masters—Joyce Carol Oates, Alice Munro, John Updike—writers who comply with the purpose of the short-story form: namely, telling a short story. This sounds trivial, but isn't. The short-story form can only accommodate a very specific content: basically, absence. Missing persons, missed opportunities, very brief encounters, occuring in the margins of "Life Itself": when the content is minimalist, then it makes sense to follow the short-fiction dictates: condense, delete, omit.

Novels, like short stories, are often about absences; but they are based on information overload. A short story says, "I looked for x, and didn't find it," or, "I was not looking anymore, and then I found x." A novel says, "I looked for x, and found a, b, c, g, q, r, and w." The novel consists of all the irrelevant garbage, the effort to redeem that garbage, to integrate it into Life Itself, to redraw the boundaries of Life Itself. The novel is a fundamentally ironic form; hence its power of self-regeneration. The short story is a fundamentally unironic form, and for this reason I think it is doomed.

When the available literary forms no longer match the available real-life content, the novel can reabsorb the mismatch and use it as material. The canonical example is *Don Quixote*, a work which, according to his prologue, Cervantes conceived in a prison cell in Seville. Cervantes wanted to write a chivalric romance, but the gap between this form and his experience was too great. Then he broke through the formal "prison": he made the gap the subject of a book.

Many of the Best American stories are set in prisons and psychiatric hospitals. They are trying to break out, but I don't think they will. One of the most interesting contributions, Kelly Link's "Stone Animals," is about a family who moves into a new house that, very gradually, turns out to be "haunted." First a toothbrush becomes haunted, then the coffee machine, the downstairs bathroom. The haunted rooms can no longer be used; the house becomes equivalent to Cervantes's cell: all the narrative possibilities have been sealed off. The family has less and less space in which to live. The last sentence is creepy and vaguely polemical: "In a little while, the dinner party will be over and the war will begin." Indeed, let the war begin.

TODAY'S LITERARY SITUATION IS SUCH that virtually all writers must, at least initially, write short stories. Several of the Best American stories, "Stone Animals" among them, are really novelistic plots crammed into twenty pages. The short story is trying to expand into a catchall genre. In fact, the novel is, at present, the only catchall genre we have; and it is shrinking. Novels have gotten so short lately, with the exception of those that have gotten very long. Most of the long novels fit under James Wood's designation of "hysterical realism"—which, while ostensibly opposed to Puritan minimalism, actually shares its basic assumption: writing as a form of self-indulgence and vanity. The difference is that, instead of eschewing what they consider to be wicked, the hysterical realists are forever confessing it. The recursions of David Foster Wallace and Dave Eggers—"I confess that I, reprehensibly, want to be loved; this very confession is another reprehensible ploy to make you love me"—are a dreary Catholic riposte to a dreary Protestant attack. It would be equally productive for every writer to start every book with an apology for cutting down trees which could have been put to better use building houses for the homeless; followed by a second apology for the paper consumed by the first apology.

Here is the crux of the problem, the single greatest obstacle to American literature today: guilt. Guilt leads to the idea that all writing is self-indulgence. Writers, feeling guilty for not doing real work, that mysterious activity—where is it? On Wall Street, at Sloane-Kettering, in Sudan?—turn in shame to the notion of writing as "craft." (If art is aristocratic, decadent, egotistical, self-indulgent, then craft is useful, humble, ascetic, anorexic—a form of whittling.) "Craft" solicits from them constipated "vignettes"—as if to say: "Well, yes, it's bad, but at least there isn't too much of it." As if writing well consisted of overcoming human weakness and bad habits. As if writers became writers by omitting needless words.

American novelists are ashamed to find their own lives interesting; all the rooms in the house have become haunted, the available subjects have been blocked off. What remains to be written about? (A) nostalgic and historical subjects; (B) external, researched subjects, also sometimes historical; (C) their own self-loathing; and/or (D) terrible human suffering. For years, Lorrie Moore has only written about cancer. In *A Heartbreaking Work of Staggering Genius*, Dave Eggers implies that anyone who does not find his story compelling is unsympathetic to cancer victims; he describes in gory detail how he plans to eviscerate such people, how he plans to be eviscerated by them in turn. For writers who aren't into cancer, there is the Holocaust, and of course the items can be recombined: cancer and the Holocaust, cancer and American nostalgia, the Holocaust and American nostalgia.

For the last combination, you can't do better than Michael Chabon's *The Amazing Adventures of Kavalier & Clay*, with its memorable opening sentence:

> In later years, holding forth to an interviewer or to an audience of aging fans at a comic book convention, Sam Clay liked to declare, apropos of his and Joe Kavalier's greatest creation, that back when he was a boy, sealed and hog-tied inside the airtight vessel known as Brooklyn New York, he had been haunted by dreams of Harry Houdini.

All the elements are there: the nicknames, the clauses, the five w's, the physical imprisonment, the nostalgia. (As if a fictional character could have a "greatest creation" by the first sentence—as if he were already entitled to be "holding forth" to "fans.") Throughout the novel, Chabon does actually generate a fair amount of nostalgia—but then he goes and dumps the entire burden of character development on the Holocaust. Joe Kavalier is a master magician, an escape artist, a writer of fabulous comic books, a charismatic and fundamentally mysterious person—until, that is, Chabon explains to us that the reason Kavalier became an escape artist was to escape from Hitler. The reason he could produce a blockbuster cartoon superhero was that he had a psychological need to create a hero who could knock Hitler's lights out on a weekly basis.

W. G. Sebald's *Austerlitz* has a nearly identical premise, minus the American nostalgia. It, too, features an authorial stand-in, à la Sam Clay, who finds in some other person a source of narrative. Austerlitz is, like Kavalier, a human enigma who disappears for years on end, leaving trails of clues; in the end, the "solution" is nothing other than the Final Solution. Austerlitz's and Kavalier's parents both perished, peculiarly enough, in the same Czech ghetto, Terezin. Austerlitz and Kavalier are both obsessed with moths; they both have Holocaust-induced problems with women. (Austerlitz's one love affair, with a woman called Marie, fizzles out during a trip to Marienbad, where he is oppressed by an inexplicable terror; later we understand that it's because he is actually Jewish, and his parents were killed in the Holocaust, and once they went on vacation to Marienbad.)

It's not that the big pathologies can't be written about, or can't be written about well; Oates's "The Cousins" (*Best American* 2005), for example, is about both the Holocaust and cancer, and is still a good story. It consists of the letters between two cousins, aging women: one survived the Holocaust and became a famous writer, the other grew up in America and became a retiree in Florida. They were supposed to meet as children, but never did. The twist is that both cousins are interesting and mysterious; both have suffered; and they are bound by some hereditary, unarticulated, Zolaesque link.

Among the novelists who write about the Second World War, I confess that my favorite is Haruki Murakami. Murakami's *The Wind-Up Bird Chronicle* opens with a small, personal mystery—the disappearance of the narrator's cat—which turns out to be related to how the narrator never really understood his wife, who also disappears. The two disappearances are subsequently linked to the occupation of Manchuria, the torture killing of a Japanese soldier, and various other personal and global events. The narrator is moved by all the big historical themes that pass through the novel, but he suffers more immediately from the loss of his cat—as in Brueghel's picture of the farmer ploughing his field while Icarus drowns. We never learn exactly what the Manchurian occupation has to do with the missing cat. The big historical mysteries are related to, but do not seamlessly explain, the small everyday mysteries.

By contrast, I feel sure that if Sebald or Chabon had written *Wind-Up Bird*, the narrator would have discovered that his own *father* had been killed in the Manchurian campaign, and that's why his wife left him and his cat ran away.

Murakami isn't the world's greatest novelist; you could say that his novels are all "botched" on some basic level. The turns in the plot are often achieved unsatisfyingly, by dreams, or by a character deciding to sit in the bottom of a well; the narrators receive an inordinate amount of oral sex from bizarrely dressed middle-aged women. But botchedness also gives Murakami's novels a quixotic dynamism. Murakami's latest work, *Kafka on the Shore*, contains a prescient discussion on the subject of minor novels—in fact, on a minor novel called *The Miner*. *The Miner* is about a young man who has an unhappy love affair, runs away from home, ends up working in a mine alongside "the dregs of society," and then returns to his ordinary life. "Nothing in the novel shows he learned anything from these experiences, that his life changed, that he thought deeply now about the meaning of life or started questioning society," Murakami's narrator explains: it is completely unclear why the author decided to write *The Miner*—which makes it particularly valuable to the narrator, by virtue of its very openness.

Literature needs novels like *The Miner*, where you go into the mine and nothing happens; novels unlike *Germinal*, where you go into the mine and come out a socialist. Perhaps modern American literature has kept the worst parts of Zola. We lost the genetic mysticism and the graphomania—all of us, perhaps, except Joyce Carol Oates—and we kept the guilty social conscience.

Dear American writers, break out of the jail! Sell the haunted house, convert it to tourist villas. Puncture "the airtight vessel known as Brooklyn New York." Write long novels, pointless novels. Do not be ashamed to grieve about personal things. Dear young writers, write with dignity, not in guilt. How you write is how you will be read.

STEPHEN BURT
POETRY

I DO THINK THERE IS A SHARP historical boundary between postwar or midcentury American writing and "contemporary" writing, what we have now. The boundary is about 1973, the year of the oil shock, the beginning of the Watergate scandal, a time by which the civil rights movement and the New Deal Democratic Party had definitively dissolved into a collection of narrowly focused movements and interest groups, and the utopian and antinomian impulses of the '60s had lost their credibility and momentum.

Before about '73, you have clearly defined generations in opposition and a clearly defined "mainstream" whose poets and novelists command public attention, a liberal consensus both in literature and in political life. Afterward you have none of those things—instead, you have a broader range of stylistic and cultural options. Few writers of consequence after 1973 think there's a powerful cultural "center" in the way that there seemed to be in '55 or '65. Even fewer people think that there's one unified thing called a "counterculture" that can turn the world on its ear. Race changes in American writing, too. The early 1970s give you more visible self-conscious groups of Asian-American and Latino writers, and debates about black writing emerge more easily from an authentic-inauthentic dipole, in part because so many more black writers get published.

It's a commonplace that postwar readers considered Robert Lowell the incarnation of their cultural "center," the guilty liberal continually surprised by the inutility of inherited forms. John Ashbery represents contemporary (post-'73) literature about as well as Lowell represents '45 to '73. He doesn't think he's going to change the political world, he doesn't give art a consistent ethical mission (though he understands that other people do), he doesn't compete with the novel or film, he envisions the limitless circulation of limitless information, and he doesn't mind that not all that many people understand him.

The Ashbery era includes the present. I'd still tell readers to start with *Houseboat Days*, but he's as representative now as he was in the 1970s—otherwise he wouldn't be the hidden hand, the stylistic innovator, two or three paces behind half the young poets of consequence I read. We're still a culture where poets feel marginal but encouraged by the coteries they form (when I say "we" I mean writers and readers of poetry), still a culture opposed to sharp, durable value judgments, and still a culture in which information circulates faster than we can process it. All those preconditions show up in Ashbery. As they affect poetry, I'm tempted to say that the cultural changes of the Reagan era and the dot-com boom, the differences in stylistic possibilities between 1979 and 2005, are small potatoes compared with the differences between 1966 and 1974.

THAT SAID, THE FIRST THING we need to remember about the writing of the present moment is that there is a lot more of it—more writers, more books published, more ways to publish, more overlapping but non-coextensive audiences for more kinds of writing—than ever before in American history (even if the percentage of the population who care about "serious writing" has also gone down). I think it's very difficult to tell a single useful story that explains most of the qualities in the contemporary writing I value. "The writing of the present moment" includes Ashbery, Rae Armantrout, Mary Jo Bang, Jorie Graham, Terrance Hayes, Juan Felipe Herrera, Thylias Moss, D. A. Powell, Donald Revell, Kay Ryan, Liz Waldner, and Greg Williamson. No single story can explain them all; and those are just some American poets I like—if you add in American novelists, comic-book writers, playwrights, and essayists, or Canadians, Australians, and South Asians writing in English, et cetera, the picture becomes too big to see.

POETRY IS NOW A MINORITY ART FORM, in some ways like contemporary "classical" music—fortunately, poetry is much cheaper to perform, distribute, and reproduce.

We sometimes hear that poetry is a protected sphere, one where production doesn't depend on consumption, where the creators get rewarded for making something whether or not anyone wants it. In that sense, yes, poetry has become a protected sphere, but there's nothing wrong with that—it just means that some select group of people who really want to make it can get paid to make it, and can therefore go on making it, thinking about it, and helping other folks make it, without having to keep an unrelated day job in order to pay for strollers, cribs, and health insurance (which is one reason why people stop making rock music). I don't know that the discipline of the marketplace would improve the product, if that's what "unprotected" means.

I can tell you a story about what status poets and poetry no longer have, but I can tell you only one useful story about what status most talented poets do have: most of them, once they have published a book or two, depend financially on institutions of higher education. That institutional dependence has certainly affected poets, but not in predictable or consistent ways. Kay Ryan, Donald Revell, and Joshua Clover all teach in universities, but academic culture has affected Clover and Revell very differently. I'm not sure if it has affected Ryan at all.

Almost all useful poetry criticism in this country since the '60s has come either from academics or from people committed to "little magazines," zines, websites, and so on. Neither source has diminished since the '60s—both have expanded. "Successful" poetry books have much lower sales numbers than moderately successful indie-rock records, unless you want to confine "successful" to Billy Collins, Seamus Heaney, Sharon Olds, and about five other people (not counting poets who are famous for something besides their poetry, such as Jimmy Carter). How many copies did *Houseboat Days* sell? What about Lyn Hejinian's *My Life*? C. D. Wright's *String Light* and *Tremble*?

Again, the shape of everything seems to change in the early '70s, after which university presses and small presses become more important, New York trade houses—for poetry—steadily less so, and the audience for the serious realist novel "tunes out" poetry more and more.

It seems to me that poets later responded by "tuning out" the contemporary novel, which is a gigantic mistake: when you're quite young, you may need to read so much poetry, and so many novels by dead people, that you have no time left for novels by the living; by the time you're 30 you should at least try.

Many poets don't seem to read literary fiction regularly, and of course many readers and writers of literary fiction don't read current poetry—sometimes they feel as separate as rock and jazz. Not only the audiences but the goals of poetry and fiction have diverged: the one increasingly resists, and the other remains defined by, the telling of stories. Conversely, there are particular fiction writers whom poets seem to read, and there's a sort of subgenre of poets' fiction (which often looks like an update on '60s-style metafiction), such as Pamela Lu's superb

Pamela: A Novel. Laura Kasischke comes to mind as someone equally capable in poetry and "mainstream" literary-realist fiction, equally at home in both genres.

I think that a lot of poets and poetry critics feel some disappointment that various waves of culturally and politically ambitious poets in the modern United States did not obviously cause cultural change. There's no *Uncle Tom's Cabin* of 20th-century poetry. The closest you get for this country in this century might be Ginsberg's *Howl,* or some portion of the Black Arts Movement, or Adrienne Rich's *Diving Into the Wreck* (published, not coincidentally, in 1973). But being disappointed that poets don't have that kind of political efficacy seems to me almost as silly as being disappointed that your dentist can't fix your car. It's a mistake to look for poetry to bear political efficacy in that way.

What stalled sometime before 1973 was the habit of reading the literature of the past on the assumption that it held lessons for the present. Too many contemporary poets (especially those who are not also critics) act as if literature began and ended with the living, or else with William Carlos Williams and Gertrude Stein. We're now in our third generation of poets who either don't know the premodernist past, or who know it in sketchy, autodidact ways. A whole lot of cool devices and formal precedents simply are not available to them.

Most poets need to get out more: not to write for a larger audience—I'm not recommending a "dumbing down," an attempt at poetic journalism (such as British poetry undertook for most of the '90s)—but to pay attention to more of the world. The interest in documentary, in nonfictional information, that has turned up in poets otherwise as different as Albert Goldbarth and Cole Swensen in the past ten years perhaps speaks to this need: we want something, anything, to counter the pressure that "theory" puts on "the self."

WHAT MODELS DO INTERESTING POETS now follow? In poetry: Wordsworth, Dickinson, W. C. Williams, Rainer Maria Rilke, Stevens, Moore, Stein, Bishop, Langston Hughes, the Federal Writers' Project, Paul Celan, Ashbery, Creeley, Adrienne Rich, James Wright. Again, "today" begins around 1973. Influential models whose careers began later than that, and who seem to matter to talented young poets, include C. D. Wright, Harryette Mullen, Lyn Hejinian, Louise Glück, Denis Johnson, and Lucie Brock-Broido. James Merrill seems to have more fans all the time, and he deserves them; he's one of my favorite poets. And yet he feels like the end of something, not the beginning.

Whom should more poets follow, or at least contemplate? Again, in poetry: George Herbert, Christopher Smart, pre-1937 W. H. Auden, Basil Bunting, Donald Davie, James K. Baxter, post-1964 Robert Lowell. Among living writers, maybe Thylias Moss, Juan Felipe Herrera, Laura Kasischke, Liz Waldner. In poetry criticism: William Empson, Donald Davie.

What current modes clog the pipeline and tire me out? (1) Quasi-automatic writing and a kind of comic quasi-surrealism, especially when the author wants to be winning, funny, "entertaining," and shocking at the same time. (2) Slack free-verse autobiography; chatty anecdote without interesting form. (3) Endless xeroxes of '50s formalist poems, copies of Anthony Hecht and Howard Nemerov. (4) "Spirituality," which, pursued as a primary goal, tends to make poems sound like bad translations.

Most poets today are writing either for a coterie of readers they know personally, who want to participate in the social circulation of new work (rather than in the rereading of old work), or else (in part) for an academic market in which the more you publish (as long as it's in semiprestigious venues), the better your chances for tenure and promotion.

Both paradigms encourage overproduction. Younger poets, in particular, seem to rush things, to make public ten pounds of cookie dough when, had they waited, they might have had five pounds of tasty cookies. I don't know what any of us can do about that, and for certain poets whose work is supposed to sound "raw" (such as Kasischke and Waldner) that may not even amount to a disadvantage.

Anything you can do 100 times in 100 poems without learning a new trick isn't worth doing more than twice. Sense is harder than nonsense; order is harder than disorder. But, as Stevens said, "A great disorder is an order"; as Dickinson said, "Much madness is divinest sense / To a discerning eye."

CALEB CRAIN
ACADEMIC CRITICISM

As a teenager, I kept a close watch over my response to music. I considered and reconsidered everything about my aesthetic development with Victorian earnestness. I had conflicting aims—to become a writer and to suppress acknowledgment of my sexuality—and so I required careful management.

I am more reckless in middle age. In the past few years I have become a fan—something I never dared in high school. In love with Belle & Sebastian, Ben Kweller, the Decemberists, and Sufjan Stevens, I have visited band websites and subscribed to band listservs. I have bought T-shirts, posters, tour-only EPs, and expensive compilation albums from Spain with only one track I can bear to listen to. I have saved old issues of British music magazines with very limited circulations. I have avidly read essays in praise of my beloveds, no matter how insipid the style or recondite the detail. I have learned about lossless file codecs in order to trade live shows. I have listened to songs recorded by one of my beloveds before he came up with his distinctive sound—before he was any good, in fact—and I have treasured them, because they are, after all, his. I have memorized lyrics. I have found obscure, probably unintentional parallels between the lyrics of one beloved's songs and those of another. I have wondered about my beloveds' personal lives and inspected their songs for hints of autobiography. If a love of mine sings a song by another musician, I buy that musician's album too, and try to like it.

Last year, at the height of my madness, I realized what it resembled: academic literary criticism of a great author. There is the same impulse to collect and the same reluctance to judge. To prove how much you love *Moby-Dick*, you read *Mardi*; to prove your love for Colin Meloy, you listen to Tarkio. There is the same fetishistic interest in variant performances and the same concern for the artist's preservation from commercial interference. The fan becomes proficient in FLAC and BitTorrent; the critic learns about copy-text and the Hinman collator. You follow Sufjan to Denison Witmer, and you follow Melville to Richard Henry Dana Jr. There is the same attenuated alliance, genial but emulous, with fellow lovers. And there is the same tolerance for trivia and banality in criticism, so long as the critic shares in your worship, and especially if he furthers it. In theory this tolerance is mystifying, since its ultimate source is an aesthetic distinction that feels particularly acute. In practice, however, it is not mystifying at all. Anyone who undams his love will end up swimming in it.

I DON'T SEE ANYTHING WRONG with fandom. However, I could only call it a science in jest, and I don't think I would ever become so confused as to think of it as morally worthy. Yet such claims were made for the academic study of literature in the course of the 20th century. To be sure, they were made after its origin in fandom was disguised by abstraction. I hasten to say that I don't think academic criticism was improved by the transformation, which I attribute to envy of science and to scorn of the fan's childlike dependency. Mere love was unprofessional; something more sophisticated was required, something less natural.

To return to music for a moment, I have been describing amateurism. For professional criticism, I have to turn to venues with the potential for disrespect, even of my idols: *Pitchfork, Blender, Spin.* Critics at these publications don't mind saying that one artist is better than another, or one album better than another. Occasionally they even try to say how. They are like ancien régime courtesans—promiscuous and expert. I hate them for their cruelty, but I go to their salons to learn refinements in love, and to meet new lovers.

The academic critics who have left amateurism behind offer no such compensations. They will not help you find new love. Northrop Frye scorned mere evaluation in 1957 as "a form of consumer's research." This is too bad, because it is the only thing most people want from a literary critic, and it is unreasonable to believe he would be competent to provide much else. For politics, ethics, philosophy, linguistics, and religion, there are more authoritative sources. With a belletristic verve that his successors rarely risk, Frye also proclaimed that "Everyone who has seriously studied literature knows that the mental process involved is as coherent and progressive as the study of science." This is nonsense, meant to flatter the professors of the Sputnik era. *Naked Lunch* is not coherent, nor is the experience of reading it; *Wuthering Heights* is an adventure in regression. Literature has nothing to do with science; it is a matter of taste.

Taste may be educated, but not with the kind of education that the most ambitious academic critics set out to provide today. In 1940, F. Scott Fitzgerald complained to his daughter that it had been hard for him to earn the money for her Vassar tuition and added that "I hate to see you spend it on a course like 'English Prose since 1800.' Anybody that can't read modern English prose by themselves is subnormal—and you know it." If literature is an art, even its difficulties should be attractive. You don't need a professor to explain indie rock to you; you especially don't need a professor to explain the songs you don't understand. And if a professor did explain them, you wouldn't think that it was the explanation that made them more worthy.

There is not any, or not much, distortion in the common assessment of the value of a degree in music appreciation or art history. But literature is thought to be improving, somehow, and the study of literature inherently valuable. The editors of *n+1* have mocked this conceit in their disparagement of the "Reading Crisis." I am afraid the crisis is real, but I agree the conceit is ridiculous. Literature is only an art. It is of course a good thing, but if it improves you, it does so the way health, riches, and elegant clothes do. It's not at all clear to me that the propagation of a taste for it needs to be federally subsidized—or that it deserves a niche in Ivy League schools, while courses in wine-tasting are consigned to institutions that place circulars in plastic bins on street corners. I'm afraid a part of me will always regard academic literary criticism the way Jeffersonians did a standing army, as an institution whose existence distorts discussion of whether it should exist, by frightening its enemies and corrupting its supporters. Long ago, Matthew Arnold argued that literature should be taught universally because it was the lingua franca of the powerful classes, and it was only fair to give everyone a chance to learn it. A lovely, democratic notion. But today the lingua franca of power is cable television, sports, and film. If a 19-year-old wants to improve his future income, he should join the college golf team. He need not read Keats.

As it happens, there is a scientific idea of literature—indeed, of all the arts. In a series of books, Ellen Dissanayake has proposed that the arts, like all aspects of human nature, are a result of evolution. Dissanayake believes that the arts evolved because they promote group solidarity; others have suggested that their function is sexual display; still others, that they render appetitive certain processes of intellectual development. The theory has not been worked out fully, especially not with regard to literature. But academic literary critics do not see an opportunity; the county school boards of Kansas are not more hostile to Darwin. I fear that some of the very few literature professors who have taken up evolution have muddled their layers of analysis: it is silly to say that novels are better when their plots exemplify evolutionary truths. Very likely, if a scientific idea of literature like Dissanayake's turns out to be true, it will be useless in evaluation. Science infers that the brilliant stripes of a male toucan's bill show off its lifelong resistance to infection; it is up to the female toucan (and the more aesthetically inclined male toucans) to notice that a band of orange beside a band of green is particularly fetching.

In toucans and in humans, criticism serves love, and in love, you want either devotion or connoisseurship—or both, if you can get it. You do not want knowledge, especially; it is not seductive. In a seminar last spring, my students noticed that ignorance was Melville's breakthrough. In *Typee* and *White-Jacket,* the narrators know everything about the worlds they describe and tell it in measured doses. But Ishmael, the hero of *Moby-Dick,* doesn't know anything that matters. He has learned about whaling exhaustively, but he has done so because he doesn't understand it. He knows something is wrong with Ahab, which he tries to describe, but he can't quite capture that, either; a piece always eludes him. And it is his ignorance that makes the novel come alive—the fact that he isn't hiding his ignorance but sharing it, elaborating it, inviting the reader to improve on it.

The journalist and the therapist know better than to finish other people's sentences. The critic, too, should accept and make use of his ignorance. He should also respect it in his readers. Not a science, criticism cannot justify specializing. Because literature is not coherent and not progressive, there is no point to criticism that only reaches professionals. The critic should at least be able to imagine a layperson who would read her work with pleasure—a fan, for example. A lover of some kind, in any case; someone who reads for mere pleasure rather than in the pursuit of tenure, which economists call rent-seeking.

And this is the root of the confusion and distortion: fewer people do read for pleasure these days. Statistics compiled by the Pew Research Center for People and the Press, the National Endowment for the Arts, and the National Center for Education Statistics indicate that Americans are steadily abandoning the practice of reading. In 1991, 56 percent of Americans surveyed had read a newspaper the day before; in 2004, 42 percent had. In 1992, 54 percent of Americans surveyed had read a work of imaginative literature the year before; in 2002, 46.7 percent had. In 1992, 15 percent of adults tested were literate enough to contrast two newspaper editorials; in 2003, 13 percent were. In the last five years, the number of books sold in America has decreased by 9 percent, although the population has grown. In the press, these dismal numbers are received with either deprecating chuckles or panicky hysteria about the internet. In fact the trends predate the internet. If a technology is to blame, it is probably television; cue the deprecating chuckles, because we're too sophisticated to become tiresome about television. But even if we weren't that sophisticated, it wouldn't change anything. In the history of the world, no one has ever hectored a free adult out of his pleasures. America is moving from a culture of reading to a culture of streaming. Even if averse to statistics, you may see the cultural signs. Fantasy books for children are popular among adults. Though it hampers communication, PowerPoint is ubiquitous, because it renders invisible the distinction between businesspeople who can write and those who can't. The young and fashionable wear glasses that are almost exclusively rectangular, stylish for watching movies but a handicap for books. The *New York Times* Styles section finds it strange and risible that Eric Anderson, brother to filmmaker Wes, protects his books with transparent plastic covers.

A RISING TIDE MAY FLOAT ALL BOATS, but a receding one grounds first those with the deepest keels. Literary scholarship has a particularly deep one. Perhaps academics stopped writing for laypeople because laypeople stopped reading them, rather than the other way around. What if the academic literary critics were atwitter in the 1990s because they were the canaries in the coal mine? What if the prestige of literature in that decade was dropping even more quickly than the prestige of literature professors, and they feuded grandiloquently in the hope that bluster would keep them aloft? The one real power they still held, that of sorting the young, it was unseemly to threaten with. After all, in the age of PowerPoint, it is not obvious that adolescents need to be credentialed according to the quality of the essays they write about books. Academic literary criticism faces, I suspect, a correction. Like the study of classic

Greek and Latin literature a century ago, it will probably dwindle in size and set down its burden of moral significance. In losing interest in seduction it seems to anticipate this fate; the group shows no wish to reproduce or recruit. Perhaps there will be compensations for the loss. To borrow a metaphor from Boswell's *Johnson*: "The flesh of animals who feed excursively, is allowed to have a higher flavour than that of those who are cooped up. May there not be the same difference between men who read as their taste prompts and men who are confined in cells and colleges to stated tasks?"

RODRIGO FRESÁN
AMERICAN WRITING ABROAD

THE FIRST IMPRESSION OF UNITED STATES FICTION seen from abroad—especially if you compare it with the space occupied by writers of other nationalities in bookstores and publishers' catalogs—is that it's everything. The eternal classics (the enormous road that begins with Hawthorne and arrives at John Updike), the quality best-sellers and the generation made up of names like Jeffrey Eugenides, Jonathan Lethem, Heidi Julavits, Rick Moody, David Foster Wallace, George Saunders, Dave Eggers, Michael Chabon, Mark Costello... they're all on Spanish shelves. The same goes for Paul Auster (a best-seller in Spain and France and Buenos Aires) or James Ellroy (one of Roberto Bolaño's favorite writers, after Philip K. Dick) or Pynchon, Denis Johnson, DeLillo, Paula Fox, Jim Shepard, Didion, Ford, Baxter, or Wolff. This doesn't prevent a more expert reader from detecting incomprehensible absences, like those of Ann Beattie or Stephen Dixon or Ben Marcus, or, until very recently, John Cheever—who had disappeared completely and now is enjoying a revival of influence in the Spanish-speaking world.

It's clear that in the US today the very lively and substantial ghosts of John Cheever and Donald Barthelme can live together without any problem—sometimes even inside the same writer. If the avant-garde impulse toward constant forward progress has been lost, it is because one can now write moving in all directions at once. Digression is like a creed. When I think of a further evolution of books as objects, or of the novel as a genre, I always remember what Kurt Vonnegut (one of my favorites) wrote about the books of the alien inhabitants of the planet Tralfamadore:

> They were little things . . . Billy couldn't read Tralfamadorian, of course, but he could at least see how the books were laid out—in brief clumps of symbols separated by stars. . . . "Each clump of symbols is a brief, urgent message—describing a situation, a scene. We Tralfamadorians read them all at once, not one after the other. There isn't any particular relationship between all the messages, except that the author has chosen them carefully, so that, when seen all at once, they produce an image of life that is beautiful and surprising and deep. There is no beginning, no middle, no end, no suspense, no moral, no causes, no effects. What we love in our books are the depths of many marvelous moments seen all at one time."

One other thing is clear: North American literature continues to be a great world power and possesses an energy and an influence that other incarnations of the American Dream no longer exhibit. I'm referring, for example, to a lot of "Made in the USA" cinema, or to the integrity of certain presidents.

VIEWING LATIN AMERICAN LITERATURE from the US side, I'm not really sure that García Márquez—a writer whom I admire unreservedly—is the most influential writer for Latin Americans. It's clear that, like Borges, he is among the best known and most respected. But perhaps García Márquez has been more influential among foreign editors, critics, and readers. The result is a reflex, or almost zombie-like compulsion, to demand Latin American novels that contain many large families and flying people and jungles and volcanos. Roberto Bolaño, on the other hand, serves as the perfect missing link between the Boom writers and those of my generation. Bolaño is an author who without renouncing classic South American literary themes—torture, exile, lyrical wandering, dictators, and writers as heroes—rearranges and reinvents them, presenting them in a way that's new and freakish and mutant. In this way Bolaño would come to be like the older brother we get to know and love.

Manuel Puig is, it seems to me, the other great presence. He is the other most vivid of our ghosts, standing to the side of the Boom and,

I think, especially novel and useful for Latin American young people (and nearly ex-young people, like me). Puig—whom the Japanese like to define as "the Argentine Haruki Murakami"—is like a practical instruction manual that clearly explains to us how to write a grand political novel without sacrificing the "pop" factor (*The Kiss of the Spider Woman* or the Warholiana of *Eternal Curse on the Reader of These Pages*); how to be David Lynch well before David Lynch (*The Buenos Aires Affair*); how to revisit the novel of initiation (*Betrayed by Rita Hayworth*); or how to play with genres and nobly take pleasure in their miscegenation (*Heartbreak Tango* and *Pubis Angelical*). More than anything, Puig is important in a literature like that of Latin America today, which still rejects the popular as a suspicious element, almost like an extraterrestrial virus—even as we struggle to understand writing in an epoch saturated with visual support, even as writing offers an idea of reality that doesn't have to contend with the unreal. To sum it up, a dead Puig is much more lively than most.

With the little that is translated into English, I fear that there's a lot for US readers to learn. Fortunately, writers like Enrique Vila-Matas or Alan Pauls or Alberto Fuguet or Edmundo Paz-Soldán have been translated recently or are in the process of being translated. Which doesn't prevent us from lamenting the absence in English of authors and books like the Colombian Juan Gabriel Vásquez (author of *Los Informantes*, a political novel à la Philip Roth) or *El Huésped*, by the Mexican Guadalupe Sánchez Nettel (a contemporary urban novel that in some way connects with the dead characters of Juan Rulfo's *Pedro Páramo*), or the Mexican Juan Villoro's *El Testigo*, or the stories and novels of the Spanish Javier Calvo. And I don't even want to think of the scant diffusion of classics like Adolfo Bioy Casares or Felisberto Hernández. To be honest, it's disconcerting.

I think everyone must choose his own models. There's no reason to submit to Stalinist tendencies. The truth is that it doesn't make sense for García Márquez imitators to keep cropping up, in just the same way that it would be a bit sad if we were to detect an increase in writers emulating Roberto Bolaño. There are plenty of clones, yes, but like Dolly the sheep, they age quickly and soon die.

In the Hispano-American world, literary supplements are ever more focused on publishing greater numbers of reviews in as little space as possible. The reviews begin sounding like slogans and synopses. There aren't many publications that publish long essays on literary matters, and the ones that exist (*La Tempestad* and *Letras Libres* in Mexico, *El Malpensante* in Colombia, *Gutierrez* in Chile, *Sibila* and *Revista de Libros* and *Lateral* in Spain) are limited in circulation and readership. It's true that recently there's been an ample boom in a crossbred literature combining fictional and essayistic forms. I'm thinking here of W. G. Sebald, the Argentine Ricardo Piglia, and the Spaniards Enrique Vila-Matas and Javier Cercas. Maybe that's an outlet for impulses that have otherwise been thwarted by the popular reviews and the academy, which is preoccupied with dead authors or with promulgating its own canon.

There's something finally terrible about naming names—praise by inclusion and censure by omission. The last things I read were Russell Banks's *The Darling*, an advance copy of Philip Roth's *Everyman*, David Foster Wallace's new book of essays, and right now I'm reading the manuscripts of new unpublished novels by Javier Calvo and Juan Gabriel Vásquez. And in between reading one thing and the next, I'm writing another novel of my own. I'm always more and more convinced that writing is nothing more than a slightly modified form of reading. Or maybe we write because otherwise the reading would never stop.

—Translated by Joshua Brau and J. D. Daniels

KEITH GESSEN
MONEY

HOW MUCH MONEY DOES A WRITER NEED? In New York, a young writer can get by on $25,000, give or take $5,000 depending on thriftiness. A slightly older young writer—a 30-year-old—will need another $10,000 to keep up appearances. But that's New York. There are parts of this country where a person can live on twelve or thirteen thousand a year—figures so small they can be written out. Of course it depends.

My wife and I moved to New York after college, at 22. We lived in Queens and paid $714 for a one-bedroom apartment (inherited, complete with artist's installation, from my friend, the poet and founder of

Ugly Duckling Presse, Matvei Yankelevich). That year, the two of us combined made $24,000. But we had a car, and on weekends we visited my father on Cape Cod. I wrote stories; she organized an art exhibit. We were young.

We moved to Boston. Our rent rose to $900, but it was 1999, even a doorpost could create "content," and I was more than a doorpost. I wrote long book reviews for an online magazine that paid 50 cents a word. Our combined income rose to $34,000. I failed to write stories, though; journalism took all my time.

The magazine collapsed with the NASDAQ. We moved to Syracuse and broke up. I stayed on at the MFA program, from which I received $15,000, then $12,000, then $15,000. I wrote stories again. My rent for a two-bedroom apartment was $435.

But I hated Syracuse. I moved back to New York; another friend, a novelist, sublet me his apartment. My rent was $550! That year, with what was left on my graduate stipend, plus some journalism and a book translation ($1,500), I made $20,000. I put $2,000 of it into *n+1*.

I turned 30. Things had to change. I moved to Brooklyn and signed a one-year contract for $40,000 to review books for *New York* magazine. This seemed like so much money that I immediately sent some to my ex-wife, who was back in Boston, with those high rents.

THERE ARE FOUR WAYS to survive as a writer in the US in 2006: the university; journalism; odd jobs; and independent wealth. I have tried the first three. Each has its costs.

Practically no writer exists now who does not intersect at some point with the university system—this is unquestionably the chief sociological fact of modern American literature. Writers began moving into the university around 1940, at the tail end of the Federal Writers' Project, which paid them to produce tour guides of the United States. The first university-sustained writers mostly taught English and composition; in the 1960s and especially the 1970s, however, universities began to grant graduate degrees in creative writing. Now vast regiments of accredited writers are dispatched in waves to the universities of Tucson and Houston, Iowa City and Irvine. George Saunders, the great short story writer and my adviser at Syracuse, told me he knew only two non-teaching writers in his generation (born around 1960): Donald Antrim was one and I forget the other.

The literary historian Richard Ohmann has argued that the rise of English departments in the 1890s, and their immediate bifurcation into Literature on the one hand and Composition on the other, emerged from a new economy's demand for educated managers. Our own age—born around 1960, and variously called post-industrial, informational, service/consumer—demanded copywriters and "knowledge workers" and, with the breakdown of traditional social arrangements, behavior manualists (*He's Just Not Texting You*). With the rise of Communications came the rise of Creative Writing, and the new split of English departments into Literature, Creative Writing, and (still) Composition. It's pretty clear by now where this is tending, and which hundred-year-old discipline will become less and less relevant from here on out. We do not have a reading crisis in this country, but we do have a reading comprehension crisis, and with the collapse of literary studies it will get much worse.

For now, the university buys the writer off with patronage, even as it destroys the fundamental preconditions for his being. A full-time tenure-track position will start at something like $40,000, increasing to full professorial salary—between $60,000 and $100,000—if the writer receives tenure. That's good money, plus campuses have lawns and workout facilities and health insurance; and there are summer vacations during which the writer can earn extra as a counselor at one of those writing camps for adults.

On the minus side, he must attend departmental meetings and fight off departmental intrigues. Worse, he must teach workshop, which means responding intelligently and at length to manuscripts. A writer who ignores his teaching duties in favor of his own writing will spend an inordinate amount of time feeling guilty; one who scrupulously reads and comments on student manuscripts will have a clearer conscience. But he will be spending all his time with children.

JOURNALISM'S PITFALLS ARE WELL KNOWN. Bad magazines vulgarize your ideas and literally spray your pages with cologne. Good magazines are even worse: they do style editing, copyediting, query editing, bullet-proofing—and as you emerge from the subway with your trash bag of books (a burnt offering to the fact-checker), you suddenly realize that you have landed a $6-an-hour job, featuring heavy lifting.

Yet the biggest pitfall of journalism is not penury but vanity. Your name is in print; it is even, perhaps, in print in the most august possible venue. But you are still serving someone else's idea of their readership—and their idea of you. You are still just doing journalism—or, worse, book reviewing. "What lice will do, when they have no more blood to suck," as the 19th century put it.

Odd jobs—usually copyediting, tutoring, PowerPoint, graphic design; I don't know any writers who wait tables but probably some exist—seem like a better idea in terms of one's intellectual independence. But these can lead to a kind of desperation. What if your writing doesn't make it? How long can you keep this up? You have no social position outside the artistic community; you have limited funds; you call yourself a writer but your name does not appear anywhere in print. Worst of all, for every one of *you*, there are five or ten or fifteen others, also working on novels, also living on peanuts, who are just total fakers—they have to be, statistically speaking. Journalism at least binds you to the world of publishing in some palpable way; the odd jobs leave you indefinitely in exile. It would take a great deal of strength not to grow bitter under these circumstances, and demoralized. Your success, if it comes, might still come too late.

AND THEN, OF COURSE, a writer can make money by publishing a book. But if it is depressing to lack social status and copyedit *UsWeekly*, it is even more depressing to talk about publishing—because *this* in fact is what you've worked for your entire life. Except now you will learn about the way of things. That book you wrote has sales figures to shoot for; it has a sales force to help it. And you are in debt. Publishers have always used anemic sales to bully their writers—Malcolm Cowley speaks of their claim that only after 10,000 copies sold could they break even; of course, says the good-natured Cowley, "they may have been displaying a human weakness for exaggeration." Now publishers come to lunch armed with Nielsen BookScan—to the same effect. The comical thing about this up-to-the-minute point-of-sale technology is how inaccurate everyone agrees it to be—"522 copies trade cloth" sold might mean 800 or 1,000 or 1,200, because so many bookstores don't participate. The less comical thing is that, as a measure of short-term popularity, it is all too accurate—*Everything Is Illuminated,* a work of Jewish kitsch, has sold, according to BookScan, 271,433 copies since it came out in 2002;

meanwhile Sam Lipsyte's *Home Land*, a scabrous work of Jewish humor, has sold 13,503 copies; Michael Walzer's *Arguing about War*, a work of political philosophy in the skeptical Jewish tradition, has sold 3,136. Of course one knew this; of course, one was not a fool; yet it's still hard to believe.

The very precision of the numbers numbs the publishers into a false sense of their finality. They cannot imagine a book good enough to have its sales in the future. Publishers wish things were otherwise, they will tell you; they would rather publish better books; *but the numbers don't lie*. The chief impression one gets of publishers these days is not of greed or corporatism but demoralization and confusion. They have acquired a manuscript; they know how they feel about it; they probably even know how reviewers will feel about it; but what about the public? Those people are animals. Over lunch the publisher tells his writer what it's like out there—"You have no idea." In fact the writer does have an idea: he lives "out there." But the publisher can't hear him; he is like an online poker player, always checking the computer. Nielsen BookScan rules.

"That equivocal figure," Pierre Bourdieu calls the publisher, "through whom the logic of the economy is brought to the heart of the sub-field of production." Yes, but he's all the writer's got. Is he looking tired? Poor publisher—last week he became so discombobulated by the "realities of the publishing industry" that he paid $400,000 for the first novel of a blogger. "He'll be promoting the book on his blog!" the publisher tells his writer over seared ahi tuna. "Which, you see, is read by *other bloggers*!" He is like Major McLaughlin, the cursed, hapless owner of the Chicago Blackhawks who once became so frustrated with his team's play, and successive coaches' failure to mend it, that he hired a man who'd sent him a letter about the team in the mail.

Once the book is published it only gets worse: the writer proceeds to the Calvary of publicity. Advances on first books vary—about $20,000 to $60,000 for a book of stories, though sometimes higher; between $50,000 and $250,000 for a "literary" novel, though also, sometimes, higher. Even the top figure—$250,000—which seems like so much, and *is* so much, still represents, on both sides of the writing and rewriting, the pre-publication and post-publication, about four years of work—$60,000 a year, the same as a hack lifestyle journalist in New York. But the costs! The humiliations! No one will ever forgive a writer for getting so much money in one lump—not the press, not other writers, and his publisher least of all. He will make certain the phrase "advance against royalties" is not forgotten, and insist the writer bleed and mortify himself to make it back.

Our forefathers the Puritans used to have, in addition to days of thanksgiving, "days of humiliation," when they prostrated themselves before God and begged for an end to their afflictions. "Before long," the intellectual historian Perry Miller wrote, "it became apparent that there were more causes for humiliation than for rejoicing." And so it is for the published author. The recent dressing-down of James Frey and his publisher by Oprah was an event that people at publishing houses gathered to watch on their office televisions as if it were the *Challenger* disaster. But this was just karmic revenge on publishers and their authors, who spend every day prostituting themselves: with photographs, interviews, readings with accordions, live blogs on Amazon.com. ("In the desert, it probably doesn't matter if the groundhog sees his shadow," went a recent entry by the novelist Rick Moody, a man who for all his sins is still the author of *The Ice Storm*, and deserves better than this. "Oh, by the way, the film *Groundhog Day* is one of my favorites!") Henry James complained about writers being dragooned into "the periodical prattle about the future of fiction." If only that were the worst of it. Consider the blurb: How humiliating that younger writers should spend so much time soliciting endorsements from more established writers, and how absurd that established writers should have to apologize for not providing them. If they'd wanted to be ad copywriters, they'd have done that, and been paid for it. But they once asked for those blurbs, too.

In the age of BookScan, only an unpublished writer is allowed to keep his dignity.

> Most writers lived as before, on crumbs from a dozen different tables. Meanwhile a few dozen or even a hundred of the most popular writers were earning money about at the rate of war contractors.
>
> —Malcolm Cowley on the book-of-the-month-club era, 1946

NOT LONG AGO I found a very interesting letter, a letter of advice, folded into one of my mother's old books. It was from the Russian émigré writer Sergei Dovlatov, to another writer, apparently newly arrived. My mother was a literary critic, but I don't know how that letter got into that book; in any case, it describes literary life here in the

States—the two clashing editors of the émigré journals, in particular, one of whom is pleasant and never pays, while the other is unpleasant and does. And so on.

Dovlatov had done his Soviet army service as a guard in a labor camp and wrote dark, funny stories about camp life—"Solzhenitsyn believes that the camps are hell," he wrote, explaining the difference between himself and the master. "Whereas I believe that hell is us." In 1979, he emigrated to Forest Hills, Queens, and began writing about the Russians there. He published some stories in the *New Yorker*, met often with his good friend Joseph Brodsky, and died, mostly of alcoholism, at the age of 48. He had liked it here. "America's an interesting place," Dovlatov concluded the letter that was folded, for some reason, into one of my mother's books. "Eventually you find someone to publish you. And you earn some money. You even find a wife. Things work out."

It's true. It's mostly true. And when you think of the long-standing idea of art in opposition to the dominant culture, if only by keeping its autonomy from the pursuit of money—the only common value great writers from right to left have acknowledged—you begin to sense what we have lost. Capitalism as a system for the equitable distribution of goods is troublesome enough; as a way of measuring success it is useless. When you begin to think the advances doled out to writers by major corporations possess anything but an accidental correlation to artistic worth, you are finished. Everything becomes publicity. How many writers now refuse to be photographed? How many refuse to sit for idiotic "lifestyle" pieces? Or to write supplemental reading group "guides" for their paperbacks? Everyone along the chain of production compromises a tiny bit and suddenly Jay McInerney is a guest judge on *Iron Chef.*

Publicity is not everything; money, also. Émile Zola was so concerned that he would lose his position in French artistic circles because of his incredible popularity that he formulated an aesthetic theory to explain his art. As recently as five years ago, Jonathan Franzen, too, worried lest his *Corrections* might seem to have fallen outside the main development of the American art novel, justified his work in aesthetic terms. (For doing so, for letting his guard down in public in tortured meditations on aesthetic value, Franzen has been made to pay, and pay again, by inferiors whose idea of good literature is German film.) Now writers simply point to their sales figures and accuse other writers of jealousy. Well, it's true. Everyone wants money, and needs it ("a woman must have money and a room of her own"). The only relevant question is what you are willing to do for it.

As for me and my $40,000, I recently went off contract at *New York* so I could finish a book of stories. My last article for the magazine, written as a freelancer, was about the New York Rangers. I received $7,000—a lot. Two weeks later I hurt my finger playing football on a muddy field in Prospect Park.

Sitting in New York Methodist, my finger worrisomely bent and swollen, I watched a man in scrubs yell into his cell phone: "1.2 million! Yeah! We put down 400!" The doctor had bought a condo.

This was the hand surgeon. After glancing briefly at my X-rays, the surgeon declared I needed surgery.

"How about a splint?" I said.

"No way."

I decided to negotiate. "I can afford $3,000," I said.

"I'm not a financial adviser."

"Well how much will it be?"

"$7,000."

Ha ha. It was like an O. Henry story: I wrote the article, they fixed my finger.

Except it wasn't like that, because I declined the surgery and kept the money. At my current rate of spending, it will last me three months. That should be enough. I hope that's enough.

VIVIAN GORNICK
MEMOIR & CRITICISM

I BELIEVE THAT LITERARY CRITICISM has most often been done best by writers themselves: Lawrence, Forster, Orwell; Auden, Woolf, Delmore Schwartz; Randall Jarrell. These are the critics whom I have prized; writers who wanted their criticism to do what imaginative writing (at its best) does: bring to consciousness the feeling intelligence trapped inside the wilderness of mind and spirit that we all stumble around in. I prize this kind of criticism because it understands intuitively that it is in an aroused consciousness that the solace and excitement of literature are to be found.

The critique must be as emotionally ambitious as the work it is interpreting if it is to give us back the taste of our own experience. The critic, like the writer, needs to perceive accurately the underlying influences in the culture and the way those influences exert themselves on the inner life of those on the ground. This is the double task for all who undertake to make or, in the widest sense, appreciate literature.

Looking back half a century, I see the same simple truths being addressed by American critics of an earlier time. In 1948, *Partisan Review* held a famous symposium on the state of American writing at a moment when the rise of middlebrow culture alarmed the pulse-taking editors of America's most highbrow magazine. In the welter of words that the symposium induced, two sets of remarks were made that still hold my attention. R. P. Blackmur said, "The elite of writers in America is at present... without adequate relation to the forces which shape or deform our culture.... If American middlebrow culture has grown stronger in this decade, I would suppose it was because the bulk of people cannot see themselves reflected in the adventures of the elite." And Lionel Trilling said, "There is in English what might be called a permanent experiment, which is the effort to get the language of poetry back to a certain hard, immediate actuality, what we are likely to think of as the tone of good common speech.... I like to think that our cultural schism may come to be bridged with the aid of a literature which will develop the experiment of a highly charged plain speech." Sixty years later, these words resonate for me. As a reader, what I look for in contemporary writing is an adequate relation to the forces that shape or deform our culture; as a writer, what I struggle to achieve is a sufficiently charged plain speech.

For me, the liberationist movements of the past forty years have been the single most powerful influence on the lives we are now living, because they drove an extraordinary wedge into the kind of coherent self-description that stabilizes a society. The current descent, in this country, into mad religiosity can be laid directly at their door. Class struggle is as nothing beside the anguish over race and sex, the real specters long haunting Western democracies. Not for the first time, the rise of feminism in America, coupled with the social progress of blacks (and this time around, gays as well), has unhinged the culture. At the end of the 19th century, the agitation caused by the great reform movements (abolition and women's rights), joined to the bitterness of the Civil War and the rise of Darwinism, caused thousands of people (many famous and accomplished) to retreat, in historic anxiety, into a belief in spiritualism (that is, communion with the dead) not so very far from where we are today. Now as then, it is as though one kind of civil order were dying, and another being born—in the midst of which we seem unable to tell the story of who we think we are; that is, to describe adequately, with intellect and emotion, how at sea we are within ourselves.

Sometimes during such a historical impasse, literature derives sufficient clarity to flourish; sometimes not. Right now, I think not. The gargantuan, language-swollen writing of the Pynchons and DeLillos declares itself an encompassing reflection of the tumult—and who knows? perhaps it is—but for me, this work is brilliant abstraction. In no way does it give me back the taste of my own experience. At the same time, the liberationist movements—which, as politics, have appealed urgently to me—have produced only novels and memoirs of testimony, not literature. I can think of no novel self-consciously feminist or gay that has achieved the kind of largeness that gives us back both world and self.

Yet not so long ago there came among us a European writer whose work, more than that of any contemporary American's, points a way out of the impasse with a kind of hybrid writing that fulfills brilliantly the demands made by Blackmur and Trilling; it also throws into question the future of well-defined literary genres. In the mid-1990s, W. G. Sebald, a German in his fifties who'd been living in England for thirty years, began publishing works of nonfiction often described as "unclassifiable" because his narratives are endowed with a power of suggestiveness we associate only with fiction.

For me, Sebald is transparently what I will call a memoirist. Every instinct for literature that I possess tells me that his is the odd but striking voice of a nonfictionist writing to puzzle out a position that will let him include himself in what he experiences as a ghost-ridden universe, at whose wavering edge he stands, alternately staring out at the emptiness beyond, and back at the silence of a world now peculiarly motionless. The "ghosts" are everything that has come before: the sum of human history, which the narrator connects to with an associativeness that is unaccountably deep, moving, mysterious. War, fable, architecture; medicine, philosophy, trade routes; old newspaper scandals, hotel lobbies, buried resort towns; literary unhappiness and political martyrdom—he remembers them all with an act of recall so strong that the connections transmute his feeling into hope rather than despair. The magic is in the transitions—as effective in Sebald as those in good poetry. They pull us directly into the marvel of human consciousness and, in a way that is hard to describe, succeed in giving us the courage to live with the fragmented civilization that is ours to endure. Everywhere in Sebald, in writing clear as water, we have the paradox of a silence and an emptiness that under the writer's calm, unafraid gaze become infused with richness and excitement. If bleakness is what we have inherited, then bleakness is what we must engage. We are here, this writing tells us, not to mourn lost worlds but to see things as they are: to take in the is-ness of what is. Consciousness is our only salvation.

At this point, it seems to me, Sebald becomes the writer for our times: the one giving us back the actual feel of experience—our experience; our moment, our world, the one we have made and are wandering forlornly about in. Alienation, his writing tells us, is a romance whose moment has come and gone. Anomie is no longer what we are about. The work accomplishes a renewal of feeling for the immensity of human existence, not its smallness or meanness or pointlessness—exactly what a writer of significance might be expected to achieve.

It is, I think, a measure of the widening gap between literary convention and sensory reality that Sebald's books are repeatedly called novels. Many readers, and certainly many critics, cannot believe that the ability to make us feel our one and only life as very few novels do these days is coming from a nonfiction truth speaker—even though it patently is.

"Give the novel back its aesthetic autonomy," says James Wood, "and we will discover... that [it] justifies itself by making an enquiry that it alone can make." But no one can *give* the novel back its autonomy (that is, its authority); it must earn it; the very thing, at this moment, it seems unable to do. Which is precisely why the memoir compels the greater interest of readers and writers alike today. It is in the void created by stasis in the novel that this genre is flourishing.

NOT TO SAY THAT MEMOIR IS THE GENRE to turn to for great writing these days—not at all—only that the present currency of nonfiction means that a sea change has taken place in literary culture. The other night I was having dinner with two friends, one of whom was recounting her harrowing experience of the past year. Her son had taken a bad spill on a ski slope that had resulted in months in the hospital, and my friend was describing—how vividly!—the terror with which she had slowly come to realize that he was permanently brain damaged. When her awful tale was ended, our other friend said, "Now, there's a memoir." I stared at her, thinking, thirty years ago she would surely have said, "There's a novel." Not that any of us thought our dinner companion might have produced a work of literature if she wrote a memoir rather than a novel; for that, we all knew a writing imagination is required, something always in short supply. But it was a sign of the times that the impulse to shape a story out of the raw material of actual event—an impulse alive in all people at all ages—suggests itself as more readily served by a memoir than a novel. I agree with James Wood that nothing can replace the novel: it occupies a position of beauty and power halfway between the poem and the essay that we can no longer do without. Nevertheless, at this moment the form does not inspire faith in its narrative preeminence.

James Wood is a strong critic because he comes alive when he is reading. He may not understand better than anyone else what his time and place is about, but he knows when the book in his hand hits a nerve. I feel the same; it's only that Wood's nerve is located in a different part of his reading body than mine. Which means that it takes a great number of critics to piece together a revealing portrait of a literary period; one that reflects the way it feels to be reading and writing at this time, in this place.

But what do I know? In the 1920s Virginia Woolf complained in print that she could not hear an authentic voice in the novels of the moment (which was why she was retreating to the literature of earlier times). In novel after novel, she said, Chloe loves John, John loves Olivia, oh dear, what to do! (Perhaps, she added elsewhere, eyes turned innocently skyward, it would be more interesting to have a novel in which Chloe loved Olivia instead of John.) In the '40s, the critics who contributed to the *Partisan Review* symposium also spoke of the retreat into the work of the past because contemporary writing was profoundly unsatisfying. Today, we look back on the '40s and '50s as a golden time for English and American literature. No doubt, in the not-so-distant future the literature that currently surrounds us will loom infinitely larger (or smaller) than it does at the moment. How could it be otherwise?

What we critics do—in the aggregate—is to provide, one hopes, a perceptive if not prophetic response to imaginative work; it either rings true or not, on the skin, in the nerve endings, at the given moment. If our responses are themselves imaginative—rich, ardent, inclusive—they will make a contribution to the record of the way it feels to be writing and reading now. Then let the literary chips fall where they may.

GERALD HOWARD
PUBLISHING

"It must be hard for you, dealing with these wretches day after day."

"No, it's easy. I take them to a major eatery. I say, Pooh pooh pooh pooh. I say, Drinky drinky drinky. I tell them their books are doing splendidly in the chains. I tell them readers are flocking to the malls. I say, Coochy coochy coo. I recommend the roast monkfish with savoy cabbage. I tell them the reprint bidders are howling in the commodity pits. There is miniseries interest, there is audiocassette interest, the White House wants a copy for the den. I say, The publicity people are setting up tours. The Italians love the book completely. The Germans are groping for new levels of rapture. Oh my oh my oh my."

Don DeLillo, *Mao II*

One afternoon in 1984, an editorial colleague of mine came back to the office hugging herself with delight at the delicious linguistic artifact her film-scout companion had bestowed on her at lunch. The wonderful new movie-biz coinage she shared with us was the phrase "high concept," which needs no explanation now, but which then contained, ab ovo, the whole subsequent history of the Hollywood film.

I can't be as specific about the year when a phrase equally full of portent for the publishing business, "literary fiction," came into use. Sometime in the early 1990s feels about right. You can't use it without feeling mentally slack and lazy, but it is ubiquitous publishing shorthand. Push in on it, unpack the forces that have made "literary fiction" a necessary formulation, and you might just see why the writers and publishers of serious fiction are unsure whether its needle points toward commerce or art.

When I first started working as an editor in the late '70s, there were categories of fiction, of course. "Commercial fiction" referred to thrillers and such aimed at the best-seller lists instead of the forebrain, and the genres and niches each had their designations—"crime" or "mystery fiction," "romance fiction," "horror fiction," "science fiction," et cetera. Everything else of a made-up prose nature was simply "fiction." Differentiating judgments were made about such works' high- or middle-browness, their appeal to a male or a female readership, but publishers and booksellers still felt comfortable with the baggy, inclusive term.

As vague a categorical designation as "literary fiction" is, it bestowed on non-genre novels the gift or illusion of a brand, a more secure niche and identity within the expanding universe of consumer goods. As critically meaningless as a term may be that can apply to such wildly disparate works as Sue Monk Kidd's sentimental blockbuster *The Secret Life of Bees* and David Markson's radical anti-novel *Wittgenstein's Mistress*, its acceptance and use signified publishers' acquiescence to and accommodation of new marketing and retailing realities. It is both a comfort and a necessity for editors anxious to know what sort of books they are acquiring and for salespeople needing to know what sort of product they are selling.

I remember the meeting at Penguin in the middle '80s when the notion of putting bar codes on our books first came up. I could see why such a thing would be helpful for our self-help and reference and practical books, but Penguin was a pretty high-toned place and for most of our titles it just seemed unnecessary. "What, do you think that *Waiting for the Barbarians* and *The Grapes of Wrath* are going to be sold in some *supermarket* or *mall*?" I sarcastically asked, demonstrating the same far-seeing percipience that a decade earlier had me predicting the swift disappearance of the newly launched *People*. Soon enough, our operations manager was reading *Barcode News*.

Both the publishing and the bookselling businesses have grown in size, complexity, and corporate sophistication ever since, in classic push-me/pull-you fashion. Most publishing houses of any size are parts of huge media conglomerates, which have imposed their own requirements for strict accounting, consistent growth, and managerial accountability. The bookstore chains now account for the lion's share of book sales in the country, much of this business fueled by the proliferation of the 50,000-title (and up) superstore, itself made possible only by the digital technology (and those bar codes) necessary to track and manage a huge product inventory. Borders and Barnes & Noble now stand cheek by jowl off the interstate next to Bed, Bath & Beyond and Home Depot, and a surprisingly wide variety of books may be found at Target, Costco, and Sam's Club (albeit saddled with a brutally short shelf life, which skews the selection decisively toward books that sell quickly—that is, already minted best-sellers). Even many independents like Powell's in Portland, Oregon, and Tattered Cover in Denver have had to hypertrophy themselves to big-box size or focus on online sales to compete and survive.

In some ideal Republic of Letters, such a situation might obtain without significant literary blowback. The novelists would toil away at their visionary labors in their cabins in the woods (or, more likely, their university writing programs) and present them to their publishers with sublime indifference to the means of cultural delivery. But, to invoke T. S. Eliot, there is the mind that creates and then there is the man that suffers—and pays the mortgage and the kids' orthodontist bills. A palpable pressure to perform presses in on editors and novelists alike, and a sense that one has to not only write and edit as well as one can but be adept at gaming the system.

In the entry "Death of Immortality" from *Minima Moralia* (1951), Theodor Adorno has some prescient insights. If the writer, demoralized by the present-day situation, no longer believes in an uncommercial future that will vindicate him, then

> something blind and dogmatic comes into his work, prone to swing over to the other extreme of cynical capitulation. . . . Writers bent on a career talk of their agents as naturally as their predecessors of their publishers, who even then had a foot in the advertising business. They assume personal responsibility for becoming famous, and thus in a sense for their after-life—for what, in totally organized society, can hope to be remembered if it is not already known?—and purchase from the lackeys of the trusts, as in former times from the Church, an expectation of immortality. But no blessing goes with it.

Ars longa no longer. The present is all there is and all that matters.

I'M A '60S DINOSAUR, and everything I've learned and observed about the machinery of culture has strengthened rather than undermined my sense that, on the subject of mass culture's designs upon us, the Frankfurt School essentially got it right. The German-émigré social philosophers developed a Marxist critique of late capitalism's mechanisms for erasing inwardness and subjectivity: coming to this country, they believed they discerned barbarism with Mickey Mouse's face. While Adorno was grotesquely off base in his disdain for jazz and popular music, it still seems to me demonstrably true that every tendency of our present culture is intended to distract us, extinguish our critical intelligence, and smoke out and neutralize those people who don't want to get with the program.

Let me plunge deeper into my shallow bath of cultural despair. I don't do well in large nonbook retail environments. I generally have the saddest heart in the supermarket—a trip to my local suburban A&P always brings on that *White Noise* frame of mind. This past Christmas, I went to a Best Buy in the Hyannis Mall in search of a portable DVD player so I could play my Netflix foreign films (I'm nothing if not pathetic) in every room in the house. Now, I am not a close follower of developments in television technology, and I was genuinely taken aback by the blooming, buzzing confusion of steroidal flat-screen high-def TVs, all sending forth eerily supersaturated images of *Finding Nemo* and *Shrek 2* and NBA highlights and Britney Spears and Shakira shaking their glutes and abs and pectorals. I was stunned by a spectacle that my fellow post-Christmas shoppers took utterly for granted; here, affordably priced, was a life of sensation rather than thought.

I'll turn the pulpit over to the Reverend Herbert Marcuse for some clarifying remarks from Chapter 3 of *One-Dimensional Man*, "The Conquest of the Unhappy Consciousness":

> In its relation to the reality of daily life, the high culture of the past was many things—opposition and adornment, outcry and resignation. But it was also the appearance of the realm of freedom: the refusal to behave. Such a refusal cannot be blocked without a compensation which seems more satisfying than the refusal. The conquest and unification of opposites, which finds its ideological glory in the transformation of higher into popular culture, takes place on a material ground of increased satisfaction.

And this was written in 1964, when Marcuse had probably not seen a color TV. Since that time, the televisual capacity for "increased satisfaction" has grown even faster than, oh, the average chain bookstore. How can literary fiction, one of whose essential qualities, I believe, is the incitement of an increased *dis*satisfication—a quarrel with the fixed conditions of human existence that has been at the heart of high culture since the Greeks invented tragedy—possibly compete with its seductions?

Television has even laid direct siege to the fragile redoubt of fiction in the formidable person of Oprah Winfrey. "This society testifies to the extent to which insoluble conflicts are becoming manageable," Marcuse wrote, "to which tragedy and romance, archetypal dramas and anxieties are being made susceptible to technical solution and dissolution." Almost single-handedly, through her passion for reading, her masterfully devised book club, and her signature template of trauma, healing, and reintegration, Oprah has retrofitted much of the corpus of literary fiction to the requirements of the culture industry. It is the triumph of the therapeutic in its starkest form, and not to be resisted. The Jonathan Franzen/*Corrections* dustup was so unsatisfying precisely because it was so enigmatic; was it a surrender, a no!-in-thunder, a rearguard action, what? What is clear is that books that insist we are not all right and probably not going to be all right are never going to be Oprah's Book Club picks.

WHAT IS TO BE DONE? I do know that such initiatives as the recent study commissioned by the National Endowment for the Arts, which discovered that Americans are not consuming their NEA-recommended daily intake of fiction, are beside the point. Why, in all the reams of commentary that this study generated, did nobody suggest that the writers themselves, not the publishers or the cultural bureaucrats, hold the solution? Nor do I feel that James Wood's plea in the pages of this magazine for a return of the 19th century and the Great Tradition is practical. Novelists simply cannot begin writing as if the 20th century hadn't altered the human prospect and the novel form beyond the dreams or nightmares of Jane Austen and Henry James. The hysterical realists have plenty to be hysterical about. I admire the energy and style (in a couple of senses) of Dave Eggers and his merry band of McSweeneyites more, perhaps, than do the editors of this magazine—they have made writing seem lively and subversive, no small feat. But the fact remains that their coy peekaboo game with the starmaking machinery is not sustainable and the movement has produced only one real book of note, Eggers's own *Heartbreaking Work*—very much an advertisement for himself.

For writers, their personal strategies must range between Pynchonian invisibility and Vidalian availability (it helps to be Gore Vidal). I believe, however, that the continuing vitality and relevance of fiction will be found in the solitary nature of both writing and reading. Marcuse claims in *One-Dimensional Man* that "solitude, the very condition which sustained the individual against and beyond his society, has become technically impossible." The stubborn persistence of the novel, the supreme solitary art, suggests this isn't true. John Updike once said the loveliest thing: that he wrote his books in the hope that they would be discovered by some kid in a library in Iowa (as, presumably, he was once a kid in a library in Shillington). When I was 12, I was such a kid in a library in Brooklyn, and with my first use of my adult library card, the discovery of William Golding's subversive caveman novel *The Inheritors* turned a switch on in my brain that has remained on all these decades later.

No American novelist has managed the present situation with more grace and dignity than Don DeLillo. I was privileged to be able to interview him on the occasion of the publication of *Underworld*, and the interview ended with these words, with which I choose to end this gloomy-hopeful meditation:

> The writer has lost a great deal of his influence, and he is situated now, if anywhere, on the margins of the culture. But isn't this where he belongs? How could it be any other way? And in my personal view this is the perfect place to observe what's happening at the dead center of things. I particularly have always had a kind of endgame sensibility when it comes to writing serious fiction. Before I ever published a novel this is how I felt about it—that I was writing for a small audience that could disappear at any minute, and not only was this not a problem, it was a kind of solution. It justified what I wrote and it narrowed expectations in a healthy way. I am not particularly distressed by the state of fiction or the role of the writer. The more marginal, perhaps ultimately the more trenchant and observant and finally necessary he'll become.

BENJAMIN KUNKEL
NOVEL

MOST NOVELISTS WORK IN A FORMAL TRADITION so conservative as to feel like second nature, and fiction as practiced as an art form over the almost two centuries since Austen and Stendhal has altered strikingly little in comparison with painting and sculpture, popular as well as classical music, poetry and even the theater, not to mention the young arts of photography and film. Considered as a form, the novel is not very accommodating to the new, and probably the most recent book to change the practice of novelists in general was *Madame Bovary*; it begins with Flaubert that today most writers suppress direct authorial commentary and avail themselves on occasion of free indirect discourse.

We can recognize something we might call *the perennial novel*. Mixing description of the world, ostensibly realistic dialogue, and psychological insight in proportions that now seem classical, and written in an often elevated but always familiar version of the language of the day, the perennial novel situates plausible human characters in a relatively narrow segment of a known society (our own or a historical one) and chronicles its protagonist's defeat by or emergence from a crisis. There is little or no essayistic component to the prose. The author may allow for a touch of allegory, but that aspect can never dominate as it does in Bunyan's or Sidney's prose romances or some of Conrad's shorter novels or all of Saramago's full-length ones. Symbols may be present, but can never loom in concentrated form above the narrative (as with Kafka's castle) or flourish in baroque profusion (as with the ecclesiastical imagery in Cormac McCarthy's *Suttree*). Likewise, the perennial novel would turn into something else if its descriptions ever attained the promiscuous exactitude of Claude Simon or Robbe-Grillet, if it were ever overrun by naturalistic speech as in Henry Green or William Gaddis, or if it ventured such speculative and exhaustive forays into psychology as Proust's or Musil's. Its signature, again, is a classical-seeming disposition of these elements, even as their proportions shift over time.

The perennial novel does not yet openly sabotage its verisimilitude in the way of much postmodernism; it seems unlikely it ever will. But its fidelity is to realism rather than reality. Describe the sensuously available world with too much accuracy, listen to speech with too keen an ear, or track the progress of a thought or an emotion too minutely and you will have immediately violated the canons of realism, as you will also have done if you leave your plot hanging too completely open at the end. And morally, too, the perennial novel tends toward a sort of stealth stylization; its apportionment of good and evil traits among its characters adheres, even now, much more to narrative tradition than to the actual distribution of virtue in the world. This is especially true of so-called genre fiction, but true enough of the perennial novel as a whole. Even the avowedly realist novel derives its realism from conventions at least as much as its conventions from reality. Its natural mode is thus to be an unconscious pastiche of itself.

Of course bad and mediocre novels belong overwhelmingly to the slow-cooking culture of the perennial novel; but who besides an ideologue feels that the mode debars greatness? There is the perennial novel and then there is another kind of novel (on which more in a moment), but these categories don't exactly correspond to high and low. Amid abundant perennial mediocrity, many impressive but formally unadventurous novels still get written, distinguished by the acuteness of perception and insight that somehow manages to elude the snares of realist convention. Very often the novelist's acuteness seems involved with the introduction of literally novel subject matter; an uncontroversial example might be the Indian diaspora of V. S. Naipaul's Trinidad, rarely if ever treated in fiction before *The Mystic Masseur*. Even John Updike's suburban rounds of adultery, material that today seems hardly to permit anything but a hackneyed treatment, was fresh and new (Updike might say "nubile") in the first decades after Levittown and the Kinsey Report. And in both *A House for Mr. Biswas* and *Rabbit, Run*, to use these examples only for their convenience, we can note the coincidence—which probably isn't one—of an acute visual sense with a notable refusal of sentimentality; we feel that the writer is being, in both senses of the term, clear-eyed.

IF TODAY THE BEST NOVELS in the perennial mode seem to come from marginal communities or peripheral countries, this certainly owes something to the metropolitan reader's flattery of the exotic; but it also has to do with the fact that standardized representations haven't yet covered all things under the sun. The notorious problem of our American generation with sincerity versus so-called irony, including the trouble in distinguishing one from the other, derives from the condition of feeling walled off from your own experience behind a barricade of *culture*, of representations, of things already achieved. Hence the strong appeal for many novelists of adopting a child's perspective or a childish one (children being seen as heroically naïve), or of taking up terrible private or historical suffering as subject matter ("I like a look of agony, / Because I know it's true—"). Unfortunately the sentimental pieties attaching to childhood and to innocent suffering make it especially hard to depict those things honestly, without recourse to cliché. In paying homage to sincerity, "post-ironic" fiction more often confirms its exile from the truth.

Another increasingly common tactic for the perennial novelist wishing to escape his own sophistication is to pastiche one or another form of genre fiction (the *policier*, historical romance, et cetera), and from behind his pages peek out at the reader with a wink. And sometimes genre pastiche will put an old form to genuinely new use: one example would be Kobo Abe's Möbius strip of a detective novel, *The Ruined Map*. More often, the winking use of generic trappings is just a flirtatious confession of bad faith. The writer *knows* he's imprisoned in generic conventions, *knows* he has no real critical perspective on these conventions, and, with the thin excuse of this knowledge, employs them all the same. Like the metafictionist, the genre pasticheur draws attention to the man behind the curtain; unlike in metafiction, the revelation of falsehood is not meant to point the way toward the reality lying, teeming, everywhere outside the book.

These are so many problems of a more or less sophisticated, more or less metropolitan novelist trying to work in the perennial mode. But there is another mode of novel writing, which might be called modernist except that it began before modernism and has long since outlasted it; which might be called "experimental" if this didn't suggest a misleading analogy with the cumulative knowledge of the experimental sciences; and which might be called formally innovative, if this didn't obscure the fact that so many innovations in the history of the novel are the result of adapting to it the techniques of other literary forms (the lyric poem, the stage drama, the prose romance, the personal essay, the journalistic report). True, the modernist novel can claim several genuine and momentous innovations, especially in the portrayal of interior states; but we feel that while this modernist technical array can still be used, it can no longer be added to. This is one meaning of postmodernism: the novel in its formally self-conscious mode has ceased to indicate a historical direction on the model of 19th-century notions of progress, and seems instead to exhibit what Fredric Jameson calls a "spatial proliferation" of formal tendencies.

Still, there plainly exists, under whatever name, a culture of novel writing, formerly modern and now postmodern, that does *not* take the form for granted, that does *not* behave simply as comes naturally, that instead finds in the artifice of the novelist's art an occasion for debilitating self-consciousness or freedom from constraint. And it happens that for this culture the last figure of widely agreed-upon significance is Samuel Beckett (whose last full-length novel, also the final volume of his famous trilogy, was called, it seems appropriately, *The Unnameable*). In sketches of the postwar history of the novel, the gaunt tall figure of Beckett stands out like no one else. What does his significance signify?

The trilogy begins in a stark enough universe, only a few props (a bicycle, a bed, some stones) distinguishing it from oblivion, and yet we listen over hundreds of pages as the already decrepit narrator relates the entire disintegration of his world and person, leaving him nattering in the void. E. M. Cioran, who knew Beckett in Paris, clearly had his friend's recent trilogy in mind when, in 1956, he proposed in his essay "Beyond the Novel" that "the only novels deserving of interest today are precisely those in which, once the universe is disbanded, nothing happens." Adorno, who died in 1969, planned to dedicate his *Aesthetic Theory* to Beckett; in the opening pages of that unfinished diagnosis of the postwar condition of art, Beckett's novels offer the prime symptom of a historical situation that overwhelms, paralyzes, and finally renders obsolete the bourgeois subject as he'd come to be known (through, in large part, two centuries of novels).

A generation later, Jameson singled out Beckett's novel *Watt* as a precursor of postmodern sensibility, with its inability to remember the past (except as simulacrum) or conceive of the future (except as disaster). It may not be surprising, then, with Adorno and Jameson in mind, to recall what Don DeLillo had his novelist character say in *Mao II*: "Beckett is the last writer to shape the way we think and see." The blocked novelist Bill Gray does not elaborate; but DeLillo's sensibility, with its attention to the attenuated life of the individual and the incommensurability of private experience with the spectacle of contemporary history, has always seemed to coincide at many points with that of the Frankfurt School and its heirs.

James Wood's perspective hardly aligns with Cioran's (Wood does not believe the novel is a spent form) or with the perspective perhaps shared by DeLillo and Adorno: in his reply to the editors of *n+1*, Wood allows that the self may change over time, but "not as quickly as our representations of the self." In this spirit he complains that there are "no human beings" in *Underworld*; the implication is that DeLillo has emphasized the novel features of contemporary experience to the exclusion of enduring human problems. And yet Wood agrees with DeLillo, and with the Marxists Adorno and Jameson, about the preeminence of Beckett. From his essay on W. G. Sebald, whom Wood praised more than any other writer active in the 1990s: "Here was the first contemporary writer since Beckett to have found a way to protest the good government of the conventional novel form and to harass realism into a state of self-examination."*

Wood and DeLillo only hint at an answer to the meaning of Beckett. Cioran and Adorno (the one an inverted vitalist praising inanition and decay, the other a late Marxist for whom only art testifies to the truth of historical experience) have more to say. For them the chief significance of Beckett's novels is that the world of objects disappears and, with it, the subject. Beckett's fiction represents the evacuation first of social, then of empirical, and finally of psychological content. The escape from other novelists could only be achieved by turning the trilogy into a true anti-novel; and reading *The Unnameable* to the end is something like watching the novel starve itself to death.

---

* Never mind for now the plain untruth of this claim: in the nearly forty years between 1957 (when the final volume of Beckett's self-translated trilogy appeared in English) and 1995 (when Sebald's *The Emigrants* appeared), not a single writer emerged to so much as *harass*—much less menace or assault—the assumptions of the realist novel? Not Gaddis or Pynchon, Sarraute, Perec, or Robbe-Grillet, Márquez or Cortázar, Grass or Bernhard, neither Abe in Japan, nor Nadas in Hungary, nor Saramago in Portugal: not one of these raised a protest against the probity and smoothness of conventional realism? (For as a political program "good government" means only that officeholders should not embezzle or take bribes and should run their administrations efficiently.) To suggest that no important departures from realism took place over the course of almost forty years is a surreal journalistic convenience; it is also, perhaps, a way to flatter *New Republic* readers for the failure to keep up, as well as evidence of the profound conservatism of Wood's tastes.

The meaning of Beckett is something like this: he represents the confessed exhaustion of the psychological novel—after Proust, according to Cioran, had rendered any further "research in the direction of psychological detail superfluous, annoying." But that would be Beckett's generally European and specifically French meaning more than his American one, in that the psychological novel has always been more of a Continental genre. Of course headlong monologues on wild or barren interior states have continued to be produced, sometimes even by Americans (e.g., Harold Brodkey), and often, as in Thomas Bernhard, Cees Nooteboom, or Javier Marías, with the shade of Beckett evidently in attendance. Which would suggest that in the end Beckett's hunger strike was more like a cleansing fast; the psychological novel emerged thinner, perhaps purer, at any rate still breathing. And yet it's hard to deny that these superb writers nonetheless feel somehow marginal, "literary" in the slightly pejorative sense of occupying a high-end niche in a mass culture they can hardly begin to reflect, much less influence—a topic for another day.

We're more concerned for now with the stateside meaning of Beckett, his meaning, if we can speculate, for both DeLillo and Wood. And this would seem to have more to do with what Adorno called his "annihilation of reality" than his whittling away of the self. Beckett's evacuation of content would then symbolize something like this: from now on, for the formally self-conscious novelist, the recovery of content or subject matter is something to be undertaken very deliberately, in the full understanding that when the reality to be represented is a social or historical reality in any of its breadth or complexity, this reality will not present itself spontaneously to the writer as the natural byproduct of his own more or less circumscribed experience, but will instead have to be sought out, pursued, willfully researched and reported on.

For it's clearly this quality of research that DeLillo (whom Wood censures) and Sebald (whom Wood praises so extravagantly) have in common, and for that matter share with the more encyclopedic fiction of Pynchon, Vollmann, David Foster Wallace, and others. We even see something similar in Roth's recent trilogy, where the narrator Zuckerman is forever being buttonholed by neighbors unloading on him the cultural-political melodramas that are their life stories; through this transparent device we easily perceive Roth's own research into McCarthyism, the Weather Underground, and so on. The disappearance of the great world as the novelist's native inheritance, his feeling of dispossession in terms of subject matter, means that the recovery of the world must be taken up as an open and deliberate project. Sometimes the research is carried out in libraries, as is made explicit in DeLillo's *Libra* (with its figure of "the Curator") and Sebald's *Rings of Saturn*. Sometimes the better term for research would be reporting, since the novelist has clearly needed to conduct interviews (as in *The Emigrants* or Vollmann's *Rainbow Stories*) or to travel widely with a notebook for the sake of his book.

Sebald thematized his research more explicitly than just about any other contemporary writer, as the psychic compulsion of his doom-haunted narrators. But this should not imply that there is no other or subtler way to do the same thing. What James Wood sees in DeLillo and describes in pathological terms as paranoia is really something else: DeLillo is not laboring under the delusion that *It's all connected* so much as he is announcing the thematic arrangement of his material, as if to say, *These things I have chosen to connect*. Surely this explains the shaggy dog quality of so many recent "social novels"; diverse people are gathered up into narrative relation by a circulating videotape, baseball, accordion, whatever, not because of the intrinsic social significance of the object, but as a way for the author to acknowledge the real uniting thing: the book itself, which stands in for the phantom public. In this way research declares itself in the service of vision, and sociology becomes lyrical. Indeed it's this manner of revealing the private sources of a public vision that makes the postmodern social novel so superior to that kind of extensively researched social panorama (one version of the perennial novel) that never accounts for its creator's subjectivity, never discloses the obsessions prompting so much objectivity.

But the postmodern social novel seems by now to have erected its monuments, in America anyway. It's doubtful that any more will appear this generation. Prophesying the future of fiction is hazardous—and self-interested—but still it's hard not to wonder whether the old form of the psychological novel doesn't offer more possibilities to younger American writers. One underexplored thesis is that the tradition of the American psychological novel that might have gotten underway after Faulkner and Ellison was badly hampered by the postwar institutionalization of psychoanalysis and its widespread public acceptance as a discourse. Now that psychoanalysis has lost so much ground to sociobiology and psychopharmacology, so that all that survives of it in public is the blunt repetition of a few therapeutic nostrums, it seems conceivable that the novel in America might achieve its old European role as the main venue for psychological investigation. In a culture where it's easier to overhear someone on his cell phone than to overhear your own thoughts, this development would have a certain usefulness.

WE MIGHT WONDER, TOO—it seems one of the biggest questions for the future of literature—whether simple, blameless ignorance on the part of readers and writers alike might not keep the novel going, and permit new instances of greatness. Perhaps a writer in 2025 or 2050, gifted with natural eloquence, fed by unsystematic reading, never having heard so much as a rumor of the mid-20th century's dream of mass higher education in the liberal arts, will want to create a single unforgettable character—an adulterer, say—or else paint some vast sociohistorical mural. He may never have heard of Emma Bovary or Molly Bloom or Rabbit Angstrom; or she won't have read *War and Peace*, *U.S.A.*, or *The War of the End of the World*, much less all three, certainly not when we haven't. "The sun shone, having no alternative, on the nothing new." So reads the first line of Beckett's first published novel. But what if the sun had no memory of what it had seen the day before? Might it not shed its light less wearily?

The novel practiced as an art form within a consciously evolving tradition was headquartered in France and may be said to have died in Beckett's room in 1958, not many more than 100 years after its birth, in whatever town you'd like to give as its *lieu de naissance*. Probably it will never regain the same centrality, the same market share. What endures is a sort of afterlife. But when does one of those ever end? Recall these lines from Beckett's play *Endgame*:

> CLOV: Do you believe in the life to come?
> HAMM: Mine was always that.

Hamm meant that he was in hell, and had been born there. But borrowed as slogan for the novel the words would mean something else; they would mean that the novel, having once died, can now live forever, or for at least as long as our civilization and the memory of it lasts.

MARCO ROTH
READER AS HERO

SOMETHING IS MISSING amid our present superabundance of new fictions, new talents, and even new seriousness. We lack novels that address the idea of literature as equipment for living. The literature of the past was full of such ideas, of characters who turn to novels to change their lives (no matter how badly things often turned out). So what would a contemporary Don Quixote, Madame Bovary, or Anna Karenina be like? The characters wouldn't make the same mistakes—trying to live their lives as though following the script of a novel—but their reading might still change them in unexpected ways. Imagine a new novel about the conflicts within our present-day readers. Call it "The Good Reader" or "The Interpreters," or maybe "The Good and the Bored." What would this novel be like, and where are the characters who will fill its pages?

Our generation seems far too aware that reading is safe and fun, that literature is spectacle. Readers of all kinds tend to feel transported or shocked, to experience a style the way people thrill to a virtuoso pianist, to have an adventure, to feel empowered (though not to *be* empowered), to get turned on. In the grip of these tendencies, we feed our voyeurism, hero-worship, lust, nostalgia, our desires to identify and project. We are vampires who yearn to warm our shivering lives with the deaths we read about, as Walter Benjamin remarked about an earlier generation of readers alienated from their communal experiences and lured into cities. We fortify our blood with ink about imaginary others. This relationship to books mirrors uncomfortably our relationship to the world: citizens of the freest of countries, yet we are wrought upon from without. We live in a cloud of vague dangers, neither clear nor present. Unelected judges appoint our president, and a man in a suit (once a Greenspan, now a Bernanke) determines whether stocks, prices, and unemployment rates rise or fall. Consent is all that is asked of us, or suspension of disbelief. And it seems that our ever increasing supply of fictions does nothing but abet the cultivation of this decadent passivity, an ideological apparatus all the more insidious for not belonging to the state.

This criticism of readers is as old as prophetic castigations of idol worshippers. The concern has usually been that reading will lead to wrong actions or no action—to immorality or passivity. So Wordsworth thought that the surge in popular novels and plays at the beginning of the industrial revolution had plunged English minds into "savage torpor." He recommended we read more to cure ourselves—more Wordsworth. Novelists too wrote against the wrong kind of novels and the wrong kind of readers. This remains one of the strongest unsettled legacies of the long tradition of the modern novel, from the era of the French Revolution, through Flaubert and Tolstoy, up through today.

The rescue of readers from their own pernicious tendencies must be counted among the many utopian projects of the past two centuries, and, like nationalism and communism, it gained an accelerated force at the beginning of the 20th. From the evident aesthetic and political failures of socialist realism onward, novelists, critics, and teachers have struggled to create readers whose aesthetic sensibilities would trigger their social responsibility and, if lucky, their mental liberation. Sometimes readers were to be dragged out of their everyday slough by an array of estrangement effects. At others, they would find freedom and enlightenment through an understanding of the arbitrary nature of the conventions governing language and narrative action. The rise of "literary theory" was aligned with these utopian hopes and movements. Looking back now, we can see the 20th century as the golden age of the reader as hero.

Where did this figure go? Like so much else, the heroic reader has succumbed to triumphal capitalism. We look around and find that we are in a consumer's world. Even those who supposedly "care" for literature have turned themselves into fans and enthusiasts. Does such and such a novel keep it real? Does it pique curiosity? Do I identify? Do I like the sound of this voice in my ear? The idea of the reader as canny consumer is so pervasive that one editor of a prominent literary magazine writes about herself as a member of "the service economy" and compares criticism to waitressing. It was undoubtedly a moment of weakness. But still: is a taste for literature nothing more than a refined palate? Is literary criticism really like being able to tell which wine tastes of wet stone and which of tart blackberry?

Banished by Amazon preferences and litblogs, the heroic reader lingers on as a memory mostly confined to academic criticism. Pick up the lit theory of the late 1960s and early '70s: There's Stanley Fish's vision of *Paradise Lost* as great test and trap for its Protestant readers; Fredric Jameson's liberation theology, in which readers bring the political unconscious of novels into the light of day; the stoical struggle of Paul de Man's "rhetorical" reading, in which the self must learn to deny that it is a self; and, most self-consciously heroic of all, Harold Bloom's quest to arrive back at "the great cyclic poem" by imagining *poets* as the best and most active unconscious misreaders. It makes sense that academic literary criticism would carry a torch for "higher reading," since these people have devoted themselves to the belief that reading is the most important thing we do.

Of course these theories never made it into broader American culture. (There was once a plan to have Andrzej Warminski, Gayatri Spivak, and a team of graduate students teach rhetorical reading in New Haven public schools, but it's not mentioned now without an embarrassed laugh.) For a while, however, there were two complementary "heroic reader" theories that did make it. These weren't necessarily the most rigorous or the most captivatingly "heroic," but they were the most directly American. They offered a sense of reading that tallied with ideas of what it means to be a good citizen in a liberal democracy. One proposed to enlarge our sympathies; the second would teach us how to overcome our own Romantic impulses and reach emotional and intellectual maturity.

THE FIRST THEORY WAS ONCE AN AXIOM of liberal-arts education back when we had liberal-arts education: reading novels could be "good for you"; it could even improve American morals. You didn't learn anything from novels exactly, not useful knowledge, not information necessarily, certainly not the Truth, but the right kinds of novels were supposed to act as a check on our freedom and selfishness by educating readers into sympathy with others. There was always something horrifying and terrifyingly banal about this assumption. Horrifying because it tried to socialize the wild imagination of readers—especially those young readers most likely to experience literature as a liberation from the limitations of place, time, social codes, their own gender, race, and class, their families, or morality itself. Terrifyingly banal because once you'd learned to read the educated way, a lot of the illicit thrill went out of reading novels. The novel just wanted you to behave. There's an analogy with the present cult of diet and exercise: the boy who runs through the grass until his lungs burn and the world looks both brighter and darker becomes a calorie counter and times himself in the mile.

The most thorough defenses of what David Bromwich nicknamed "literature as moral vitamins" appeared on the scene in the late 1980s and early 1990s, a time that can now be seen as the death throes of American liberalism and the liberal arts. (Then, it was thought of as a mere crisis period; the enemies were presumed to be the antiliberal left and French theory, rather than fundamentalists, demagogues, and rampant consumerism.) Richard Rorty and Martha Nussbaum both attempted to make the case for reading novels as a socially desirable and even necessary activity for a society that would be both good and just. For Rorty, the relation of reader to novel and also of author to character demonstrated the kind of solidarity that could hold secular and democratic countries together even if we accepted that truth was unknowable, shot through with irony and contingency. Nussbaum thought novels could offer revisions to liberal utilitarian calculations. They would rehumanize a technocratic elite and teach them to account for exceptions to the sort of generalized rule-making that prevailed among professional ethicists and lawyers. Not just any novel would do, of course. A canon was available and it appeared to be a closed one: adapted, with variations, from F. R. Leavis's older "Great Tradition," it often sounded like Austen, some Dickens, George Eliot, and Henry James. Instead of Leavis's favorite, D. H. Lawrence, Rorty substituted Nabokov and Orwell; Nussbaum offered Beckett and also stepped back to Shakespeare and the ancient Athenians. One became an ethical reader, in short, by reading ethical writers—writers devoted to the task of creating characters who were, as much as possible, autonomous.

Despite this late attempt to rescue the liberal view that, in John Dewey's phrase, "art is more moral than moralities," the model already had encountered serious opposition. Crucially, it bred a feeling of superiority among novel-reading liberal-arts types that had first been exposed during the '60s revolt of the antiliberal left. It turned out that characters who existed in novels as objects of sympathy (put-upon women, poor people, colonial subjects, prisoners) had ideas of their own about life. They didn't want sympathy, they wanted power. And so, at the high school level, the whole post-1968 model of reading for group empowerment and identity formation supplanted the cult of sympathy and devolved into niche marketing (chick lit, anyone?). On the political level, the short-lived triumph of minority politics was followed by the long counter-revolution in whose shadow we've spent our lives. One of its major triumphs has been the careful corruption of minority "Yes We Can!" rhetoric of empowerment into an excuse for majority bullying. Liberals are now told that corporate bosses, policemen, and politicians have feelings that must be respected; that we must care for the strike-breaker, the prison guard, and the executive's wish for privacy. To do anything else would be elitist.

BUT WOULD IT BE UNCIVILIZED? Becoming a responsible citizen and even an adult is precisely about knowing when to judge and condemn and when to sympathize and care. Yet how does one know what is real, what romantic? What a true judgment and what an act of faith or misplaced trust? To try to answer these questions, the second type of American heroic reader was called forth in the aftermath of World War II amid a host of European influences. In his 1948 essay "Art and Fortune," Lionel Trilling argued that we needed novels to make us feel fully alive; he proposed that we read novels precisely in order to re-experience a developmental process and win our way to full adulthood. The aim was to achieve knowledge without loss of power, but with a recognition of limitations.

The right new novels in the hands of the right new readers could bring about a change, a synthesis in the ongoing "dialectic of reality and illusion." In Trilling's account, the novel that best staged this multi-layered dialectic between worldly and literary experience was Stendhal's early-19th-century "novel of ideas," *The Red and the Black*. In the character and fate of Julien Sorel, Trilling saw the heroic readers of the future as well as hope for novels.

For Trilling, when Julien borrows a gardener's ladder to climb into the bedroom of his boss's daughter, with a pistol in his pocket and a knife, pirate-style, between his teeth, he rises to the level of a novelistic objective correlative. Within a single action, Stendhal captures the farcical elements of Liberal France in the 1830s, a culture in which a young man's dream of romantic heroism had been degraded to one of upward mobility. Julien isn't just an idea himself; however, later in the novel, as Trilling reads it, he becomes exactly the adult enlightened reader who learns to recognize his past actions as misguided—motivated by the pursuit of "specious goods." Julien, though, doesn't quite make it. (He gets bored of the aristocratic girlfriend he's seduced, but he never manages to figure out what he wants.) And that failure too is a parable.

This kind of reading, let's call it allegorical transumption, depends on the reader's will to pass through identification into interpretation; call it a will to grow up. This reader—while we're at it, let's call him he—with his novel (and friends to argue about it) would be allowed fantasies of seductions, rope-ladders, murders, strapping men, and women "in all ways shapely"—the trappings of old romances endlessly updatable for new situations. But he would also have to understand that these demons must be sublimated into thoughts and arguments about the state of the world and the condition of his life. By plunging into the lives of fictional others with all reckless abandon, he'd yet emerge clutching a pearl of greater price, a fuller understanding of himself, his motives and wishes. He'd do this not necessarily to act on them, but to bring them to light and expose them to a world shared with others.

Both the will to interpret and the will to grow up flagged in the '60s, epitomized by Sontag's essay "Against Interpretation" and its argument for endless surface textual pleasure. Sontag's call for an "erotics of art" anticipated and echoed sexual liberation's promise of eternal youth as well as the growing suspicion of psychoanalysis. Yet, against Sontag, we can once more recognize hermeneutics as a kind of erotics, albeit more *Civilization and Its Discontents* than "zipless fuck."

DESPITE OUR CULTURE'S BEST EFFORTS—from left and right—the liberal hero-readers of both the "moral vitamins" and "allegorical transumption" accounts can never be fully liquidated—even when History itself seems to have no more use for them. They've been driven underground in a curious inverted repression, but they may return as characters again. No character returns unchanged from the underworld or from exile. We shouldn't expect our new heroic readers to be as innocent in their quests for spiritual upward mobility as their many precursors. The liberal hero reader is different from Emma Bovary, Anna Karenina, or Don Quixote—those overly active readers betrayed into becoming characters in someone else's novel—but there's still a story to tell.

A contemporary novel that could dramatize the life of one heroic reading consciousness or even one reader's struggle between heroic reading and the impulses so effectively tapped by consumerism might just be the sort of novel to save us from our own savage torpor. It would still be a novel, of course—just as *Anna Karenina* remains a novel critical of novels and already points the way to Tolstoy's ultimate renunciation of art. The struggle would have to be set in one of the great metropolitan centers of our global commercial culture, New York or London. Curiously, it seems difficult to write anything but minor novels and satires about these places now. It used to be that the metropole was defined as the place everyone went to write and the place everyone wrote about. The former still holds, for the most part, but the metropolis now lies shrouded in myths of its boringness, its unrepresentability. The inhabitants of these places who want the news from novels get "realist" writing purchased from developing countries or America's expanding borderlands and hinterlands. We metropolitan readers have lives no less real for taking place within this history of reading. Let us turn the gaze upon ourselves, if only the better to focus it again. +

THE GAMATS GROUP, *CHURCH OF THE REDEEMER, ANI RUINS, KARS PROVINCE, TURKEY*, 2005,
MANIPULATION OF DIGITAL PHOTOGRAPH, 6 X 4". COURTESY OF THE ARTIST.

WHY REPEAT THESE SAD THINGS?

Meline Toumani

PART ONE

I HEARD SARKIS BEY TALK ONLY TWICE about what happened to the Armenians. The first time was at Van Castle, in southeastern Turkey, where most of the Armenians had lived under the Ottoman Empire. The second time was much later.

At Van Castle we met a group of little boys. Sarkis Bey walked up to them and presented a pop quiz: Why were there three different kinds of stones in the castle walls?

"I know," one of the boys said. "First it was Byzantine Turks. Then it was Seljuk Turks. Then it was Ottoman Turks."

"What about the Armenians?" said Sarkis Bey.

"I don't know."

"Does anybody know what happened to the Armenians?" Sarkis Bey asked.

Another boy spoke up. "Yes. Half of them left, and half of them dropped into foreign lands."

Sarkis Bey took aside this boy, a 10-year-old named Ridvan who had brown skin and brilliant green eyes, and told him that in fact the first layer of rocks was the work of the Urartians, who were the ancestors of the Armenians. The second layer was probably the work of the Armenians themselves, who lived here in great numbers during the Byzantine era and were known for their stonemasonry. He pointed out the site, in the distance, of the old Armenian quarter, and said that in 1915, to protect themselves from the advancing Ottoman army, the Armenians took refuge in this very castle where we stood. "Many, many Armenians were killed," he added.

Then, one by one, the little boys sang us love songs in Kurdish and Turkish. Sarkis Bey put an arm around Ridvan. "This boy is especially bright," he told me, and asked me to take their picture together.

I HAD NEVER EXPECTED to end up in southeastern Turkey, an area the Kurds consider Kurdistan and the Armenians regard as the heart of *Medz Hayk*: Great Armenia. And it had been great, once—in the first century B.C., to be exact—when the Armenian Kingdom stretched from Syria to Azerbaijan. It's a long story, but things went downhill from there. Two thousand years later, in the United States, I grew up surrounded by an unabashed hatred for Turkey and Turks. We referred to Turkish coffee, which we drank every day, as "Armenian coffee," and we refused to buy products labeled "Made in Turkey." My mother once spent weeks trying to buy a new bathrobe, but at store after store, every single robe declared its Turkish origins: the Turks had cornered the market on terrycloth. One evening, my mom returned home, exhausted, with a large bag from Sears. "Don't tell anyone," she warned me, and then held out her plush, pale yellow purchase.

My ancestors, though full-blooded Armenians, came from Georgia, Azerbaijan, and Iran, where I was born. Nobody in my family was directly affected by the massacres of 1915 (which is probably why my mother was able to buy the bathrobe, in the end). Even so, I was immersed in anti-Turkish sentiment at Armenian school, Armenian church, and Armenian summer camp. In the woods just outside Boston, we'd line up in front of our cabins each morning and raise the Armenian flag while singing "Harach Nahadag," an anthem of the Armenian Revolutionary Federation, the century-old political party whose youth branch ran the camp:

> Forward, immortals of a martyred race!
> Armored in six centuries of unforgotten vengeance,
> Upon the far mountaintops of our fatherland
> Let us go plant the tri-colored flag!

At least half of the kids didn't speak Armenian—they were chanting memorized sound fragments day after day—but their zeal was no less for it. Those who did understand the words also understood that the "fatherland" in question was not merely the one currently delineated on the map as the Republic of Armenia. And I, it should be said, sang louder than anyone.

UNTIL LAST YEAR, I had encountered three Turks in my life. The first was a girl named Ellie, whose family lived down the street from mine when I was in elementary school in New Jersey. Ellie had blond hair and blue eyes, so I had no idea she was from the same part of the world as I, much less that she was Turkish, until one morning she arrived at the bus stop and announced, "My dad says your family is Armenian."

"Yeah."

"He says that seventy-five years ago we had your heads on sticks."

I don't remember how I answered this, but Ellie's family moved away soon after.

The second time was during college, when one of my roommates went on a couple of dates with a Turkish guy. He stopped by our house one night, we made small talk for a few minutes, and then they left for dinner.

The third time took place five years ago in San Francisco, where I lived at the time. My then-boyfriend and I hailed a cab to go see a movie at the Opera Plaza Cinemas, which is located at the intersection of Van Ness Avenue and Turk Street. We were a little drunk, so when the cab driver asked whether we'd like to be dropped off on Van Ness or on Turk, my Irish-American boyfriend replied: "Van Ness, please. We don't travel on Turk Street."

We had never discussed Turk Street before, as such. In truth, I'm not sure I'd ever even made the connection. But the two of us collapsed into giggles, and I kissed him on the cheek for being such a loyal friend to the Armenians.

Then—in my memory this happens in slow motion—the driver turned around in his seat and faced us. He had thick black hair and a wide handlebar mustache that was pulled down at the edges by his frown. As I looked at his face, I somehow knew what was coming, even though it was impossible.

"I am a Turk," he said.

Emboldened by alcohol and set loose by awkwardness, I didn't let it end there. I said, "Do you realize that in 1915, your people massacred two-thirds of the Armenian population?"

I thought that his voice held more weariness than anger when he finally answered: "Things that happened such a long time ago should be left in the past."

THE PROBLEM WAS THAT, IN TURKEY, the Armenian genocide was left in the past almost before it ended. In 1923, which was the final year of the massacres, General Mustafa Kemal—later called Atatürk, "Father of all Turks"—came to power. He abolished the Caliphate and established the modern Republic of Turkey on a platform of Westernization and secularization—a platform for the future, he said. In 1928 he outlawed the Arabic alphabet, effectively putting into a foreign language all the records of Ottoman Turkey—including, of course, the contemporary evidence and accounts of the genocide. Atatürk's ideas, which were embraced by a beleaguered population, came to be known as Kemalism. At the heart of Kemalism was a principle called *milliyetçilik*, or nationalism, based on the idea that in the wake of the multinational empire, the Republic of Turkey needed a unified national identity to protect itself against imperialist threats. In the story Turkey began to tell about itself, everybody was Turkish, and always had been.

In the story Armenians tell, one of Ottoman Turkey's largest ethnic groups had faced genocide. On April 24, 1915, the army rounded up 235 of the leading Armenian intellectuals in Constantinople, held them for three days, and then exiled them to the country's interior, where most were slaughtered. In the years that followed, even after the cessation of hostilities between the Ottomans and the Allies, province by province Armenian populations were ordered to leave their homes and join caravans, often on foot, into the desert. Men were usually rounded up first, and shot in groups outside of town. Women, children, and the elderly were considered a waste of bullets, so if they were not dismembered or burned by the Ottoman army, they arrived in camps where many starved to death. Between 1915 and 1923, approximately one million Armenians were murdered.

Ninety years later, Turkey has not acknowledged, much less apologized for, what happened. As a result, the quest for Turkish government recognition of the genocide has become an obsession for Armenians in the diaspora. Each year on April 24, Armenians gather in cities worldwide to review the progress: a city council in Oklahoma has passed a resolution calling it genocide; a newspaper in Italy has dropped its usage of the modifier *alleged* in describing the events. The climax of these rituals—Armenians will chant it backward in their sleep—is always the recitation of a quote from Hitler: "Who today remembers the extermination of the Armenians?"

After faithfully participating in the commemoration routines for many years, I started to feel ridiculous. It's not that I doubted what happened—although I did occasionally find it strange that everybody from the Armenian grocer to the heavy metal band System of a Down felt themselves credible arbiters of history. But it was impossible to attend any Armenian event, no matter what the occasion, without encountering the same passion play. It was all we could talk about. I began to find it insincere, histrionic, and hateful.

So when I actually visited Armenia for the first time, I was surprised, and a little relieved, to find that genocide recognition was not nearly the priority there that it was in the diaspora: the biggest issue was the economy, in particular the closed border with Turkey. There were various reasons for Turkey's decision to seal the border; officially it was in protest of the Armenian occupation of Nagorno-Karabagh, an enclave in Azerbaijan. But unofficially, according to some Armenian politicians I spoke with, the problem was that the Armenian diaspora had created a hostile climate by relentlessly vilifying Turkey.

So was the Armenian diaspora's recognition campaign actually bad for the Armenians? When I wrote an essay in the *Nation* arguing that it was, a Turkish nationalist website—www.tallarmeniantale.com—hailed me as a "contra-Armenian"; my fellow diasporans sent me hate e-mails. By this time, I felt so alienated from the community that I had folders on my computer with labels like "EXAMPLES OF ANNOYING EMAILS FROM ARMENIANS" and "ARTICLES DEMONSTRATING OBNOXIOUS ARMENIAN RHETORIC." I consoled myself by listening to a CD by a nihilistic Soviet-Armenian folk singer, over and over and over again. The folders grew. I wanted nothing more to do with any of it.

THEN I LEARNED ABOUT MÜGE. Fatma Müge Goçek (pronounced "meugeh go-chek"), a professor of sociology at the University of Michigan, was born and raised in Turkey but earned her doctorate at Princeton. She is 100 percent Turkish—the family fortune came from a flag-making factory her grandfather founded in 1919—but she had nonetheless come to the conclusion that the 1915 massacres were genocide. I had never heard of such a thing. Scholarship on this issue followed blood lines. A quick glance at the relevant shelf in any library showed that Armenian scholars called it the Armenian genocide, and Turkish scholars called it the Armenian question, the Armenian problem, or the Armenian propaganda.*

When I contacted her for an article I was writing, Müge explained to me that, growing up in Turkey in the 1960s, she'd understood that the Armenians had second-class status, but she hadn't known why. "There was such control over the information that one never knew anything," she said. "I got the best education Turkey had to offer, and I still didn't know."

That changed quickly when she came to the US. "Every time I mentioned that I was a Turk," she said, "I had to account for why I had killed all of the Armenians!"

Now Müge's work analyzing Turkish historiography was coming to life in a debate over minority issues that had just begun in Istanbul. Thanks in part to pressure from the European Union to improve treatment of minorities and guarantee freedom of speech, Turkey was changing. A handful of brave Turks were speaking out about the Armenian issue—what the radical Turkish historian Taner Akçam has called one of the five taboos on which the modern Turkish state was founded. Not surprisingly, those publicly challenging the state position on 1915 ran into trouble right away with the courts, which are known to be aligned with the nationalist "deep state," the Turkish military.

Throughout 2005, various friends of Müge's were sued for "insulting the Turkish judiciary"; many other Turkish citizens—most famously the novelist Orhan Pamuk—were sued for "insulting the Turkish nation." Most of the offenses, like Pamuk's, amounted to saying or writing anything that implied that the Armenians had been deliberately massacred. One of the more prominent defendants was a Turkish-Armenian named Hrant Dink, the editor of a little newspaper called *Agos*.

The paper, which was created in 1996, is at the heart of the minority-rights debate in Turkey. Unlike the two older Armenian papers in Istanbul, which mostly print wedding announcements and ads for Armenian dentists, *Agos* is explicitly political: its stated mission is to

---

* The main exception to this rule, until very recently, was a Turkish historian named Taner Akçam, one of Müge's close colleagues, based at the University of Minnesota.

expose the problems of the 60,000 Armenians remaining in Turkey to the rest of Turkish society. Unlike the two other papers, it is published in Turkish, with only a small Armenian insert, and often read by the Turkish liberal intelligentsia. Now and then it is also read by Turkish ultra-nationalists, who like it so much they sometimes take piles of issues away from newsstands and once left a gift, a black wreath, outside the *Agos* office door.

The publisher of *Agos*, Sarkis Seropyan, a 70-year-old former refrigerator salesman, is a good friend of Müge's. He is also an amateur archaeologist who for years has been collecting old maps, books, postcards, and photographs to help him track down and identify Armenian sites throughout Turkey. In reaction to the massive body of literature produced by the Turkish state to retell centuries of history with little if any mention of the Armenians, there has arisen a kind of volunteer brigade of enthusiasts working to record evidence of the former Armenian population. Their efforts are not exactly coordinated, but in his office at *Agos*, Sarkis Bey (Müge addressed him with the Turkish honorific) is the closest thing Turkey has to a one-man clearinghouse. People write to him with bits of information—the partial name of a village, or an old family letter in Armenian that they can't read—and he writes back.

Müge, meanwhile, had been doing research for a scholarly book about what she calls "the silences in Turkish history." Last year, she wanted to see the southeast of Turkey, the heart of historic Armenia, but there was no easy way to find the old Armenian sites: everything had been renamed. So she convinced Sarkis Bey to go exploring with her—he had been there once before, thirty years earlier—and during one of our long phone conversations, she asked me if I wanted to come. By then, I had mostly gotten over the strange exhilaration of talking on the phone with a Turk—not just that, but admiring and trusting her, considering her a friend—but to actually go to Turkey? Was it safe? Of course, said Müge. Could I bring a tape recorder? Bring a whole camera crew, she said. And what if they found out I was Armenian?

"So I understand you're going to Istanbul," an Armenian friend in New York said to me as I was preparing for the trip.

"I'll start out in Istanbul, but then I'm going to Van," I replied.

"*Oh,*" she said. "You mean you're going to Western Armenia."

"Actually," I said to my friend, "Van is in Turkey."

But then, she already knew that.

PART TWO

When I emailed Yavuz Bey, Müge's travel agent, to purchase a ticket from Istanbul to Van, I received the following reply:

> thy flight is confirmed.
> we will issue e-ticket.
> pls inform payment details (credit card).

I informed them of the payment details and immediately began to worry. Not about my card, or that I was going to enemy territory, but because I had learned my lesson about e-tickets the last time I went east of Frankfurt, when I spent hours in the airport in Yerevan trying to convince a bemused clerk that my ticket was "in the computer." Only after tears and an expensive cell phone summons to Delta customer service had I been allowed on board. The same thing had happened in Moscow more than once.

Maybe e-tickets were part of Turkey's EU reform package, I hoped. But the first thing I saw in Istanbul's airport was a huge banner with the words "I ❤ THY." Absurd signs in public places—this was too familiar. It did not bode well. I approached the check-in desk, ready to defend myself.

And then I learned my first Turkish: THY was not a biblical pronoun, but the acronym for Türk Hava Yollari, Turkish Airlines. And there was a good reason to "heart" THY: e-tickets were standard procedure, and I was whisked to my gate with a smile and a perfect "Have a nice trip, Miss Toumani."

It had been my mistake to expect Turkey to be anything like Russia or Armenia, or for that matter like Iran or Georgia or any of its other Eastern neighbors that I knew and loved in spite of their decrepitude. Istanbul was glorious: a seaside city with hills and bridges and water everywhere. Evenings on roof decks with wine and meze, mornings in gardens with elaborate breakfasts, universities bustling with PhDs, heated conversations about global politics—in the Queen's English if you needed it—and two or three newspapers in each person's hands, it seemed.

I had arrived in Istanbul a few days earlier, so I could meet some friends of Müge's before setting off for Van with her and Sarkis Bey. Müge's friends, many of them outspoken critics of the Turkish government, received me with extraordinary warmth. I wasn't prepared for that. I was less prepared still to fall for Istanbul. If this was the enemy, I thought, I would wave my white flag while riding a ferry across the Bosphorus at sunset.

Then I went to see one of Müge's old family friends, a man named Nihat Gökyiğit, the founder and president of the Tekfen construction company. After building a business empire, Nihat Bey had become a patron of the arts and created a multicultural music group called the Black Sea Orchestra. I would be going to Georgia in a few weeks to write about a music festival there, and I wanted to interview Nihat Bey for background. He had attended college in the US and spoke very good English. "I think you will find him *very* interesting," said Müge.

Nihat Bey, who was nearing 80, had white hair, a white mustache, and bright blue eyes. We sat in his office, facing each other on velvet armchairs, with a large square coffee table between us. An assistant carried in cups of Turkish coffee on a tray, and Nihat Bey told me that his Black Sea Orchestra brought together Iranians and Iraqis, Greeks and Turks, Israelis and Palestinians, Armenians and Azerbaijanis.

"Why should these civilizations, East and West, ever clash?" he said. "They can get together and share their talents! You see that painting?" He pointed to one of the forty or so canvases covering his walls. "I got that at the outdoor market in Yerevan."

So Müge had told him that I was Armenian. It was a painting of Mount Ararat, the twin-peaked mountain that Armenians consider their national symbol. Mount Ararat, which Turks called Ağri, lies on the Turkish side of the border. I looked carefully at his painting. When one looks at the mountain from Armenia, the smaller peak is on the left. From Turkey, the smaller peak is on the right. Nihat Bey's painting looked from Armenia. This seemed like a good sign, and so, though I hadn't exactly planned to talk about politics with Nihat Bey, I suddenly found myself asking: "Do the Armenian and Turkish musicians ever discuss the Armenian issue?"

He looked at me for a moment.

"I'll tell you a story," he said.

"I came from the town called Artvin. About 1921, the Armenians started leaving for Batumi. My grandfather told me that he wanted to buy a store in town from an Armenian. He wanted it for his two sons. So he went to the Armenian and said, 'I want to buy this store,' and the Armenian said, 'Sixty golds.' My grandfather gave him the money. But later he thought about it and he said, 'That was not the proper price for this store.' It was not enough. Probably the Armenian wanted to be sure that he would sell it because he had to leave anyway. So he went back to the Armenian man and said, 'I have changed my mind. I do not want to buy this store.' 'But why?' the man said. And my grandfather said, 'You did not ask for enough money. I do not want my two sons to live with this in their hearts. I have brought thirty more golds. If you take this, I will buy. Otherwise the deal is off.'"

Nihat Bey waited, to let his message sink in, then he asked me, "How could such people make harm to each other? Impossible!"

"That's a nice story," I said, but I was annoyed by it. His grandfather was the hero, and the Armenian guy was a poor schmuck. I tried again. "Did you know all your life that there was this question—this issue about what happened to the Armenians?"

"In my family it was not an issue," said Nihat Bey. "We always talked about how good the Armenians were."

"Really?" I said. "Do you believe that the Turkish government is being honest about the information they have?"

"It is my sincere belief," he said.

"So, what do you think is motivating the Armenians who say that it was genocide and ask for recognition?"

"Hm?"

"Why do you think that they need—I mean, want—"

Nihat Bey cut me off. "I don't know. It doesn't make sense. If they want to be friendly with their neighbors, they shouldn't bring up old issues and go into every parliament in Europe and the United States and always try to push it. Why? I'm asking the question to you now. Why repeat these sad stories over and over? The Turkish side never makes an issue of this with the Armenians.

"It's history," he went on. "So what do the Armenians want to do? They want the Turkish government to accept that we have done such a terrible thing, and that we are going to pay for it? They will never have that."

I didn't say anything.

"They will never have that," he repeated.

And then he told me about Armenian terrorists and Armenian assasins, and how there were two sides to every story.*

"So you are a bit mixed up now," Nihat Bey concluded.

And I was. Walking out of his beautiful office, I was confronted with a country that had well-paved highways, innovative environmental projects, and a first-class tourism industry—a country that could remember that you had a ticket "in the computer," but could not remember that it had murdered a million Armenians. While the 70 million citizens of Turkey went about their business, across a sealed border the 3 million citizens of Armenia counted their pennies for bread. Their diaspora, meanwhile, 5 million strong, chanted in public squares worldwide about genocide recognition.

AT THE GATE FOR OUR FLIGHT TO VAN stood my group, none of whom I'd ever met. Müge had said it would be easy to spot them, and she was right. They were four Armenian men and a woman who looked ethnically Turkish but carried herself like an American: it was Müge, who spoke loudly, laughed even more loudly, and—unlike the other women heading to Van—didn't wear anything over her head.

Müge had invited along two other diaspora Armenians, both middle-aged men whom she'd met at an academic conference. Leo was an orthopedic surgeon from Boston, and Ara was a human-rights-policy analyst from Canada. They were grandchildren of genocide survivors, and their fathers had been active in the Armenian Revolutionary Federation, but now both were politically moderate and kept up with liberal Armenian intellectual circles.

I didn't need to be told who the other two men were; I'd been looking forward to meeting them for months. The younger one was a tall, awkward guy in his mid-thirties, with a huge, kinky beard of the sort worn by Orthodox priests. This was Sarkis Bey's son, Vagharshak, who

---

* In the 1970s and '80s, a terrorist group called the Armenian Secret Army for the Liberation of Armenia carried out a series of attacks against Turkish targets, especially diplomats, in Europe and the Middle East, killing about fifty people, and wounding another couple of hundred. A comparatively milder group, the Justice Commandos for the Armenian Genocide, also attacked Turkish targets during this period. For many Turks, the activities of ASALA and JCAG, still in recent memory, are a reference point with which all Armenian diaspora agitations are conflated.

was a deacon—a priest in training—at the Armenian Patriarchate in Istanbul.

And then there was Sarkis Bey himself. He was shorter than his son and more round. He wore a Michigan T-shirt (a gift from Müge) and a Yankees cap over his thinning gray hair. He held an unlit pipe in his mouth. He and Vagharshak sported matching fanny packs around their bellies. Perhaps I had expected a saintly man, a Gandhi? At the very least, I thought he would carry a cane. But here was Sarkis Bey. After we'd all introduced ourselves, he pulled out a box of cookies and offered them around. A few minutes later he handed me the entire box and said, in Armenian, "Müge doesn't need any more cookies, but you should eat some." This comment would have been our little secret had he not then gestured toward Müge—she was standing next to me—and used both hands to indicate a large pair of hips.

THE CITY OF VAN IS THE CAPITAL OF THE VAN REGION, near Turkey's border with Iraq, Iran, and Russia. Armenians were a majority there before the genocide. That, and its proximity to the Russian border, meant that if Armenians were inclined to side with Russia, as the Ottoman government had feared, this was where they'd do it. In April and May of 1915, the Armenians of Van, supported by Russian forces, withstood a six-week-long siege by the Ottoman army before capitulating. As a result, Turkish denialists point to Van as evidence that the Armenians were rebels who got what they deserved.*

Now Van is a dismal place, with high unemployment, crowded streets, and poor infrastructure. We'd been there about ten minutes when a young man, Suat Atan, showed up at our hotel looking for Sarkis Bey. Suat was the son of the mayor of the Gürpınar district and was creating a website to track down Armenian sites in the area. I didn't understand why he was doing this, as he was Kurdish, but he was, and Sarkis Bey was helping him.

It went on like this all day, Sarkis Bey holding court with people he'd been corresponding with from Istanbul: a local journalist who was following EU developments; a kilim designer who had explored the mountains of Van in search of authentic rug designs. Each of these people

---

* There were indeed incidents, along the Eastern Front, where Armenian armed bands, sometimes working with Russian troops, raided Muslim villages killing Turks and Kurds. But for the most part, the Ottoman Empire's Armenian subjects remained loyal, and many fought for the Ottoman Army.

possessed a few key pieces of information, like the location of a specific Armenian church or the Kurdish translation for a particular Armenian name. Nor was Sarkis Bey empty-handed. For the young webmaster, he deciphered some Armenian inscriptions. For the reporter, he offered a business card and a promise to run one of his stories in Istanbul. And to the kilim maker, Sarkis Bey delivered a photocopy of an entire book about kilims—in Russian, which neither man could read.

At his kilim studio, Enver Bey, who was also a Kurd, offered suggestions for our stay in Van. "Be sure you go to our local historical museum," he said, and winked. "You will learn about how the Armenians massacred us," he added, and winked again.

Müge and I laughed, but Sarkis Bey did not. This was my first clue that in the great Armenian-versus-Turk matchup, there is a third party, performing what is known in psychoanalysis as triangulation: the Kurds might be counted as friends or enemies by either side, depending on the circumstances. During the genocide, they were encouraged by Turkish soldiers to rape and steal from the Armenian deportees. But many of them also saved Armenians from death, often by marrying the women or adopting the children.

The Kurds in the southeast had huge problems of their own with Turkish authorities, so it seemed to me that there should be a kind of fellowship of suffering between us. But Sarkis Bey's manner with the Kurds we met was awkward at best, icy at worst. As we got up to leave, Enver Bey urged us to stay for lunch, but Sarkis Bey shook his head. "We have work to do," he said.

We spent the rest of that day hunting down a handful of sites with Armenian significance: the monastery of Surp Bartoghomyos, the Urartian fortress of Çavuştepe, the ruins of Narek, and Van Castle, where Sarkis Bey gave the little boys a history lesson. Most of these sites, abandoned with no signs and no explanations, were located near tiny mountain villages overlooking Lake Van, a stunning volcanic lake. Often, there were piles of broken pottery or other artifacts strewn around, untended and ignored. As part of our getting-to-know-you ritual, Sarkis Bey kept handing me choice fragments of the pottery, until I had to refuse. It was like collecting seashells at the beach; after a while, you're not sure what to do with them. Except unlike seashells, these ignored relics would, upon inspection at any airport, gain the status of antiquities and require a steep penalty.

Everywhere, there were Armenian inscriptions, written in classical Armenian script, which only religious people can read. (We had Vagharshak to help us.) The region was like a giant open-air museum.

The actual museum—the Van Historical Museum, which Enver Bey had recommended—was another story. It was small, unembellished, tucked away on a side street. In a corner of a room upstairs, a huge yellow and black sign hanging from the ceiling bore the words "KATLIAM SEKSIYONU"—Massacre Section.

By this was meant: the massacre of the Turks. A display case presented books with titles like *The Massacres Committed by the Armenians* and *Setting the Record Straight on Armenian Propaganda Against Turkey*, written by Turkish government officials. Another case, containing some bones, was labeled "IN 1915 BURNED AND MASSACRED OF TURKS SKELETONS." It included a long report about an aborted archaeological dig where, it said, the remains of Turkish women and children were found.

We took turns entering and exiting the massacre section. I read notices into my tape recorder and photographed the display cases. Leo, suddenly very clinical, made his rounds from skeleton to skeleton and mumbled about the shapes of the bones and their characteristics. Sarkis Bey didn't say anything at all. He took a quick glance around, then waited in the courtyard out front while the rest of us finished.

In our hotel room that night, Müge and I slept with the window open so that we could hear the gentle sound of Lake Van lapping against the shore just a few feet away. But I was woken around sunrise by the most awful, unpleasant crowing sound I had ever heard. I couldn't imagine what hideous birds were making this noise, and my reaction was not annoyance so much as disgust. I knew something really twisted was happening in my mind when, caught between dreaming and waking, I registered a thought that would have made me groan if I'd heard it from anybody else: that this must have been the way Armenians sounded to the Turks.

That day, we were headed to an island in Lake Van called Akdamar (Akhtamar in Armenian), which is home to a 10th-century Armenian church, Surp Khatch, or the Church of the Holy Cross. Surp Khatch had recently become a big political issue in Turkey. For the first time ever, the Turkish government—under pressure from the EU—had agreed to work with the Turkish-Armenian community to restore an Armenian historical site. Sarkis Bey had arranged a meeting with the architect who was managing the reconstruction.

Besides being the name of the island, Akhtamar is also the name of an epic poem by Hovhannes Toumanian, the Armenian author from whom my grandfather borrowed our last name. In Toumanian's poem, a beautiful maiden named Tamar lives on this island. Each night, she lights a lantern and carries it to the edge of the shore, so that her true love, a strong young man who lives on the mainland, can swim across the lake and find her. But then the stars and the waves gossip about Tamar's sins, so the young men on the island find out about these late-night meetings and extinguish Tamar's flame. That night, her suitor swims and swims to reach her but can't see any light. As he drowns in the waves, he calls for her: "Akh, Tamar! Akh, Tamar!"

My mother used to read me this story when I was a child, and each time she reached the part where the stars start to whisper about Tamar's transgressions, she would sob so dramatically that she couldn't finish. For years I never really understood what happened to Tamar's love affair. I only knew that this island, this Akhtamar, meant something large and important to us.*

A Turkish flag waved on the mast of the small, rusty boat that would carry us across Lake Van to the island—a bit of a taunt, I had to admit. But we were immediately distracted by something much more surprising: a group of about ten people were already on the boat, and they were speaking Armenian—Eastern Armenian. They were from Yerevan.

Traveling to Turkey from Armenia is a bit like traveling to Cuba from the US: the border between the two countries is sealed, diplomatic relations do not exist, and you generally need to take a roundabout route through the mountain roads of Georgia. Weekly flights between Istanbul and Yerevan were instituted recently, but they serve foreigners and businesspeople more than ordinary tourists.

---

* So important that decades after the Armenians were expelled from the Van region, some enterprising patriots turned their attention to Lake Sevan, in Armenia proper, and renamed an island there Akhtamar; it was home to its own old church, Surp Karapet, whose silhouette bore an uncanny resemblance to the church on the real Akhtamar Island. But the fantasy was soon fouled: thanks to an ill-conceived drainage plan designed by the Armenian Supreme Soviet, water levels in Lake Sevan dropped so low that Akhtamar II revealed itself to be a peninsula. Tamar's young lover would simply have walked.

So I was delighted by this chance encounter with the group from Yerevan: after being surrounded by Turkish and Western Armenian for several days, I could speak to them in my own dialect.

"Vordegh'its ek?" they exclaimed when we greeted them. "Vordegh'its ek?" Technically this means "Where are you from?" but I knew in a situation like this it meant much more: Where were your grandparents from, why are you here, what is your political affiliation? And, are you married?

It was easy to explain that Ara was from Canada by way of Kessab, Syria; that Leo came from Boston via Beirut; that Sarkis (I didn't make the mistake of adding "Bey" then) and Vagharshak were *Bolsa-hye*, Armenians from Istanbul. As for me, my accent was evidence enough that I was an Iranian-Armenian from America. But what about Müge?

I couldn't figure out a way to explain who Müge was without using the word *Turk*—which sounds like "toork" in Armenian. I didn't want to use it, because in Armenian, the word is less an indication of nationality than it is an all-purpose insult, applied liberally to describe liars, penny-pinchers, and people with dirty kitchens. So I geared up with a big smile and some acrobatics of the eyebrows, which I hoped would convey that there was a good, deep, important reason why we had a Turk with us.

"Yev eenkuh Toork-eh," was all I needed to say—"And as for her, she's Turkish." But I was nervous that as soon as Müge heard the word "toork" she would know that I was talking about her. I watched Müge reclining in the sun on the bench across from us, and wondered what to do.

But Müge is perceptive. She saved me from my bumbling explanation by stating firmly, with a smile, "I'm Turkish." And then she got up and went to the other end of the boat.

Now that they knew Müge was Turkish, I had to explain how it had transpired that we, a group of Armenians, were traveling with her. My Armenian is OK—it's something like talking to a precocious child, or an enthusiastic peasant—but sometimes I can't achieve the nuance I need. And so: "Well, Müge is a *friend* of ours from America. She is a professor at a *very good university* there, and she is a *very interesting, very unusual person*. She has done a lot of *work* on the *Armenian issue*," I said, "and she is *friends* with *a lot* of Armenians."

I was trying to figure out how to convey the point without saying, plainly, "Don't worry, she believes it was genocide!" But I could tell they thought I was crazy, so I gave up and joined the rest of my group at the front of the boat. Sarkis Bey had been there all along; he seemed to want nothing to do with the *Yerevan'tsis*.

I DIDN'T UNDERSTAND SARKIS BEY—and not just because we spoke two different dialects of Armenian. He was the publisher of a confrontational Armenian newspaper, but as we entered one formerly Armenian village after another, he never seemed interested in confronting anyone. He was taking us to church after church, and his son was pursuing the priesthood, but I had it on good authority—Müge's—that Sarkis Bey, an old socialist, was having a hard time dealing with Vagharshak's decision. Müge said that Sarkis Bey had told the Patriarch that if he ordained his son, Sarkis Bey personally would convert to Islam.

He had spent seventy years living quietly in a place he was supposed to have been erased from, and it had left its mark. One day, when a village guard in the town of Muş asked him why we were interested in seeing a structure—it was a church converted to a mosque—Sarkis Bey snapped: "Who are you that you need to know? I've got as much right to be here as you have, by my lineage." But he never, ever said what that lineage was.

As for the *Yerevan'tsis* on the boat, I wondered if Sarkis Bey resented the unspoken assumption that they were somehow more Armenian than he. The Armenians of Istanbul had suffered considerable hostility from Armenia proper as well as from the diaspora, where younger generations bristled at hearing them speaking in Turkish or using Turkish names. Their loyalties were mixed: they were Turkish citizens, after all, and it was a pretty nice country if you managed to stay out of trouble.

AKHTAMAR CAME INTO VIEW as a green mass on the lake with a domed, stone church perched on its edge. As we pulled up to the shore, Sarkis Bey got off the boat first, and standing on a large boulder, bowed and said, to nobody in particular, "Hametsek"—which is how, in Armenian, you welcome somebody to your home or to your table.

The Yerevan group scattered up the hill to get as close as possible to the church, which was completely fenced off to visitors, and I wandered around for a few minutes until I found Sarkis Bey sitting on a low, square wooden stool under an almond tree. He handed me a little branch holding a cluster of three almond pods. "Take this to your mother. Tell her they are almonds from Akhtamar," he said.

Oh, how we understand each other, we Armenians. My mother collects things in threes, especially things relating to pomegranates, figs, apricots, and almonds—the symbolic bounty of Armenian soil—in the form of paintings, figurines, Christmas tree ornaments, you name it. These are talismans for the fertility of her three daughters.

Then Sarkis Bey told me to sit down and keep a low profile, because once the *Yerevan'tsis* had their fill and got back on the boat, the architect, who was expecting us, would unlock the gate and take us into the church.

Cahit Bey, the architect, turned out to be an extremely charming, handsome man. He was also, he told us, a Kurd. This was no longer surprising information. At the start of the trip, I had asked Müge about the ethnicity of every person we met in Van (Turkish? Kurdish? Assyrian, maybe?), but then I stopped asking. Everyone we met—everyone—was Kurdish. Every village that had been occupied by Armenians was now populated by Kurds. Cahit Bey told us he was a fellow minority as a kind of reassurance; it seemed he wanted the newspaper publisher from Istanbul to feel that the church was in good hands. That didn't work, though, and finally Cahit Bey obliged Sarkis Bey in a lengthy discussion about hydraulic lye, the proper spacing of stones, and the difference in materials used over the centuries.

On the boat ride back to the mainland, their diplomatic summit concluded, the two men shared a cigar. Sarkis Bey examined the burn pattern for a long time, and then announced, "You'll go on a journey." He meant himself.

High on a hillside, the words VATAN BÖLÜNMEZ were carved into the brown grass. "The motherland cannot be divided." For a moment, this was confusing: we were in Kurdish territory, so was this a protest from the Kurds against the state? Müge told me the words were a quote from Atatürk, a standard message from the government. Kurds, I later realized, would have written it in their own language, although it was against the law to use Kurdish in public demonstrations. A court recently fined twenty people in the city of Siirt 100 lira each for holding up signs at a Kurdish New Year celebration containing the letters *q* and *w*, which are not a part of the Turkish alphabet.

The motherland cannot be divided, except that it is. I thought of all the words I'd been seeing on storefronts throughout Van, words that explained the names of Armenians I had known: a tailor, *terzi*, for Sandy Terzian, a girl from summer camp; a jeweler, *kuyumcu*, for Dickran Kouyoumdjian, an Armenian professor I had at Berkeley. Kassabian, Ekmekjian, Momjian: the butcher, the baker, the candlestick maker—I knew them all.

WE CONTINUED TOURING THE REGION. The white van we drove around in like an Armenian indie rock band was hot, and dirty, even though poor Refik, our driver, washed it down every day, and the floor was covered with our empty water bottles. At first we would just kick them toward the back, but pretty soon the entire thing was water bottles, two or three deep. This was bad enough, but then we'd pass by a spring or a fountain of some sort, and Refik or Sarkis Bey would start filling up the bottles, to drink from, after we'd been kicking them around for a few days already. And then I didn't dare complain about being thirsty, because somebody would try to hand me a beaten-up, refilled bottle that had been rolling around in the sun for God knows how long, and I'd be a real jerk to refuse it.

We drove from Van to Tatvan, where we stayed in a dismal hotel for a night, and then moved on to Kahramanmaraş (formerly Marash), where instead of Armenian churches we were seeking the famous Marash ice cream, so thick the vendors sometimes hung it from hooks outside. We found ancient villages, like Çangli, where elaborate Armenian tombstones were placed sideways or upside down in the walls of Kurdish houses, rode boats to still more distant outposts like Altınsaç, and, in the mountain town of Suleymanlı (formerly Zeitun), we found a village guard who told us he'd written a poem about the Armenians. ("Oh, it wasn't interesting," Sarkis Bey dismissed it when I asked for a translation.)

Strange things happened to us in the places we visited, but more often they happened on the road. A couple times a day we were stopped at checkpoints to make sure we weren't carrying any bombs or trying to smuggle petroleum from Iran. Once, a solider pulled us over and, seeing that we carried nothing suspicious, asked if we knew the time. In a similar vein, we were given directions to a village by a man in a donkey cart who said it was "just one cigarette away," prompting a lengthy anthropological debate, when we did not soon find the village, as to whether he meant one cigarette walking, or driving, or riding the donkey cart, and what kind of cigarette anyway? Another day, a man chased us down after we stopped to photograph a sign for a church, on which the word *church* had been scratched out. He asked us to come to his village and translate an Armenian inscription on a stone above his stable door. It turned out the stable had been a chapel. The man, who was the head of the local prison, was pleased by this news and told us that there were still a few very old people in the village who were said to have Armenian blood. "Does everybody know who is who?" Müge asked him. "We don't distinguish very much," he answered. "We live near the road, so we are more civilized than most."

In the van that we climbed out of every hour or so, I wanted to sit next to Sarkis Bey, and also I didn't. On the one hand, he wasn't a typical Armenian man of his generation, the kind I found intimidating: he endured teasing from Müge, who had been charged, by his wife, to keep him from eating or smoking too much, and he also let Müge handle all the money and most of the arrangements. And he had a daughter just about my age who had moved to Switzerland with her husband, and he spoke of her often. On the other hand, our Armenian dialects were pretty far apart, so it was exhausting to communicate. On the back of his business card for *Agos*, Sarkis Bey had written down all three of his personal phone numbers for me. The first two were followed by the words, in Armenian, *summer house* and *winter house*. The third number was followed by one word, in English: "hand." If you count it, "hand" was the only conversation that Sarkis Bey and I ever had in English.

But Sarkis Bey and I had the bond of journalists, and in his way he understood that I needed facts. Many of our interactions consisted of Sarkis Bey turning toward me in the van and saying two names in succession: the name of a village in Turkish, and then the original name, in Armenian: "Haşköy, Hatsik!" or "Pertek, Pertag!" Now and then, when he could find it, he threw in the Kurdish name, too, and his eyes lit up, like he'd hit three cherries on the slots.*

---

* When we approached the town of "Harput, Kharpert!" which had been an intellectual center for Ottoman Armenians, Sarkis Bey sounded his call, and Vagharshak woke abruptly from a nap. He said hopefully, "Karpuz?" which is not the name of a town, but the Turkish word for watermelon. Unfazed, Sarkis Bey explained that, as it happened, an Armenian was responsible for bringing melons to Europe and the rest of the world. This couldn't be true, I was certain; Armenians believe Armenians invented everything. In my notebook, I

And when we got to Muş, which is 200 kilometers west of Van and hasn't changed its name, Sarkis Bey announced our arrival by launching into "Zartir La-o," a song about the woes of the Armenians of Muş. It's one of the most forceful Armenian nationalistic songs there is—I don't know if it's the aggressive marching rhythm that does it, or the fact that the word "Turk" appears in almost every verse, instead of euphemisms like "evil one" or "our enemy"—either way, Ara, Leo, and I joined Sarkis Bey exuberantly.

But then I became worried that Müge would feel hurt by our Armenian-bonding sing-along. We were getting sloppy about maintaining our previously admirable Armenian-Turkish goodwill. So, to make her feel included, I began to translate. "The mob of patriots has gathered," I said, "come to surround the battlefield of Muş. The sultan wants to erase us!"

The second verse was worse:

> The poor Muş'etsi died crying,
> Wandering around in foreign lands;
> He died paying taxes to the Turk!

Müge nodded with interest; it was all sociology to her. I recalled the day we'd seen the horrible Van Historical Museum, and had gotten back in the van afterward, depressed. At that moment, it had taken some self-control for a carload of recovering nationalists to avoid saying something inappropriate. Müge had saved us then: "Look what I bought at the gift shop!" she said. She handed Sarkis Bey a necklace bead, about an inch long. Sarkis Bey studied it and then his shoulders shook in a deep, rhythmic laugh. "It's a reproduction of a typical Urartian design," she grinned. The drawing depicted one Urartian taking another Urartian from behind.

I also remembered the story she had told me a few days earlier, about the first trip she had taken with Sarkis Bey, two summers ago, to

---

wrote "Papa Cantalupe, 17th C., Italy," and tried not to laugh out loud. And when we got back to Istanbul, I entered "cantaloupe" into Wikipedia: "Cantaloupe was named after the commune Cantalupo in Sabina, in the Sabine Hills near Tivoli, Italy, a summer residence of the Pope. It was originally cultivated about the year 1700 from seeds brought from Armenia, part of the homeland of melons." What do you know? (Then again, Wikipedia entries can be written by anyone, even an Armenian. Is there something suspicious in the misplaced zeal of those final words, "homeland of melons"?)

a town called Kemaliye (Agn in Armenian), where both of their ancestors had lived. "We found exactly where my relatives had lived," Müge told me. "It was easy: the names, the information, it was all there. But we couldn't find any trace of Sarkis Bey's family." Eventually they found a tombstone with some Armenian writing on it, in a dumpster. It was the only evidence they saw that Armenians had lived in Kemaliye. We were lying in the dark in adjacent twin beds in our hotel room as she told me about it. "History belongs to the victors," Müge concluded, and we nodded off to sleep.

AND THEN THINGS GOT REALLY STRANGE. On the way to a village that the Turks call Yedi Kilise and that the Armenians call Varakavank, we wound our way into the mountains, farther and farther from the lake. Yedi Kilise means "Seven Churches" in Turkish, while Varakavank is the Armenian name for the monastery, or *vank*, which comprised those churches and was the seat of the Armenian Patriarch in the 10th century.

In the distance, another minivan headed toward us. It was identical to ours—the angular shape, the off-white paint dusted in brown, probably a mountain of water bottles in the back. We hadn't seen anything but donkey carts in hours, so when the van pulled up alongside us it was natural for the two drivers to lean out their windows and greet each other.

Suddenly a man in the passenger seat of the other van called out, in Turkish, "Is there a priest among you?"

Then several things happened at once.

Vagharshak, sitting in the middle section of the van, sat up straight. His hand went to his wannabe-priest beard.

"Dook hye ek?" Sarkis Bey called back in Armenian. Are you Armenian?

And Ara, who had been squinting through the two layers of tinted windows, shouted, "Gavin! Is that you?"

The passengers of both vans climbed out to get to the bottom of all this. I started talking with a guy named Paul, 24 years old, who explained to me that they were members of the youth branch of the Dashnakstutiun, the Armenian Revolutionary Federation, from Los Angeles. "We've been here in Western Armenia for about a week now," Paul said.

I couldn't believe it. These were the people who ran my childhood summer camp and made me sing those songs of Armenian liberation. I wanted to know what they were doing here, but also I had to be careful, because I didn't want to explain to Paul that I considered his group a borderline terrorist organization.

But Paul seemed to trust that the very fact that we were Armenian and we were here meant that our mission was the same as theirs. He told me that they had spent months researching the sites they wanted to find. "We figured it was important to know what these places look like, if we're ever going to get them back."

Ara introduced me to Gavin, not an Armenian at all, but a full-blooded Scottish Armenophile who had hitched a ride with Paul's group on the road to Yedi Kilise. Ara had met Gavin in London once, through friends. For the past ten years, Gavin had sought out Armenian sites all over Turkey and taken photographs of every single cross, inscription, corner, ceiling, whatever. His pet project was the ruins of Ani, the medieval Armenian citadel outside of Kars, and to that end he'd created a remarkable website, VirtualANI, which stood in stark contrast to the state-issued Ani guides.*

Meanwhile Paul had learned that Ara was from Canada. "Oh," he said to Ara, "did you see our play?"

"What play?"

"In 1989 our group went to Toronto and did a play about Karekin Njdeh," Paul said, referring to one of the dead heroes of the Armenian nationalist movement.

"Uh, no, I guess I missed that," said Ara.

As we concluded this summit, Paul told me he wanted to invite me to one of his group's meetings in Los Angeles, so that I could see "what we're all about." I thanked him politely, but he asked me to promise that I would come.

So I said I would. I wanted very much to understand how he and his comrades—that is what they call one another in the organization—had come to believe that it was their destiny to one day leave Los Angeles and reclaim southeastern Turkey as their own.

* If you would like to see this website, go to www.virtualani.freeserve.co.uk. Whatever you do, don't go to www.virtualani.com, especially if you're at work.

"I want to give you something to hold you to your promise," Paul said. He removed a bracelet from his wrist and handed it to me. It was a black rubber band engraved with the words "NEVER AGAIN."

He told me that he and his friends had them made for Armenian-genocide recognition. He really wanted me to have it. "You can give it back to me when you come to LA to see us," he said. "I just need you to promise that."

Müge and Ara watched me. I should have refused the bracelet; I hated this bracelet. But there Paul stood, a sweet Armenian boy, the kind I never spoke to anymore, and finally I took it and thanked him and told him I would see him in LA.

"There's just one more thing you have to promise," he said. "You can't take it off your wrist until I see you." So I promised that, too, and Paul gave me a big hug good-bye.

When we finally reached Yedi Kilise, we found an old Kurdish man who seemed to be some kind of self-appointed proprietor of the Armenian monastery, a cluster of ancient stone buildings with fallen ceilings and crumbling walls. He was immediately annoyed by our presence. "I think I'm going to tear this down," he said.

Refik, our driver, who occasionally acted as an ambassador of sorts since none of us spoke Kurdish, asked him why.

"It costs money to maintain it," he said. "Give me some money so I can maintain it, then."

"Hold me back so I don't hit this guy," Sarkis Bey said to us. He put his hands behind his head like he'd just finished running.

Later, I learned why the proprietor had been hostile. Paul's group from Los Angeles had been returning from Yedi Kilise when we ran into them, and they'd had a fight with the same old man. Apparently the whole group of them had strolled right into the main church, set up a portable stereo playing Armenian hymns, and lit candles all around. Then Paul had read out loud from Saint Grikor Narekatsi's 10th-century Book of Lamentations. They had been performing this routine at churches all over Eastern Turkey, and they'd even made it onto Turkish CNN after one of their vigils was broken up by the police.

ONE BY ONE, my traveling companions had revealed their idiosyncrasies—most, though not all, endearing ones. Ara was witty and cheerful, though when we neared the border, and the Syrian town of Kessab, where he'd grown up, he became very nervous because, it turned out, he'd never fulfilled his military requirement. "I want to see it," he said when we suggested a quick visit, "but that doesn't mean I want to stay." Leo, though magnanimous and enlightened, hated Kurds: he considered them unscrupulous freeloaders and often said so. Vagharshak was silent, especially with me; he seldom spoke except to translate religious inscriptions, and often, while we explored various ruins, he'd wander off alone, quietly humming old church hymns. Müge, I thought, could do anything. She cracked jokes, translated, and expounded on political theory, and her cell phone rang constantly as friends, family, and colleagues called her to check in. The only remaining mystery—not including Sarkis Bey, that is—was Refik, our driver. We knew almost nothing about him. Besides the minivan itself—and the creaky tapes of Kurdish pop music that he blasted in it—Refik hadn't brought anything with him on this trip. At night, when Müge and I would retreat to our hotel room to wash off the day's grime with our sweet shampoos and expensive lotions, Refik would walk silently a few steps behind Sarkis Bey and Vagharshak into their room, and take off his shoes, and sleep on the floor.

So when Refik invited us to visit his family, who lived in a village near Yedi Kilise, we enthusiastically agreed, even though Sarkis Bey considered it, as always, a waste of time.

In the two-room mud house of Refik's family, we sat on kilims while his nieces spread out a large vinyl tablecloth on the ground. They brought us cold barley soup, goat meat stew, rice with bits of noodles, and *ayran*, a yogurt drink.

Refik's uncle, Izzettin Bey, a tiny man with brown skin and perfect posture, wore a tasseled fez over his white hair. He told us that his grandfather bought this village in 1945, which led Müge to ask whose village it had been before that.

"Before that, the state owned it."

"And before that?"

"I don't know."

"Was it the Armenians?"

"Well, I guess that's right. Now that you mention it, it makes sense. No wonder there are all those churches up the hill."

Refik's uncle had an elementary school education and did not speak any Turkish until he joined the military. He had five sons and six daughters. As we started to eat, he asked us a question.

"So, how does it work with your group?" he said. "Do the two of you"—nodding toward me and Müge—"cook for the four of them?"

There was another reason for inviting us to lunch, we discovered. Izzettin Bey's wife, an old woman with a smooth, pale face, was escorted into the room, bent over a knobby tree branch for a cane. She had some kind of medical problem and they hoped that we might be able to help. "Because you are learned people," said Izzettin Bey.

Leo finished eating and moved across the room to sit closer to the woman. He spoke Turkish, but not quite enough to conduct an accurate medical examination, so there ensued a game of telephone—Leo speaking in English, Müge translating to Turkish, Refik translating to Kurdish, and then Izzettin Bey repeating Refik's words to his wife—as Leo inquired about her energy, her breathing, her appetite, and so on.

"It is not a neurological problem, and I think her lungs are clean," Leo eventually said. He needed to take her pulse, so he bowed slightly toward Izzettin Bey and asked, "May I touch her wrist?"

Two small girls spied from the doorway. It was impossible not to stare. The woman herself turned away while Leo took her hand, looked at his watch, and counted to himself. Then, as if he hadn't already stripped her naked with the pulse count, he asked Izzettin Bey if he could see her ankles, to know whether they were swollen. Slowly she moved aside several layers of skirts while Leo inquired about her age.

"I am more than 70," said Izzettin Bey. "Her age we don't know, but we have been married forever!" He gazed at his wife.

Leo asked whether she had taken any medication, and somebody came into the room with a large plastic bag filled with tubes and bottles. "Aspirin, gingko biloba, antibiotic ointment," Leo read them aloud one by one. An admirable collection, he said. But there was nothing that looked relevant to this case.

"It could be a lack of sugar," said Leo, "or bad circulation. Or something to do with progestin and menopause." The woman watched as he wrote a series of explanations on a piece of paper, which Müge rewrote in Turkish. "They should take the note to a pharmacy in town," he said.

° ° °

As we drove away, I thought about something that had happened the night before at dinner. We had been guests of a Kurdish member of parliament, and Leo had spent the meal ranting to me about how much he distrusted the Kurds. Yet he had just treated this Kurdish woman so tenderly.

"You know," Sarkis Bey said suddenly, "my mother's father was a doctor."

Sarkis Bey had been quiet throughout the medical examination. Now he nodded, as if confirming to himself the truth of what he'd just said.

"He was a military doctor from Izmit, near the Black Sea. He married my grandmother when she was 15. They had a horse and two servants, and he was stationed in Gümüshane, where he was a high-ranking colonel and a surgeon.

"In 1915, when they gathered up the men, they also gathered my grandfather. He had some tension with the mayor of Gümüshane. So you see, even though during the deportation, all the Armenian doctors were spared so that they could treat wounded Turkish soldiers, they slit my grandfather's throat right away. They didn't even bother to send him into exile.

"Zarouhi, my grandmother, had a 15-year-old son, a 7-year-old daughter, a 3-year-old daughter, and an infant daughter. They were all sent to Der Zor, to the desert. My grandfather's aunt and mother had been visiting the family when the deportation orders came, so they had to go, too. But my grandfather's aunt couldn't walk anymore, so she jumped from a bridge into the Euphrates.

"She was like a water lily, with her dress floating up around her. The 3-year-old thought she was swimming.

"Then my great-grandmother asked a soldier to shoot her, and he said that the bullets would cost her money. He shot her from behind, and my grandmother told the children not to look back.

"When the caravan reached Agn, halfway to Der Zor, my grandmother had the idea to pretend that she was Greek. A cable was sent back to Izmit, asking, Is the doctor's wife Greek? Izmit had been a Greek city, Nikomedia, during the Roman Empire. My grandmother had learned Greek growing up in order to communicate with the shopkeepers. The answer came back from Izmit that nobody was sure of her origin, but that she was known, for sure, to be fluent in Greek.

"So she and her children—my mother was 7 at the time—stayed in Agn, and then moved on to Malatya, where the two girls were accepted in an orphanage and my grandmother became the orphanage nanny. Her son, who was 15, was sent to Yerevan. They never spoke to him again."

Sarkis Bey told the entire story from the front seat, looking straight ahead. Now he turned his body around to face us, and said, "My grandmother and my mother each told me this story on their own, but I didn't want to believe it."

So in 1965, he decided to go to Yerevan for the first time in his life. There, he found his uncle, the one who had left Malatya as a 15-year-old boy and had not been heard from since.

"We sat down together, and he told me the exact same story."

IT HAD TAKEN THIS LONG FOR SARKIS BEY to tell his family's story, and there it was. It's not that I hadn't asked him before. But after hearing variations on the same story since I was ten, eight, five years old—I used to read and re-read them as bedtime stories, and cry—it was surprisingly awkward, just as it should be, to ask Sarkis Bey to tell me how his relatives had suffered. Each time I asked him to tell me what had happened, he'd put me off somehow. He liked to blackmail me by insisting that I write an article for *Agos* about what I had learned on this trip. If I tell you, he'd say in any number of situations—if I tell you about this village, this church, if I tell you about my family—you have to write me that article about your impressions of Van. And I kept saying I would, though I knew I wouldn't. Now, hearing his story, I knew exactly why. I didn't really care what village we were in, or what had happened there, and I wasn't filled with some sense of wonder at the sight of the ancestral homeland. I had come to Turkey because I wanted to find out what Turks said about the genocide. I didn't expect them to say much. But it was the reticence of an Armenian, Sarkis Bey, that had been the real surprise. How could I write in *Agos* that what I had discovered on this trip was him? So I didn't say anything when Sarkis Bey finished telling us what happened to his family in 1915. I only asked him how to spell Gümüshane, and what year they had made it to Malatya.

ON THE LAST NIGHT OF OUR TRIP, after everybody had gone to bed, I stayed up and had one more raki on the rooftop with Sarkis Bey.

In eight days we had gone from Van to Muş, Marash to Zeitun, Elazığ to Antakya, and to about thirty towns and villages in between. I asked Sarkis Bey if he was happy with the trip.

He told me a couple of discoveries we'd made had meant a lot to him: a monastery near a village that used to be called Gandzak, which had been almost impossible to find, and a chapel he called Garni, which he hadn't known existed. "You can't know how happy I was," said Sarkis Bey, and he was right about that. He'd given no indication.

He told me he'd planned our journey based on the novels of the great Armenian writer Khachik Dashtents, who was born in a village in the mountains between Van and Muş, and who fled during the genocide. When he was 25 years old, Sarkis Bey read *Khodedan*, in which Dashtents wrote about life in the Armenian villages of this region. He wrote with a level of topographical detail that was almost incantatory in its reverence for each hill, each tree. Ever since Sarkis Bey read about these places, he wanted to see them for himself. "If you can't recognize your homeland, you can't love it," he said.

If you can't recognize your homeland you can't love it. Sarkis Bey sounded exactly like Paul, from Los Angeles—and yet utterly unlike Paul at the same time.

"Baron Sarkis," I began. (I traded *bey* for *baron*, the Armenian honorific, now and then when we were alone. Sarkis had been my grandfather's name, and my dad had always addressed him this way.) "What do you think of the fact that some Armenians around the world believe they have the right to take back these lands?"

Sarkis Bey put down his drink and leaned forward. "Let me ask you a question," he said.

"Would you go live in Varakavank?" He used the Armenian name for the broken-down village of Yedi Kilise, where Paul's group had held their candlelight vigil.

"Come!" he called out, beckoning grandly with his arms. "Please, come live on this land!" He was talking to all of them—to all the Armenians in the diaspora, the ones who hate Turkey, who have never been to Turkey, who—when they think about them at all—feel that the Istanbul Armenians have sold out the Cause by living quietly among the enemy.

"Don't tell me you want them to give back Kars, or Ardahan, or Van. Don't tell me you want them back unless you're ready to get up and go live there," he said.

"First, we just wanted an independent Armenia. Now we have that country, that flag, and so? Nobody wants to stay there. All the Armenian girls are prostitutes in Trabzon.

"Don't misunderstand me, OK? I love Van more than you and more than any of them. But I'm not looking to take it back. I only wish they would open up the borders so that an Armenian from Yerevan might be able to open up a shop here and earn some money."

POSTSCRIPT

FOR THE NEXT FEW WEEKS, I enjoyed the Istanbul high life, staying out late at clubs with American expats, visiting Sarkis Bey's summer house and meeting his wife, talking to the *Agos* staff in their unmarked marble office building. Then it was time to leave Turkey, and, as it happened, I did so by taking a boat from Trabzon, on the Black Sea coast, to Russia. Sarkis Bey was right: there were a lot of prostitutes—although, since all of them had dyed yellow or orange hair, it was hard to tell which ones were Armenian.

A few months after that, on a weekend trip to Los Angeles for a friend's wedding, I called Paul. I still had his "NEVER AGAIN" bracelet, and it was time to give it back. We met near the pier in Santa Monica, on a clear, sunny day not unlike the one when we'd first bumped into each other—except that now we were looking at the Pacific instead of Lake Van, and instead of donkeys and sheep we were surrounded by people with J. Crew shopping bags.

Over lunch at a Greek restaurant, Paul told me there had been a big change in his life since our encounter in the summer. After nine years, he had stepped down from his post as the head of the local chapter of the Armenian Youth Federation. In fact, he'd left the group entirely. There were personal differences, he said. Besides, he was busy, working full time as a loan officer and finishing his master's degree in finance.

Would he go back to Van? I asked him. "No," he said. "Now I've seen it, and I know I can't do anything." He had decided to focus on Armenia itself, he told me, and had contacted various government ministries in Yerevan to see if they needed an intern. They did not.

On Christmas Day, I got bad news from Turkey. The courts had opened a new lawsuit against Hrant Dink, the editor-in-chief of *Agos*, because he'd written an editorial criticizing the court decision to cancel an academic conference about the Armenian massacres. As the publisher of the paper, Sarkis Bey was also named in the suit. If found guilty, he could face up to four and a half years in prison.

I e-mailed Sarkis Bey expressing my concern about the lawsuit; it was impossible to imagine such a thing. "Please send good news," I wrote. He wrote back and didn't mention the charges at all. He told me he had just returned from Switzerland, where he had visited his daughter and her husband and their brand-new baby—a boy. "Finally, we are grandparents," he said. He also asked me why I'd never written that article for *Agos* that I promised him. "Get ready for this year's trip," he signed off.

A month later, the lawsuit against Orhan Pamuk was dropped, after a massive international campaign on his behalf. But the suit against *Agos* was not. Hrant Dink, Sarkis Bey, and two colleagues will be tried in May. +

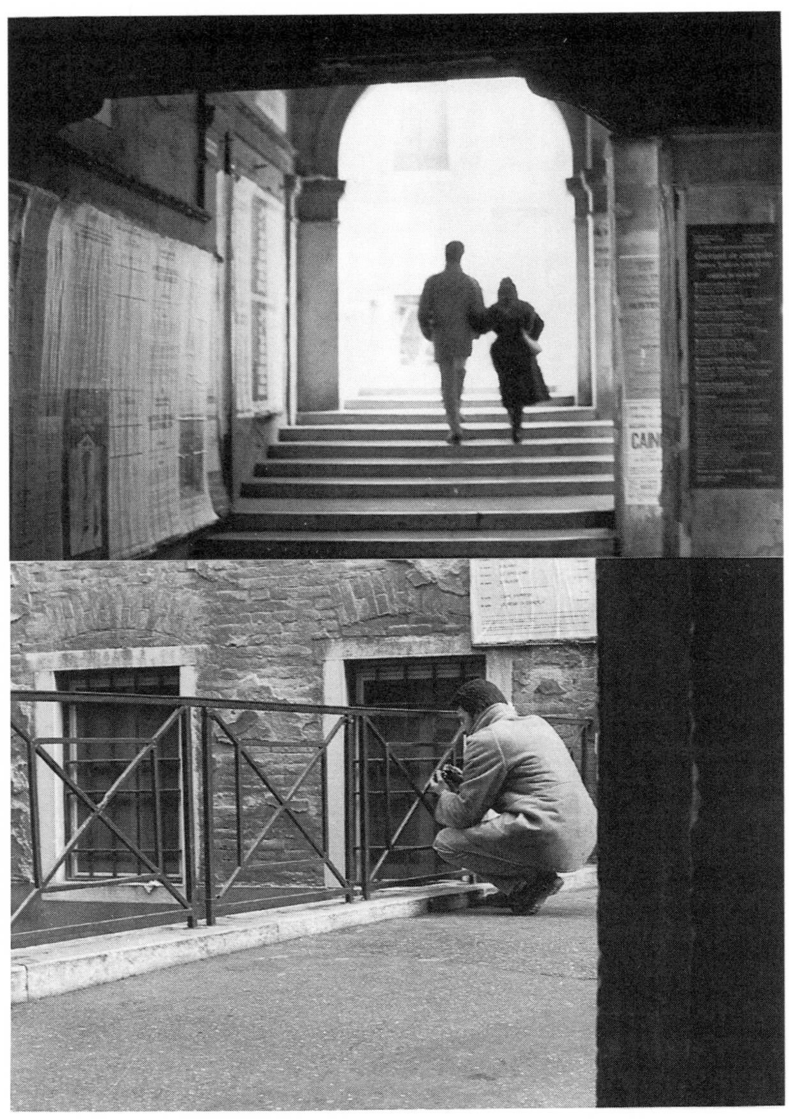

SOPHIE CALLE, IMAGES FROM *SUITE VÉNITIENNE*, 1980,
B/W PHOTOGRAPHS, 9 X 7". COURTESY OF THE ARTIST.

THE MYSTERY GUEST

Grégoire Bouillier

The following is a partial translation of L'Invité mystère, *a memoir by Grégoire Bouillier and the first of his works to appear in English. Bouillier was born in 1960, in Algeria. He was raised in Paris. His previous book,* Rapport sur moi *("Report on Myself"), tells the story of his childhood, his first loves, and his parents' open marriage. (Bouillier begins by explaining that he was conceived during a threesome.) "Boccacio and Aristophanes have always struck me as coming near the truth," he writes, "as do Sade and Georges Bataille." Yet the writer who exerts the clearest influence over Bouillier's work is Michel Leiris, an anthropologist associated with the surrealist movement, whose memoirs were translated by Richard Howard and Lydia Davis (and celebrated by Susan Sontag in* Against Interpretation*). Like Leiris, Bouillier revisits past humiliations in search of the secret, fairy-tale logic that governs his inner life. In* The Mystery Guest *the humiliation begins with a phone call from his ex-girlfriend, the great love of Bouillier's youth, who had left him abruptly ten years before.*

IT WAS THE DAY MICHEL LEIRIS DIED. This would have been late September 1990, or maybe the very beginning of October. The date escapes me—whatever it was I can always look it up later on—in any case it was a Sunday, because I was home in the middle of the afternoon, and it was cold out, and I'd gone to sleep in all my clothes, wrapped up in a blanket, the way I generally did when I was home alone. Cold and oblivion were all I was looking for at the time. This didn't worry me unduly. Sooner or later, I knew, I'd rejoin the world of the living, just not yet. I had seen enough, I felt. Beings, things, landscapes... I had enough to last me for the next two hundred years and no inclination to go hunting for new material. I didn't want any more trouble.

I woke to the ringing of the phone. Darkness had fallen in the room. I picked up; I knew it was her. Even before I was conscious of knowing, I knew. It was her voice, her breath, it was practically her face, and along with her face a thousand moments of happiness came rising from the past, gilded with sunlight.

I sat up in bed, heart pounding in my chest. I actually heard this going on, this unnatural pounding, as if my heart were electrified. I heard it thudding in every corner of the room—and this was no illusion, I wasn't dreaming, there wasn't any question it was her. The senses don't lie, no matter how unlikely it was to be hearing her voice now, after the years I'd never heard from her, ever, not once. *How appropriate* flashed through my mind. *And on the exact same day Michel Leiris died* was my next thought, and the coincidence struck me as so outlandish it was all I could do to keep from laughing. I felt as if I'd plugged into the inner hilarity of things, or else brushed up against a truth so overwhelming only laughter could keep it at bay—but maybe it wasn't a coincidence at all! Maybe she wouldn't have called, it occurred to me, if Michel Leiris *hadn't* died. Of course that's what happened: she'd heard about Michel Leiris and somehow the fact of his disappearance had made her reappear. However obscurely the one fact figured in the other, I sensed a connection. The significance of a dream, we're told, has less to do with its overt drama than with the details; a long time ago it struck me that the same was true of real life. Or of what passes among us for real life.

But this was no time for a philosophical discussion, and besides, I was in no shape to bandy wits. I could hear how soft and gummy my voice was, how drowsy-sounding, and somehow I just knew that she must under no circumstances be allowed to know she'd woken me up. That was crucial, even if it meant sounding cold and detached—and why on earth did she have to call, not just on the very same day Michel Leiris had died but when I was fast asleep and at my most vulnerable, my least up to answering the phone, when in a word I was completely *incapable* of appreciating this miracle for what it was? In real life, it goes without saying, the ideal situation eludes us, and no doubt that's a good thing for humanity in general, but just then I'd have done anything to keep her from guessing that she'd caught me sound asleep in the middle of the afternoon. It was out of the question. Either it would look like a sign of weakness or else it would make me look churlish, to be caught napping the one time something exceptional actually happened; or, then again, she might draw certain conclusions—I didn't know what conclusions, exactly, but still, I'd just as soon she not draw them. And no, I wanted to protest, it wasn't as if my life had devolved into one long slumber. It wasn't as if I'd been languishing, stricken and alone, since she'd left me. On the contrary. I just happened to be leading a life of leisure.

The strangest part was how I completely forgot that I'd sworn never to speak to her again, and that she'd left me years before without a word of explanation, without so much as saying good-bye, the way they abandon dogs when summer comes (as I put it to myself at the time), the way they abandon a dog chained to a tree for good measure. And I'd circled my tree in both directions and climbed up into it and spent a long time—spent millions of hours, years—in the void, cursing her name in the darkness. Yes, cursing her, because her disappearance had taught me that I was a less exemplary person than I'd previously supposed; but now the whole thing might as well never have happened and all that mattered was the fact of her calling, and that the day for action had come.

How I had yearned for this moment. I'd been looking forward to it so long I already knew how it would go. I even knew what she was about to say because I'd rehearsed it all in my head, could see myself explain softly that the past was the past, that the statute of limitations had expired, that it didn't matter that she'd left me (or that she'd left me the *way* she'd left me), it was ancient history. Really and truly. I'd dug down to the root of my unhappiness and it had nothing to do with her, I didn't blame her in the least, and in this cruel world we're all innocents, we do the best we can, and worse things are happening all around us even as we speak. Just this morning Michel Leiris had died, and yesterday the last of the Mohawks had laid down his arms, and tomorrow a war and/or scandal would break out and be replaced by something else, and in the end the world would turn the page before I did, and it didn't exactly speak well of me that I'd taken years to get over her, and it's not as if I was talking about the Movie of the Week, where love triumphs, justice gets handed down, liberty's reestablished in the hearts of men, humanity regains a name and a face and the whole thing happens between 8:45 and 10:30, 10:35 at the latest—once I watched them save the earth from a giant meteor and even *that* didn't take two hours—and I'm not the sort of person who mixes up real life and fiction, no more than anybody else does, but the conviction had snuck up on me that I, too, would smile again in my own ninety minutes, give or take. Yes, I'd be smiling again in a more or less similar lapse of time; her leaving had been a blip. There was something crazy about how far it had set me back. In retrospect, the insane way she'd disappeared actually seemed for the best. It showed panache, at any rate. Most stories just fizzle out as if they'd never happened. And I *agreed* with her, that was the thing, I agreed that she'd been fighting for her life. We couldn't go on the way we'd been, and she'd been driven to get out by nothing less than the survival instinct, and she was sorry, so she told me she was sorry and asked me in a whisper to forgive her, and it made me want to cry, to let the tears flow down my face, hearing her ask over and over how she could have just up and *left*, after four years together, after all we'd lived through, all we'd shared; but she'd had no choice. She was hurting so bad back then. And she was so young and felt so guilty, without knowing why, she felt guilty all the time—I'd never know how guilty she felt—and maybe it was society's fault, maybe it was the fault of her family, she didn't know, but in the end she did the only thing she could and went off with the first man who wanted her. And he was a nice man, and he loved her, and she loved him, too, despite his age and the fact that he was short, and now they had a little girl, and she was happy I saw it the way I did because (and she knew I'd laugh) she kept worrying that I might have turned into a bum. Sometimes on the bus she'd look out for me on city benches. She had this feeling that things had gone badly for me and it scared her. For years she'd been afraid of bumping into me. I had no idea how long it had taken just getting up the nerve to call, and tracking me down wasn't easy either, and in the end she just wanted me to know how sorry she really was and to forgive her. I had to understand, it meant the world to her. And I understood. I was all understanding. And I forgave, for in my dreams I was great and magnanimous. And besides, what else could I say or do?

But this was her actual voice, not just some figment that I'd invented to fill the void and salve my wounds, as they say; finally I'd hear her version, finally she'd come out and ask my forgiveness and acknowledge the thing she'd done. I pictured her hand gently shutting my eyelids so I could open them freely on other sights and love again with no second thoughts. Yes, she owed me an explanation—she owed me *something* at any rate. I wanted to know the truth of our story, its truth and its meaning. I wanted to cast off my burden. And I was ready.

But she hadn't called to talk about the past. She didn't even refer to the past, much less clear things up the way I'd hoped, and my heart leapt with anticipation, crowed with joy, rose high over my head only to plummet back into the shadows, burrowing down in shame before the dawning truth that she was calling simply *to invite me to a party*—and will it never end, this continual pinching of the flesh in disbelief?—a "big party," to be precise. She was counting on me to come. It was important. She was asking as a favor, and she laughed faintly on her end while silently I kept telling myself that she had, in fact, called after all these years just to ask me to a party. As if nothing had happened and time had laid waste to everything and Michel Leiris were still alive.

Eyes closed, I listened. It was a birthday party for her husband's best friend, her husband who'd finally married her and was the father of her child, and every year Sophie—that was the friend's name, she was a "contemporary artist" (she said this in quotes), maybe I'd heard of her? Yes, exactly, Sophie Calle, the one who followed people in the street—anyway, every year this friend had a birthday party and invited as many people as she was years old plus a "mystery guest" who stood for the year she was about to live, and this year *she* was in charge of bringing the mysterious stranger and she couldn't say no, and so she'd thought of me (another faint laugh), and that was the reason, the one and only reason, for her call.

On my end I was stern. Galvanized steel. Clearly I was the one person she could think of who'd go along with this little charade of hers, and besides I made an ideal candidate seeing as how no one had ever heard of me. What's more, I thought, the mission must have actively appealed to her since, by picking up the phone just to invite me to a party, she'd overcome certain obvious objections raised by what I thought of as "our story." She could hardly have acted in a spirit of pure disinterestedness, put it that way. But couldn't she have come up with a better pretext to see me—and did this mean she *wanted* to see me? Anything was possible. But why did she need a pretext? All she had to do was call and say "Let's get together" or even "We should get together" or better yet "Could we get together?" and if only she'd put it that way—any of these ways—she'd have acknowledged the ties that bound us, ties that would never come undone in a thousand years, and then I'd have come running with a beating heart. But invite me to a party? Who did she think I was? It was absurd, and I'd been kicked around enough, and yet I heard myself answer, in a voice that was almost chipper, that I'd be there. Consider it done, I told her. She could rest easy, I'd be her mystery guest, even as I was gnashing my teeth with every fiber of my being. She sounded unaccountably relieved. No sooner had I spoken than her voice regained its air of gardenias, and I took down the time and address on a scrap of paper; then, without my knowing how it happened, she'd hung up, not that we had anything left to say that could have been said on the phone.

My hand shook as I set the receiver down. The room was silent, the air livid, and the telephone sat chuckling on the bed until in my rage I lobbed it across the room; but it didn't even come apart, and for long seconds I lay there listening to the dial tone in the dark, and that was even worse than before; so I got up to put it where it belonged and hang it up, and I didn't know what to do, and I took a walk from one end of the apartment to the other, and that didn't take long, and—that took the cake. No other words came to mind but "That takes the cake. That really takes the cake." For a good hour I paced the apartment repeating those words out loud as if they were the sum total of my vocabulary. All the same, the blood was fizzing in my veins: I couldn't stifle a thrill at the thought that I was finally about to have the meeting she'd owed me all these years. I was happy to make a fool of myself at some glamorous party. I'd gladly undergo much more painful transformations just to see her and hear her finally explain what she'd been thinking and cut the leash that bound me to her vanishing and put an end to this strangulation once and for all. I wanted answers. The rest of my life depended on that party, I knew that for a fact, and that night I dreamed of a horse trampling coattails in the dust.

THE DAYS AND WEEKS THAT FOLLOWED were unspeakable. Her call had plunged me back into a hellish slough that I'd considered well behind me, and that all of a sudden wasn't, and I slid back into sickening black thoughts I thought I'd exorcised, and was prey to grinning fiends, my old familiars, as if all my efforts to escape and move on had been worthless, as if nothing would ever come of anything. I felt like tearing the skin off my face. For a long time I'd considered the case closed, as they say. I could go and buy bread at the bakery without thinking about her the entire time, and for this and plenty of other reasons the affair seemed, as they say, laid to rest. I seemed to have turned the corner, as they say, and surfaced the way people tend to surface even if they come back utterly changed, wrecked, the change belied by a fold of the mouth, by something about their shoulders or hair, something unmistakable in the depths of their eyes, or the way they walk, or the way they laugh and talk and stand and—well, just look around you. You'll see what I mean.

Unless, as sometimes happens, the change is in the person's clothes. Since I'd always hated turtlenecks worn as undershirts, and despised the men who wore them as the lowest kind of pseudo-sportsmen with, as they say, the lamest kind of collar, I'd started wearing turtlenecks as undershirts the moment she left. Basically, I never took them off. No doubt this was magical thinking on my part (if I never took them off, nothing would ever take off on me); at any rate these turtleneck-undershirts erupted into my life without my noticing until it was too late and I was under their curse. You could even say they'd *inflicted* themselves on me, so that now I hardly remembered the wind on my neck, which is the very feeling of freedom. But if that was the price I had to pay, I told myself, so be it. We brick ourselves up in prisons of our own devising; we spend our lives losing touch with ourselves, disappearing behind what negates us. I took comfort in the thought that others had it even worse than I did, and I looked and saw people covered from head to toe in far weirder Band-Aids than mine. Yes, I told myself, my case was far from hopeless. In the end, I'd found a workable way of moving incognito through the world and keeping up appearances, just like everybody else, and I moved freely, unbruised. Impunity was mine, and I was at peace. I'd even started seeing someone.

Yes, despite my turtleneck-undershirts a woman had taken an interest in me of late. And to my shock the turtlenecks didn't put her off, even though most women feel an instinctive, to my mind legitimate, revulsion toward men in turtleneck-undershirts, unless somehow they find them attractive—but I gave those women a wide berth then and still do. At any rate she wasn't one of those; she just seemed not to notice my sartorial neurosis, for which I was profoundly grateful. At the same time it frustrated me. I was unnerved that my turtleneck-undershirts didn't bother her, never even gave her pause, when it would have made me feel so much less burdened and alone, would have meant such a sharp rise in the value of her affections, if I'd only known that she loved me with open eyes. But no, she saw no secret meaning in my layered look, so there I was, misunderstood at her side, furious, divided, unfairly and hatefully demanding that she *adjust* to my turtlenecks when it was exactly her easy acceptance of them that had brought us together in the first place, and, screwed-up as we are, doesn't every stroke of luck come with some kind of catch?

It's the worst, I told her. The worst in the sense that I can never get free and I keep looking like the person I seem to be and never was and never had been and never *would* have been except by force, as they say, of circumstance. Meanwhile she fell into the habit of rubbing her right cheek as if she were always trying to rub away—what?—some kind of permanent irritant, a slap that kept on stinging and had left her dazed and dumb. But when I pointed out that she hadn't exactly been born with this gesture she laughed and shrugged and told me I was making a mountain out of a molehill, as they say, and she refused to see this cheek-rubbing as anything more than a harmless idiosyncrasy (even though she couldn't stop doing it), and I didn't press the point because I didn't want to spoil the evening or poison things and because, in any case, none of this would have happened if, years before, this other person hadn't just up and left without a word of explanation, et cetera, et cetera, and because, all things considered, I preferred to sleep in the afternoon when there was no one around, and because *she* found me that way and asked me to a "big party." And on walls all across the city large posters were announcing the opening of *Die Hard*, and I was in despair.

But I'd gotten over her disappearance, and no one was going to say her reappearance did me in. I refused to give up. I wanted to understand, and while I stood there clinging absurdly, instinctively to this desire—to understand—as my sole support and the last vestige of my humanity, it hit me. She'd called late on a Sunday afternoon and she'd left me in the middle of the afternoon, also on a Sunday. Coincidence? Hardly. From that moment on, I knew I couldn't possibly be dealing with a coincidence. I knew something else was going on. It was too beautiful, I couldn't get over it, and really the truth was plain enough to see: by calling me on that day of the week, at that hour of the day, she was trying to pick up the thread of our story at exactly the point where it had been snapped in two, as if to say that all the intervening years had lasted a matter of seconds. And this changed everything. Suddenly time meant nothing and there was nothing final about her disappearance either, so our love had never ceased to be—all the rest was straw in the wind—and this business about the party was a pretext, a lure. After all, if all she'd wanted to do was invite me to the party, she'd have called on a Monday morning or a Wednesday night or Friday in the middle of the day or possibly on a Saturday in the middle of the day but never late on a Sunday afternoon. Miracles do occur between people who've been in love, we all know that, and inwardly I exulted, I quivered, and her call, which at the time had struck me as the last word in brutality, suddenly made a kind of clear and overwhelming sense; such are the loopholes that reality offers us from itself.

For once I wasn't cooking the data. Not this time. Appearances never deceive (I told myself), they are their own meanings and there's nothing to look for behind them, and I rejoiced, and the reasons for her call rose up more and more vividly and gloriously into view. And the thing was, the reasons had nothing to do with her. Because it wasn't as if she had *decided* to call late in the afternoon on a Sunday and send me a coded message. No one was that roundabout, I told myself. At least not that pointlessly roundabout. So there had to be something else—call it a force—a force seeking some means of self-expression, struggling to give me a sign, and unbeknownst to her this something had told her to pick up the phone and dial my number at that moment, of all moments, the meaning of which apparent coincidence only I could discern. Yes, I was convinced that this had to be the explanation: for reasons unknown to me, but which might have had something to do with the death of Michel Leiris, something in her clicked and, taking advantage of her need to find a "mystery guest," the force stole this chance to slip her hand into mine, to wave a handkerchief like a prisoner locked in a tower. The force trusted me to hear the call within her call, in spite of everything. How could I explain her years of silence without positing a counterspell that had finally lifted the curse? How else could I explain her complete failure to allude to the past during our conversation, the way any normal person would have done? This in itself proved she wasn't behaving normally, that some larger power was working its will through her. And no doubt the psychoanalysts would speak of the "unconscious," but I told myself that this force was nothing more or less than our love.

Any last doubts I had melted away. I was going to the party. How could I not? At the same time I jeered at my own idiocy—my insanity, too, but mostly my idiocy—and despised myself for going and looking for trouble like some kind of dime-store Don Quixote. Just what did I think I could achieve? Despair has a force of its own, and out of my despair I'd created a universe in which I was the star, and I was about to see this universe for what it was. This party would be the death of all my illusions, it would tear me to shreds and cripple me for life. Didn't I see the trap I was striding into? She was making a fool of me, a laughingstock, and no one cared because I was such a nobody, I had nothing to look forward to but disaster and humiliation and more bitterness. I was like that general Aoun, shouting defiance from the rooftops of Beirut long after anyone could see it was in ruins. But I stopped my ears against my own misgivings, in which the voices of my mother and father and grandparents and great-grandparents and all my ancestors in every generation since biblical times were mingled, warning me in vain again and again (while I stuck to my guns) that I shouldn't come crying to them when I was a wandering shade: I had a rendezvous, even if I didn't know just what I was rendezvousing *with*. Nothing else counted and nothing could change my mind or turn me around, not when the great mystery of her leaving was about to be unveiled: I'd always thought I must be missing something. After all, no one just up and leaves another person, a person she's loved, without some very specific, in the end very particular reason of her own. No matter how unhappy she may be, a woman at least says *good-bye* on her way out the door. There had to be more to the story, and I had to know what it was, and when I did, I too would be unmasked and the curse of the turtleneck-undershirts would be abolished!

All the same, I was feverish and uneasy and in a state of absolute heartache and helpless rage at the prospect of showing up at this party where I was clearly supposed to play the part of a sentimental curiosity, where I'd be a stuffed monkey—where I'd be a dwarf, a dwarf to be thrown as far as possible so as to beat some dwarf-throwing record the precise nature of which eluded me. And I thought of Flint, Michigan, where the local directors of General Motors organized a big party as a consolation for everyone laid off after the "outsourcing" of some plant, and on the grounds of the mansion that sat on the heights above the town they paid the laid-off workers to play living statues and hold poses while men in tuxedos with cigars squired women in silk gowns sipping flutes of California champagne, and I thought of Baudelaire cutting the Belgians to pieces and Rimbaud insulting the literary men of his time and Thomas Bernhard and Artaud and Alfieri and Paul mailing off his epistles, and it made me happy just to know they'd existed. Suddenly

I felt less alone. I felt emboldened by their example, as if somehow I shared in their refusal to be debased, to be robbed of their souls and selves. When my own turn came I would rip the mask from the face of our era and its most visible spokesmen. Yes, I, too, wanted to bolt from the ranks of the assassins and their cronies, and if I was going to be the "mystery guest," well, they had no idea just what a mystery guest I'd be! Because I was 30 years old and the time had come for me to make my presence felt. And I didn't see anything vain or vapid about this line of thinking. Far from it. Just when circumstances were least favorable (I told myself), that was the moment I'd turn them to my advantage, when no one was looking, and like a jack-in-the-box I'd spring the first chance they gave me. The moment they let down their guard I'd make them dance.

To say I was afraid would be an understatement. As the day and the hour of the rendezvous (or The Reckoning, as I'd come to call it in my darker moods) drew near, I seemed to be running helplessly toward my doom. I felt my strength fail, I wavered in my determination, and the certainty that I was going to lay bare the "figure in the carpet" faded, so great was the task before me, a task I'd have to perform all alone. At least Ulysses had his son by his side and the swineherd Eumaus and what's-his-name, that cowherd, and the old servingwoman and most of all Athena, who helped him beat the suitors and get Penelope back in the end. As for me, I had nobody, I was going in alone, and the opposite of courage isn't cowardice but discouragement, at least that's the opposite in French.

By now all my euphoria had vanished, and I was furious with myself all over again and dead set against the part I'd been assigned. Who did they think they were? More to the point, who did they think *I* was? I had a name. She couldn't take that away too! I had to protect myself; yes, there are limits to what a man can agree to suffer, and I couldn't always just sit there and let other people prey on me with their desires and all their obscure machinations. I was going to show them who I was. They'd see, the world would see—it would see and *then* some. In the first place, I wasn't about to show up empty-handed. Because it hadn't been lost on me that this was a birthday party, in fact I'd spent hours racking my brains to figure out what a "mystery guest" should bring a person he doesn't know, a person who is, what's more, a "contemporary artist," and, from what I could gather, a "well-known contemporary artist," and this made me even angrier and more resentful and set the bar that much higher, as they say. But I couldn't come up with a present, and I tore my hair out, pacing the length of my bedroom for the thousandth time, and besides I had no money. I mean nothing: I was so broke I wore secondhand shoes from the flea market at Clignancourt—but what was I doing, thinking about money and shoes, when the situation undermined the very *idea* of present-giving, and the connection it implied between two individuals, a connection that meant more than just handing over some object (as I said, gnashing my teeth)? Unless I was supposed to come up with the world's most transcendent present—the present that symbolized The Gift, independent of any particular recipient or giver. Maybe that was what this Sophie of hers expected of the "mystery guest": to arrive at the highest possible conception of presenthood. Could that be what she had in mind? And so I kept walking the streets and going up and down the avenues and looking in every storefront; but wherever I looked all I saw was merchandise and more merchandise and nothing of any value except the value assigned to each thing in its turn by society, and nowhere I looked did I see any object that seemed to incarnate anything more than profit and gain, and in every direction lay stacks of products expressing nothing so much as a degraded idea of The Gift, an idea contrary and, in a word, hostile to the idea of The Gift rightly understood, and the last thing I wanted was to arrive at that party bearing a gift that would shed its mystique the moment the colored paper and ribbon had been torn aside. And all at once I saw why our societies cover presents in gift wrap: not for the sake of surprise but rather to cover up the fact that the gift is based on a lie, as we inevitably discover every time somebody gives us something. What happens is we open it and, after that microsecond when we expect the fulfillment of our deepest desire, disgust and sadness wash over us and we smile as fast as we can and say thank you, the better to bury deep within ourselves our chagrin at never once in all our lives receiving something more than what we'd hoped for. And this evanescent joy, forever disappointed, remains incomprehensible to us.

For a while I toyed with the idea of giving her a book by Michel Leiris. At least it beat flowers or candy, I told myself. It would be dull and anticlimactic, that went without saying, but it seemed like the least worst option I had—and, after all, haven't we spent years in default mode, in *faute de mieux* mode, following the path of least badness as if nothing nowadays merited our full and utter and joyful consent? And how long, I began to wonder, can this go on? How long can we go around economizing our desires? And that's when I stopped short, right there in the middle of the street. I'd give her wine! It was so obvious I couldn't think why it hadn't occurred to me before. What could be better? My search was over, I'd bring her wine. A very good bottle of wine, the oldest and most expensive wine that money could buy. And this idea struck me as nothing short of brilliant, as if, coming from the depths of my being and my heritage, it battened on my energies and desires until it grew huge and glorious, until I could no longer contain it, and I burst out laughing, still standing right there in the street. Yes, if they wanted my blood, I thundered to myself, I'd give them vintage blood, and a very good vintage at that, and they would drink it in remembrance of me—and wasn't Christ himself a model mystery guest? The more I thought it over, the more dazzled I was by my plan. For once I'd come up with the perfect thing. And in a wine store near Saint-Lazare I found a 1964 Margaux. I remember it perfectly. It was the best bottle in the store, and it was way beyond my means and I exulted, I pranced with delight in front of the clerk, who looked at me suspiciously, nervously even. But that was just it: I wanted to sacrifice everything, I wanted to shame them as I climbed up on the pyre. We'd see how haughty they looked then. We'd see whether they had brought anything beyond their means—in a word, I challenged them to a potlatch and for once put all social chicanery aside, and they would know who'd really give all for love, and the bottle cost more than my rent, a lot more, and that didn't matter. On the contrary, I'd crossed the Rubicon, as they say. The so-called die had been cast, and the rent could wait. (Which in fact it did.) On my way out of the store, as I cradled my tissue-wrapped bottle to my chest like a talisman, the city seemed to have changed its aspect. It was all light farce, and I felt tall enough to cross outside the crosswalk. I could stop cars with a glance, I could contend with their bumpers and hulls, and I no longer had any fear that the distress and indigence of the world might rub off on me. No, never again would my own opulence be reduced to begging, I chanted to myself, for at that moment it seemed to me that I had earned the right to quote Hölderlin, a thing that doesn't happen every day.

How much had changed since her phone call! I'd been at loose ends and now I was on a mission. And I wasn't alone anymore, I contained multitudes, and I had to go, the hour was upon me. To hell with the expense, I told myself, hailing a cab to the party with no more thought for the future than a condemned man accepting his last cigarette. Leaning my head against the window, the bottle of '64 Margaux resting on my knees and my hands resting—brooding—on it all the way, I watched the lights and the shadows go by and I remembered how it all started with the death of Michel Leiris.

Then the driver ventured to say something about its being chilly for early October and how you couldn't predict the weather anymore. And I didn't feel like talking, but there was no stopping him, he was in a confiding mood, and he told me that after his wife left him two years earlier he'd lost seventeen kilos. Seventeen kilos. He still couldn't believe it. And he chuckled in quiet alarm as if it haunted him even now; and I said maybe that's how much his wife weighed for him, seventeen kilos. He glanced at me in the rearview mirror. Clearly, he'd never seen it that way before. It had never occurred to him that love might not just feel like a burden, that it might also have an actual, physical weight. Then I let him in on the secret of my turtlenecks so he'd know we were in the same boat, but he seemed distinctly unimpressed and just nodded and turned up the radio in time to hear a voice introduce "the last recording of '*L'aigle noir*' by the immortal Barbara." And for the duration of the ride, which took forever, I couldn't stop thinking that the black eagle had come back, come back out of nowhere; and we all have our mystery guests; and the fare was ninety-two francs.

SHE WAS STANDING WITH TWO MEN, one of whom was laughing at something, and a smile crossed her own lips, and she hid her mouth with her hand the way I'd always seen her do when she laughed. This came back to me. And her hair was still as blond as I remembered but shorter now. Or she was wearing it differently, I couldn't think which, and if I'd expected to feel overwhelmed, I didn't. I couldn't feel anything, really. The ground stayed put beneath my feet. In fact it was oddly familiar to have her there in front of me, familiar but strange, and I pushed open the French door, careful not to bump the bottle of Margaux. Seeing me come in from the cold, a woman turned and smiled at me, and I smiled back and happened to notice the shape of her small breasts and, from that moment on, everything unfolded as if someone else were acting in my place. That's how it felt. As if by entering the room I had also entered into a character, someone who hadn't been there a second ago, someone who took up the baton and composed my facial expressions so as to ward off any prying glances, someone who'd keep me from looking ridiculous, on the one hand, but also from making a scene or doing anything untoward. I wouldn't be allowed so much as a faux pas. I had been changed, despite myself, for better and for worse. It was as if I had no continuous inner life, whatever I might have thought, and I cursed my own sense of decorum. What was I waiting for? Well, I told myself, let them make one false move and all bets were off, I'd blow this little charade of theirs sky-high. The game, as they say, wasn't over. In the meantime I took off my coat with the air of a man who knows how to take off his coat wherever he happens to find himself and rolled it up into a ball and stuck it next to a great big bouquet of red and white roses. They were spilling out of a vase that had been planted there on the floor, and it crossed my mind that this bouquet took up an amazing amount of space. And despite myself I started to count the roses. All of a sudden it seemed absolutely necessary that I find out, then and there, how many roses were in the vase, so that at least some part of my surroundings wouldn't remain unknown to me, since sometimes just knowing *something* is enough to lull you into believing that you *know* something, and it turned out there were thirty-seven roses, and this had to be the number of candles that would later be blown out. And at the prospect of seeing a cake brought in and people singing "Happy Birthday" I felt defeated before the fact.

No one paid any attention to me and everything happened exactly the way it does in real life: enigmatically, without your being able to put your finger on the enigma. And I lit a cigarette to keep my hands and lungs and all the rest busy while, with an air of unconcern, as they say, I threw myself into the fray, sure that everyone had already noticed my turtleneck. Without meeting anyone's eye I marched straight ahead and cleared a path as if I knew exactly where to go and how to get there, and it worked: underneath a big iron staircase that led to the upper floor I found a place where I could observe things from out of the way, without anyone slipping behind me, and just then it seemed to me that the hardest part was over, so I looked up and took in the proceedings.

The room was enormous. In its center a table advanced endlessly toward the walls, laying down mile after mile of knives and forks, and a dazzling white tablecloth made up of several sheets lay like a bridal train under the bright track lights up above, and chairs and stools were drawn up all around it. At the foot of the stairs a stuffed cat was pouncing without ever touching down on its forepaws, and farther off a pink flamingo stood on one leg, and the atmosphere was cheerful. It was festive. Everywhere men and women discussed and conversed and were generally moving around, and some went and others came, and many of the guests wore black and smoked, and some were sitting and had their elbows on the table and picked at saucers holding little canapés or slices of dried sausage, and most were drinking champagne, and one woman was insisting that they put on some Spanish music while a man in a white panama hat seemed to be sulking over in a corner. In other words, it was a party. There was no doubt about it. It was a party like any good party, and in a sense this was reassuring. All the same, I fought back an urge to howl while I beamed an utterly false smile back and forth at no one in particular. At some point a woman carrying a large platter toward the table slipped and fell, and this piece of slapstick drew people's attention, heads turned, and that's when she saw me. Her gaze crossed the room and landed where I was, and she interrupted the man who'd been laughing, she laid a hand on his arm and murmured something in his ear, and the man glanced up in my direction while she moved away from him and came toward me. And the way his eyes followed her from behind kept me from enjoying this moment which I'd promised myself as recompense. Yes, it spoiled everything, but no more than everything else did in the end. And I stood there, stock-still with a frozen smile the whole time I watched her coming nearer. And she was very beautiful, I had forgotten just how beautiful she was, and at the same time I didn't remember her having been beautiful in quite this way, or ever having worn this dress. It bared her shoulders and made her instantly desirable and, so to speak, sexual. So sexual that, as she passed, all the men and the women, too, caressed her with their glances, and thousands of feelings and impressions came washing over me, all of them tending toward the question whether she'd chosen this dress for my sake, to seduce me—to bring me, as they say, to my knees—or else to show me that we moved in different worlds now and she belonged to somebody else. Not that the two scenarios were mutually exclusive. Maybe she wanted to exert her powers of seduction over everyone and no one. And I know as well as anyone that a woman never chooses her clothes haphazardly, at least not in a situation such as this. But whatever motives had gone into choosing her outfit, I couldn't sort them out in the folds of her dress; they all kept jangling together in my mind. The mere act of keeping myself in one piece seemed like a kind of magic trick, and I felt a trapdoor give way beneath my feet when she came up and leaned in to kiss my cheek as if it were the most natural thing in the world. And that was the last straw. How dare she? It wasn't just inappropriate, it was obscene, it was phony through and through, as if our story could ever, even conceivably, degenerate into—into what? Friendship? Camaraderie? Whatever she had in mind, it was out of the question. She could save these affectations, these empty shams of hers for other men, or else love meant nothing and our story had never happened and she herself didn't exist, and just then I could have torn her face off, I could have ripped it from her neck and stamped on it before she made a sound. How was I supposed to accept that what had bound us together, and still did despite everything, should moulder away into anything as reasonable and pitiful as a kiss on the cheek, into something that had nothing to do with us? We deserved better and she knew it, and inoffensive was the last word you could ever use to describe our story, and what begins in beauty, as they say, can only end in beauty—otherwise what was the point of Michel Leiris dying in the first place and what was the point of her inviting me? But maybe all she wanted was to catch a secret whiff of my scent after all these years and relive, for an instant, the touch of her skin against mine without laying herself open to reproach. It was true that her attitude gave me some cause for hope. In any case, it was too late. I'd already kissed her cheek, closing my eyes and clenching my fists and fighting the urge to seek her lips and find and open them and taste her tongue and lose myself there the way I used to do—and so to put an end to this charade I placed the bottle in her hands, saying, "From the mystery guest." And I hope no one else ever has to smile the way I smiled then. +

—Translated by Lorin Stein

ROSWITHA HUBER, 06 _ *SHE SUDDENLY SAID. . .*, 2005,
MIXED MEDIA ON PAPER, 16 X 23". COURTESY VG BILD-KUNST BONN.

AFTERNOON OF THE SEX CHILDREN

Mark Greif

NOT LONG AGO I TOOK PART IN ONE OF THE CONVERSATIONS you're not supposed to have. It turned on whether Vladimir Nabokov, author of *Lolita*, really desired underage girls. The usual arguments came out: Nabokov was a master of personae, and Humbert Humbert a game to him. Kinbote, analogous narrator of *Pale Fire*, didn't make you think Nabokov loved boys. The late novels were Nabokov's allegories of the seductions of aestheticism, which transfigures the forbidden into the beautiful; or moral paintings of our acceptance of crime, when crime is presented alluringly. So love of the wrong object becomes a metaphor for art, ethics, personality, and so forth.

I was reluctant to say that I felt these explanations were inadequate and even in bad faith. The trouble with *Lolita* is plainly its ability to describe what a sexual 12-year-old looks like. What her dress is like when it brushes her knees, what her toes are like with painted nails, how the color sits on the plump bow of her lips—the phrase for this is that it is "too real"; that's the scandal. It continues to be the scandal fifty years after publication, and it will be a scandal whenever any adult acknowledges the capacity to upend his vision and see a child, protected larval stage of the organism, as a sexual object. The girl is still a child, only now she is a sex child. Yet this makes me feel Nabokov was not a pedophile, but something he is not credited with being—a social critic.

You, too, see it, or should. The trend of these fifty years has been to make us see sexual youth where it doesn't exist, and ignore it as it does. Adults project the sex of children in lust, or examine children sexually with magnifying glasses to make sure they don't appeal to us. But these lenses became burning glasses. The hips of Betty Grable melted and disappeared. The breasts of Marilyn Monroe ran off and were replaced with silicone. The geography of fashion created new erogenous zones—pelvic midriff, rear cleavage—for dieters starving off their secondary sex characteristics, and for young teens, in the convergence of the exerciser and the pubescent child. The waif and the pixie became ideal. Mama and daughter look the same again before the bedroom mirror—not dressed up in Mama's pearls and heels, this time, but in children's wear. The dream belongs to 16, or to those who can starve themselves to 16.

The critic Philip Fisher used to note that *Lolita*, tightly plotted as it is, repeats one scene twice. Humbert spies a lit window far opposite. Because he longs to see a nymphet, he sees one. The wave of arousal returns, its tide dampening him up to his knees. As he nears the climax, the form is refocused as an adult woman or man. Disgusting! But this is a simple inversion of a characteristic experience of our time. A man will see a distant form, in low-cut top and low-slung jeans, and think he is on the trail of eroticism; draw near, and identify a child. Revolting! The defenses against it continue the problem. The more a whole nation inspects the sex characteristics of children to make sure it is not becoming aroused by childishness, and slyly hunts around to make sure its most untrustworthy members are not being so aroused, the more it risks creating a sexual fascination with the child. However you gaze, to accept the fantasy, or to assure yourself you see nothing, you join in an abomination.

WE LIVE IN THE AFTERNOON OF THE SEX CHILDREN; Nabokov just saw the dawn.

Now children from junior high to high school to college live in the most perfect sex environment devised by contemporary society—or so adults believe. Now they are inmates in great sex colonies where they wheel in circles holding hands with their pants down. Henry Darger, emblematic artist of our time with his girl armies, made for our sensibilities what Gauguin's Tahitian beauties were to the French 19th-century bourgeoisie—repositories of true, voluptuous, savage, inner nature.

Yet in public we want to believe that children are not prepared for sex as we are, do not understand it, and have a special, fragile, glassy truth inside them that will be endangered by premature use—as if the pearls of highest value for us, our chase after sex, our truth of "sexuality," should not also be the treasure for them.

It took the whole history of postwar American culture to make the sex child. It required a merging of old prurient fantasies, dating from the Victorians and Progressives, with the actual sexual liberation of children after mid-century. You needed the expansion of the commercial market for children—selling to kids with sex as everything is sold with sex. You needed the bad faith of Madison Avenue advertisers and Seventh Avenue fashion writers. You needed the sinister prudery of Orange County evangelicalism and the paraliterature of child sex that arises in antipedophilia crusades (*Treacherous Love*; *It Happened to Nancy*)—erotica purveyed to middle-school libraries. You needed the internet.

Victorian child-loving is only loosely the background for our current preoccupation with the pedophile and the sexual child. With Lewis Carroll and Alice, John Ruskin and Rose La Touche, the fantastic young bride and her gauzy innocence, we know we are in the realm of adult prurience. It is *child sexual liberation* that transforms the current moment. We can no longer say it is *only* fantasy that exists about the sex lives of children. Or, rather—maybe this is the better way to say it—children have been insistently invited into our fantasy, too, and when they grow up they'll furnish the adult continuity of this same madness.

Is it necessary to say that the majority of the sex children we see and desire are not legally children? The representatives of the sex child in our entertainment culture are often 18 to 21—legal adults. The root of their significance is that their sexual value points backward, to the status of the child, and not forward to the adult. So there is Britney, famous at the age of 18 for a grind video to "Oops, I Did It Again" (*I'm not that innocent*), and Paris, 19 years old in her amateur porn DVD (*1 Night in Paris*); alumnae of the Mickey Mouse Club like Christina—licking her lips at 20 on the *Rolling Stone* cover, miniskirt pulled open above the headline "Guess What Christina Wants"; and Lindsay, veteran of Disney children's films, whose breast size, extreme dieting, and accidental self-exposures on the red carpet are the stuff of *Entertainment Tonight*. It's important that these are not adult "stars" in the way of Nicole Kidman or Julia Roberts; not called beautiful, rarely featured in adult films. Instead they furnish the core of entertainment news to two distinct audiences: children 9 to 14, who enjoy their music and films on these works' own terms, and adults who regard them—well, as what?*

---

* The entertainment does not seem to be only for adult men. It's a difficult question whether there is strict symmetry by gender, so that boys should also become sex objects for adult women, and adult male fashion regress to youth. In the private realm, school teachers keep being revealed as molesters when they get

CONTINUED ON NEXT PAGE

Oddly, those of us who face these questions now have been sex children ourselves; we come after the great divide. You would think we'd remember. Our sex was handed to us, liberated, when we appeared in the world. We managed to feel like rebels with all the other 12-year-olds, deluded, but not to be blamed for that. A great tween gang of sexual ruffians, trolling the basement TV for scrambled porn, tangling on couches, coming up for air in clouds of musk, shirts on backward; what did we learn? Having lived in the phantasm evidently does not diminish the phantasm. One still looks at those kids enviously; that is one of the mysteries to be solved. It is as if crossing the divide to adulthood entailed a great self-blinding in the act of seeing what is not, precisely, there; and forgetting what one oneself experienced. If we turn to the sex children as avidly as anyone, it must be because they are *doing something for us, too,* as participants in this society and as individuals. And the supplement will not be found in their childhood at all, but in the overall system of adult life.

THE LURE OF A PERMANENT CHILDHOOD IN AMERICA partly comes from the overwhelming feeling that one hasn't yet achieved one's true youth, because true youth would be defined by freedom so total that no one can attain it. Presumably even the spring-break kids, rutting, tanning, boozing with abandon, know there is a more perfect spring break beyond the horizon. Without a powerful aspiration to become adult, without some separate value that downplays childhood for sharper freedoms in age and maturity, the feeling of dissatisfaction can proceed indefinitely, in the midst of marriage, child rearing, retirement, unto death.

The college years—of all times—stand out as the apex of sex childhood. Even if college is routinized and undemanding, it is still inevitably

---

CONTINUED FROM PREVIOUS PAGE
pregnant by their seventh-graders; so that is one kind of appeal. And in the popular culture, "Abercrombie & Fitch" names a certain iconography of high school musclebound male toplessness, teen depilation and wrestling as signs of eros—an eroticism drawn from gay men's pleasure in the college boy and teen, repurposed for heterosexuality. But it does seem the popular culture is still just testing the waters to find the extent of adult women's desire. This is the meaning of the aphasic silences, for example, around Demi's Ashton and Gabi's lawn-boy lover on *Desperate Housewives*. The logic of our society should ultimately even out private fantasies between the genders. But perhaps because there is always so great a capacity for fantasy and pleasure in self-display—not just in pursuit of one's opposite number—for now adult women's investment in the sex children, at least in public, remains largely oriented to youthful girls.

residential, and therefore the place to perfect one's life as a sex child. You move away from home into a setting where you are with other children—strangers all. You must be patient for four years just to get a degree. So there can be little to do but fornicate. Certainly from the wider culture, of MTV and rumor, you know four years is all you will get. The semester provides an interruption between institutionalized sex jubilees: spring break, or just the weekends. The frat-house party assumes a gothic significance, not only for prurient adults but for the collegians themselves who report, on Monday, their decadence.

As a college student today, you always know what things *could* be like. The "Girls Gone Wild" cameras show a world where at this very moment someone is spontaneously lifting her shirt for a logoed hat. You might think the whole thing was a put-on except that everyone seems so earnest. The most earnest write sex columns ("Sex and the Elm City") in which the elite and joyless of Yale aspire to be like the déclassé and uninhibited of Florida State. The new full-scale campus sex magazines (e.g., Boston University's *Boink* [2005] and Harvard's *H Bomb* [2004]) seek truth in naked self-photography and accounts of sex with strangers as if each incident were God's revelation on Sinai. The lesson each time is that sleeping with strangers or being photographed naked lets the authors know themselves better. Many of these institutions are driven by women. Perhaps they, even more than young men, feel an urgency to know themselves while they can—since America curses them with a premonition of disappointment: when flesh sags, freedom will wane.

From college to high school, high school to junior high, the age of sex childhood recedes and descends. "The Sexual Revolution Hits Junior High," says my newspaper, reporting as news what is not new. Twice a year *Newsweek* and *Time* vaunt the New Virginity. No one believes in the New Virginity. According to polls of those who stick with it, their abstinence is fortified with large measures of fellatio. Eighty percent of people have intercourse in their teens, says the Center for Disease Control. (Why the Center for Disease Control keeps records of sexual normalcy, unsmilingly pathologized as an "epidemic," is its own question.) My newspaper tells me that menstruation starts for girls today at 11, or as early as 9. No one knows why.

Yet the early reality of sex childhood is its restrictive practical dimension. It exists only in the context of the large institutions that dominate children's lives, the schools. In these prisonlike closed worlds of finite numbers of children, with no visible status but the wealth they bring in from outside (worn as clothes) and the dominance they can achieve in the activities of schooldays (friend making, gossiping, academic and athletic success), sex has a different meaning than in adult licentiousness or collegiate glory. Sex appeal is demanded long before sex, and when sex arrives, it appears within ordinary romantic relationships. New sexual acts are only substitutes for any earlier generation's acts, as you'd expect. Where petting was, there shall fellatio be.

It will simply never be the case that children can treat sex with the free-floating fantasy and brutality that adults can, because we adults are atomized in our dealings with others as children in school are not. If I do something rotten on a blind date, I never need to see the only witness again. A child does something rotten, and his date is sitting next to him in homeroom. The adult world sends down its sexual norms, which cannot blossom in a closed institution (though alarmists say they *originate* there), but which the children tuck away to fulfill just as soon as they can. Children are the beneficiaries of a culture that declares in all its television, jokes, talk, and advertising that if sex isn't the most significant thing in existence, it is the one element never missing from any activity that is fun. They are watchers, silent, with open eyes, and they grow in the blue light.

So much for the decadent reality of childhood.

BUT ADULTS THEN LOOK BACK FROM EXILE AND SEE WRONGLY, thinking the children are free because we've hemmed them in with images of a transitory future freedom. Never mind that we ourselves led carnal lives that would make old men weep. Those lives hardly counted: inevitably we were caught in actual human relationships with particular people, in a matrix of leaden rules and personal ties. Envy of one's sexual successors is now a recurrent feature of our portion of modernity. Philip Larkin:

When I see a couple of kids,
And guess he's fucking her and she's
Taking pills or wearing a diaphragm,
I know this is paradise

Everyone old has dreamed of all their lives—
. . . everyone young going down the long slide

To happiness, endlessly. I wonder if
Anyone looked at me, forty years back,
And thought, *That'll be the life . . .*
He
And his lot will all go down the long slide
Like free bloody birds.

("High Windows")

Larkin's solace in the poem was high windows and the icy blue; in real life, an enormous collection of pornography.

The dirty magazines and their supposedly legitimate counterparts in fact play a significant role in the system of sex childhood. In Larkin's life, the poetry of longing went hand in hand with the fulfillments of porn, and all of us share in this interchange at a more banal level. The colloquialisms "men's magazines" and "women's magazines" generally seem to name two very different sets of publications. "Women's magazines" are instructional—how to display oneself, how to serve men, and nowadays (maybe always) how to steal sexual and emotional pleasure from men, outwitting them, while getting erotic and affective satisfactions, too, in the preparations for your self-display. "Men's magazines," for their part, are pornographic—how to look at women, how to fantasize about women, how to enjoy and dominate, and what one becomes while fantasizing this domination. The two genres are distinct, but continuous.

The women's advice and fashion magazines, *Cosmopolitan, Glamour, Elle, Vogue,* hold a permanent mandate for an erotic youthfulness, though not literal sexual youth. They provide shortcuts to staying young for old and young alike: how to keep your skin young, how to keep your muscles young, how to keep your ideas young, how to feel perpetually young, how to siphon vitality from elsewhere to be "young" even if you're not, literally, young, and how to use your youth if you are. You learn early what you'll lose late, and get accustomed to denying the aging that you might never have minded as much without this help.

Men's magazines fix readers' desires in the range of women's shapes and bodies and modes of seduction and subordination—fragmenting the market by body part and sex act and level of explicitness, but also by age. Pornography has a special investment in youth. The college girl is a central feature of *Playboy* in its "Girls of the Big Ten" pictorials; *Hustler* has a relentless *Barely Legal* franchise in magazines and videos, aped by *Just 18* and *Finally Legal* and all the bargain titles behind the convenience-store counter. In the demimonde of the internet, an even more central category of all online pornography is "teen." Of course it is profoundly illegal in the United States to photograph anyone under 18 sexually; in what is called 2257 compliance, producers of pornography must keep public legal records proving that every model is 18 or older. Technically, therefore, there are only two ages, 18 and 19, at which "teen" models can be actual teens. Nor do the models ever seem to be sexually immature; child pornography doesn't seem to be what the sites are for. Rather, putative teen models are made *situationally* immature—portrayed with symbols of the student life, the classroom, the cheerleading squad, the college dorm, the family home, the babysitting, the first job; not the husband, not the child, not the real estate brokerage or boardroom or bank office, never adult life.*

Thus a society that finds it illegal to exploit anyone beneath the age of legal majority is at the same time interested in the simulation of youth—often by people who are sexually mature but still only on the cusp of adulthood. And in its legitimate publications, as in its vice, it encourages a more general, socially compulsory female urgency to provision youth across the life span, and a male rush to take it.

Though the young person has never been old, the old person once was young. When you look up the age ladder, you look at strangers; when you look down the age ladder, you are always looking at versions of yourself. As an adult, it depends entirely on your conception of yourself whether those fantastic younger incarnations will seem long left behind or all-too-continuous with who you are now. And this conception of yourself depends, in turn, on the culture's attitudes to adulthood and

---

* Feminist critiques of pornography rooted in an idea of male violence and revenge against the threat of women's liberation might have predicted a different outcome in our age of equality: wider representations of the literal humiliation or subordination of adult women in power. What they did not anticipate was a turn to sexualized youth. Though the two lines of critique are not at all incompatible (i.e., youth still may be a way of denying adult equality), one sees now that feminist critiques of youth and aging are proving to be more significant historically than the MacKinnon-Dworkin line of pornography criticism.

childhood, age and youth. This is where the trouble arises. For in a culture to which sex furnishes the first true experiences, it makes a kind of sense to return to the ages at which sex was first used to pursue experience and one was supposedly in a privileged position to find it. Now we begin to talk, not about our sex per se, but about a fundamental change in our notion of freedom, and what our lives are a competition for.*

We must begin to talk directly about the change that was well begun in Nabokov's day and is well advanced in ours, the transformation

---

* I want to acknowledge two popular lines of thought that insist on the attraction to sexually mature children as natural not social, contravening my account. One is the commonsense historical argument that until recently sexually mature children of the middle teen years *were* adults, because human beings used to marry in their teens. Natasha, the dream of Russian womanhood in *War and Peace*, one of the greatest novels of the 19th century, set in that century's early years, is 14 when she becomes the object of her first suitors' attention—and admirable suitors too: hussars in the Czar's army, and a count. Her girlishness is treated matter-of-factly by those who are drawn to it as an appealing aspect of her personality, and it is considered realistically by her parents, who are concerned she may be too immature yet to leave home and run a household. In the United States, as the historian Philip Jenkins has summarized, the standard age of sexual consent was 10 years old until the 1890s, when it was raised to 16 or 18 depending on the state.

The other argument is one occasionally offered explicitly, but much more often implicitly, in the field of evolutionary psychology. Evolutionary psychology explains behavioral dispositions in modern human beings by the optimal strategies for passing on genes, through patterns hardwired into our brains by our evolutionary past and the continuing reproductive demands of the present. "Youth is a critical cue," writes evolutionary psychologist David M. Buss in the standard book on the subject of sex, "since women's reproductive value declines steadily with increasing age after twenty. By the age of forty, a woman's reproductive capacity is low, and by fifty it is close to zero" (*The Evolution of Desire*). The desire for children from the moment of visible pubescence (say, 12 today) to the maximum age before reproductive decline (age 20) may therefore be the best means for passing on genes. This inclination would be set beneath the level of consciousness, as men's desire is targeted to females who are fertile, healthy, and poised for the longest period of childbearing possible before the decline sets in. On evolutionary-biological presuppositions, it ought to be the case that human males today and yesterday, and in every society, should be maximally attracted to newly postpubescent girls unless it be determined statistically that there is some ramping-up of reproductive success in the years after menarche—in which case, certainly, no later than 14 or 15.

Neither the historical nor the biological argument seems to meet the problem of the sex child as we now know it, because I think neither captures our current experience of desire, in which the sex children come in only secondarily, through some kind of mediation of fancy; in our real lives adults feel the sexual appeal of other adults. Unless sexual desire is wholly unconscious, not plastic and social, and the social level entirely a screen or delusion—a very complex delusion to cover biological determinism—then with the sex children it's my sense that we are dealing primarily with the sexual appeal of *youth* rather than the actual determinative sexual attractiveness of *youths*. It would be something like a desire for the sex child's incipience, the child's taste of first majority before the rules clamp down: youth as eternal becoming, in eternal novelty of experience. Apart from such fancies, the appeal of sexually mature children seems to me particularly weak, not strong. But I understand that introspection is not science and I am aware this may not satisfy partisans of the "natural" views.

that created the world in which we are both freed and enslaved. That was sexual liberation.

LIBERATION IMPLIES FREEDOM TO DO what you have already been doing or have meant to do. It unbars what is native to you, free in cost and freely your possession, and removes the iron weight of social interdiction. Even in the great phase of full human liberation which extended from the 1960s to the present day, however, what has passed as liberation has often been *liberalization.* (Marcuse used this distinction.) Liberalization makes for a free traffic in goods formerly regulated and interdicted, creating markets in what you already possess for free. It has a way of making your possessions no longer native to you at the very moment that they're freed for your enjoyment. Ultimately you no longer know *how* to possess them, correctly, unless you are following new rules which emerge to dominate the traffic in these goods.

In sexual liberation, major achievements included the end of shame and illegality in sex outside of marriage (throughout the 20th century); the disentangling of sex from reproduction (completed with the introduction of the oral contraceptive pill in 1960); the feminist reorganization of intercourse around the female orgasm and female pleasure (closer to 1970); and the beginning of a destigmatization of same-sex sexuality (1970 to the present). The underlying notion in all these reforms was to remove social penalties from what people were doing anyway.

But a test of liberation, as distinct from liberalization, must be whether you have also been freed to be free *from* sex, too—to ignore it, or to be asexual, without consequent social opprobrium or imputation of deficiency. If truly liberated, you should engage in sex or not as you please, and have it be a matter of indifference to you; you should recognize your own sex, or not, whenever and however you please. We ought to see social categories of asexuals who are free to have no sex just as others are free to have endless spectacular sex, and not feel for them either suspicion or pity. One of the cruel betrayals of sexual liberation, in liberalization, was the illusion that a person can only be free if he holds sex as all-important and exposes it endlessly to others—providing it, proving it, enjoying it.

This was a new kind of unfreedom. In hindsight, the betrayal of sexual liberation was a mistake the liberators seemed fated to make. Because moralists had said for so many centuries, "Sex must be *con-*

trolled because it is so powerful and important," sexual liberators were seduced into saying, in opposition, "Sex must be *liberated* because it is so powerful and important." But in fact a better liberation would have occurred if reformers had freed sex not by its centrality to life, but by its triviality. They could have said: "Sex is a biological function—and for that reason no grounds to persecute anyone. It is *truthless*—you must not bring force to bear on people for the basic, biological, and private; you may not persecute them on grounds so accidental. You must leave them alone, neither forcing them to deny their sex nor to bring it into the light."

This misformulation of liberation only became as damaging as it did because another force turned out to have great use for the idea that sex is the bearer of the richest experiences: commerce. The field of sex was initially very difficult to liberate against a set of rival norms which had structured it for centuries: priority of the family, religious prohibitions, restraint of biology. Once liberation reached a point of adequate success, however, sex was unconscionably easy to "liberate" further, as commerce discovered it had a new means of entry into private life and threw its weight behind the new values. What in fact was occurring was liberalization by forces of commercial transaction, as they entered to expand and coordinate the new field of exchange. Left-wing ideas of free love, the nonsinfulness of the body, women's equality of dignity, intelligence, and capability, had been hard-pressed to find adequate standing before—and they are still in trouble, constantly worn away. Whereas incitement to sex, ubiquitous sexual display, sinfulness redefined as the unconditioned, unexercised, and unaroused body, and a new shamefulness for anyone who manifests a *non*sexuality or, worst of all, willful sexlessness—that was easy.

Opposition to this is not only supposed to be old-fashioned but also joyless and Puritanical—in fact, ugly. Sex talk is so much a part of daily glamour and the assurance of being a progressive person that one hates to renounce it; but one has to see that in general it is commercial sex talk that's reactionary, and opposition that's progressive. Liberalization has succeeded in hanging an aesthetic ugliness upon all discussions of liberation, except the purely ornamental celebrations of "the Woodstock generation" one sees on TV. Original liberators are ogres in the aesthetic symbolism of liberalization. They don't shave their legs! They're content to be fat! They have no fun. To say that a bodily impulse is something all of us have, and no regimentation or expertise or purchases can make one have it any more, *is* to become filthy and disgusting. It is to be nonproductive waste in an economy of markets, something nonsalable. It is not the repression of sex that opposes liberation (just as Foucault alerted us), but "inciting" sex as we know it—whatever puts sex into motion, draws it into *publicity*, apart from the legitimate relations between the private (the place of bodily safety) and the public (the sphere of equality).

THE QUESTION REMAINS WHY LIBERALIZATION turned back to gorge itself on youth.

How should a system convince people that they do not possess their sex properly? Teach them that in their possession it is shapeless and unconditioned. Only once it has been modified, layered with experts, honeycombed with norms, overlaid with pictorial representations and sold back to them, can it fulfill itself as what its possessors "always wanted." Breasts starved away by dieting will be reacquired in breast implant surgery—to attain the original free good, once destroyed, now recreated unnaturally.

How to convince them that what appears plentiful and free—even those goods which in fact are universally distributed—is scarce? Extend the reach of these new norms that cannot be met without outside intervention. Youth becomes a primary norm in the competition for sex. The surprise in this is not that youth would be desirable—it has always had its charm—but that you would think youth ought to be competitively *ineffective*, since it is universally distributed at the start of life. Yet youth is naturally evanescent, in fact vanishing every single day that one lives. It can be made the fundamental experience of a vanishing commodity, the ur-experience of obsolescence. Plus, it was everyone's universal possession at one time; and so artful means to keep it seem justified by a "natural" outcome, what you already were; and youth can be requalified physically as an aspect of memory, for every single consumer, in minutiae of appearance that you alone know (looking at yourself every day in a mirror, you alone know the history of your face and body) even while other people don't. We still pretend we are most interested in beauty, and it covers our interest in youth. Beauty is too much someone else's good luck; we accept that it is unequally distributed. Youth is more effective precisely because it is something all of us are always losing.

From the desire to repossess what has been lost (or was never truly taken advantage of) comes, in the end, the ceaseless extension of competition. It is easily encouraged. It doesn't require anything nefarious or self-conscious, certainly not top-down control, though it's sometimes convenient to speak of the process metaphorically as a field of control. All it requires is a culture in which instruments of commentary and talk (news, talk shows, advice magazines) are accompanied and paid for by advertisers of aesthetic and aestheticizable products—everything from skin-cream to Viagra to cars. This is supremely prosaic; but this is it. Once people can be convinced that they need to remain young for others to desire them, and that there are so many instrumentalities with which they can remain young; once they can be encouraged to suspect that youth is a particularly real and justifiable criterion for desire, then the competition will accelerate by the interchange of all these talkers: the professional commentators and product vendors and the needy audiences and ordinary people. Norms will not be set in advance, but are created constantly between the doubting individual and the knowing culture; or between the suddenly inventive individual and the "adaptive" and trend-spotting culture; a dialectic ultimately reproduced *inside* individuals who doubt ("I'm growing old") but seek know-how ("I'll be young")—in the channeling of desire in the bedroom, in conversation, in the marketplace.

For our object lessons and examples, it becomes advantageous for those searching for sexually desirable youthfulness to follow the trail to those who actually have youth. Thus young people in all forms of representation—advertising, celebrity-following, advice literature, day-to-day talk and myth—augment the competitive system of youth whether or not they are the "target market" of any particular campaign.

And yet the young are off-limits sexually, by law and morality and, more visibly, because of institutions that instruct and protect them. An adult simply will not get his or her hands on a college student—in large part because that student is in a closed institution. Professors have increasingly learned to stay away from students by threat of firing and public shaming. An adult should never wind up in sexual contact with a high school student unless conscience is gone and jail holds no fear; but neither will he run into many of them. The real-world disastrous exceptions of abuse, as we well know, come from those inside the institutions which instruct and protect the child: teachers, priests, babysitters, and, far and away most frequently, parents and family members. This criminal subset has an ambiguous relation to the wider fascination. For society as a whole, gazing at those youths who are sexually mature but restricted from the market institutionally or legally, sex children become that most perfect of grounds for competition, a fantastic commodity unattainable in its pure form.

Hence the final double bind of social preoccupation with the sex children in a commercial society regimented by a vain pursuit of absolute freedom. On one side, the young become fascinating because they have in its most complete form the youth which we demand for ourselves, for our own competitive advantage. They are the biologically superrich whose assets we wish to burgle because we feel they don't know the treasures they keep; they stand accidentally at the peak of the competitive pyramid. *Desire for sex childhood is thus a completion of the competitive system.* On the other side, the sex child as an individual is the only figure in this order who is thought to be *free* from competition; who holds sex as still a natural good, undiminished, a capability, purely potential—not something ever scarcer and jeopardized by our unattractiveness and our aging. For sex children, sex remains a new experience of freedom and truth that retains its promise to shape a better self. The kids are not innocent of carnality but they are innocent of competition. *Desire for sex childhood thus becomes a wish for freedom from the system.* The sex child can be a utopia personified, even as she props up the brutal dystopia to which her youth furnishes the competitive principle.

AS I ATTEMPTED THE FIRST DRAFT OF THIS ESSAY, the news was filled with reports about a 22-year-old North Dakota college student, Dru Sjodin, who was abducted and murdered as she left her retail job at Victoria's Secret. Police arrested a 50-year-old "Level Three sex offender" who had been identified in the mall parking lot though he lived thirty miles away in Minnesota. The man had Sjodin's blood in his car; police couldn't find the girl. But the news kept showing a college glamour picture, comparing her to other abducted youths, and dwelling on her workplace with its lingerie.

At the time, I thought: We can expect this to keep happening as long as sex with the sex children is our society's most treasured, fantasized consumer good. There was something inevitable about a murderer going to the mall to abduct a sex child—though under the circumstances it seemed terrible to say so. The whole tragedy was too depressing. So I stopped writing.

During the second attempt, I reached the clinical literature on child molestation. Some of it is tolerable. This includes the accounts of abused children who enter therapy and meet child psychologists who then record their cures in a whole hopeful literature on the side of healing. What is mostly intolerable, on the other hand, is the literature about child molesters. There are valuable contributions to criminology and psychology on the library shelves, which outline the problems of pedophilia and sexual abuse and molestation, often with in-depth interviews. I couldn't read very much of them. Sorry as I felt for these men, it seemed clear to me they should be destroyed. But this was really insane, and went against my other beliefs. So I began to consider: What is the meaning of abomination today, in a nonreligious age? It must be that there are points of cultural juncture at which phenomena are produced that, though explicable, are *indefensible* in the terms of any of the structures which produce or analyze them. You don't want to appeal to trauma, rehabilitation, socialization, or biological inclination. You can't just run away from the phenomena, and yet they can't be brought into the other terms of social analysis without an unacceptable derangement of values. This explains the impasse in which the annihilative impulse takes hold. So I stopped a second time.

In an increasingly dark mood, I came to the darkest way to frame the enigma of the sex children. A fraction of young people are extraordinarily highly valued, emulated, desired, examined, broadcast, lusted after, attended to in our society. These legal ex-children are attended to specifically as repositories of fresh sexuality, not, say, of intellect or even beauty. As their age goes up to 17, 18, and 19, the culture very quickly awards them its summit of sexual value. Yet as their age goes down from some indefinite point, to 16, 15, 14, and so on, the sexual appeal of childhood quickly reaches our culture's zone of absolute evil. Worse than the murderer, worse than the adult rapist of adults, and even worse than the person who physically and emotionally abuses children, is the person who sexually tampers with a child in any degree—who can then never be reintegrated into society except as a sex offender—or is simply the author of monstrous thoughts, a cyberstalker netted in police stings in chatrooms, or found downloading underage images to his hard drive. This is the "pedophile" whether or not he acts. Since the two zones—maximum *value* of sex, and maximum *evil* for sex—are right next to each other, shouldn't we wonder if there's some structural relation in society between our supergood and absolute evil?

The most direct explanation is that we may be witnessing two disparate systems as they come into conflict at just one point. System A would be the sexual valuation of youth, spurred by the liberalization of sex and its attachment to youth in a competitive economy. System B would be adult morality, the moral impulse to shield beings who need protection from sexual tampering and attention—because of the cruel nonreciprocity inflicted on a young child who doesn't yet have sexual desire (in true pedophilia, molestation of those beneath pubescence); the equally cruel coercion of those old enough to desire but not to have an adult's power to consent or to see how their actions will look to a future self (molestation of adolescents); and the deep betrayal, in all acts of sexual abuse, of the order of society and of its future, in something like a society-level version of the taboo on incest. Now, System A (sexual value, commerce) possesses a major flaw in its tendency to drive sexual attention down the age scale relentlessly—even to those legal children who hold sex in its newest and most inaccessible form. System B would fight this tendency, trying to provide necessary restraints; but perhaps it becomes most destructively punitive just where it refuses to disavow System A entirely. By otherwise accepting the sexual value of youthfulness, in other words—with such threatening possible side effects—morality would have to narrow itself vengefully upon the single point of visible contradiction, and overpunish whomever pursues too much youth, or does so too literally.

What's really striking to anyone who watches the news is of course the *intensity* of punitive violence where the two systems clash. From the point of view of morality, the overpunishment of the pedophile and the sex offender (barred from living anonymously, unrehabilitable, hounded from town to town unable to return to society) makes perfect sense, because of the extreme moral reprehensibility of abusing a child—combined with a dubious contemporary doctrine that *desires* can never be rehabilitated. It would also make sense, however, if we feared that the ruthlessness of this interdiction of pedophilia helped rationalize or reinforce the interests which confer extreme sexual value on youth just a bit up the ladder. *One fears our cultural preoccupation with pedophilia is not really about valuing childhood but about overvaluing child sex.* It would be as if the culture understood it must be so ruthless to stop tamperin with real children, just because it is working so hard to keep afloat the extreme commercial valuation of youth and its concrete manifestations in the slightly older sex child. Does the culture react so vehemently at just this point because were the screen of morality to collapse, the real situation would have to be confessed—the child's extreme uninterest in adults; the child's sexual "liberation" as a sub-effect of our own false liberation; the brutalization of life at all levels by sexual incitement?

One further step into the darkness has to complete the critique. The most pitiful and recondite form of pedophilia is sexual attachment to children below the age of sexual maturity—true pedophilia, which seems so utterly unmotivated, a matter of strict pathology. But a certain amount of the permanent persistence of child molesting as a phenomenon must not come from a fixed psychic category but from the misdirecting of sexual impulse to young people who temporarily fill a place of temptation or fascination—especially in desire for teens who are sexually mature, but whom an adult may still do a profound wrong by addressing sexually. It seems likely that an incessant overvaluing of the sex of the young will *train* some people toward wrong objects. This should swell the numbers of the class of incipient or intermittent wrongdoers who might no longer see a bright line between right and wrong—because social discourse has made that beam wobble, then scintillate, attract, and confuse.

If this is so, such immoral attention is not just a matter of a "loosening" of morality, but the combination of liberalization (*not* liberation) with a blinkered form of cultural interdiction. The pedophilic sensibility of the culture is strengthened. Thus we may produce the obsession we claim to resent; the new pedophile would become a product of our system of values.

ONE REHABILITATIVE SOLUTION WOULD BE to try to extinguish the worship of youth. Childhood is precisely the period when you can't do what you like. You are unformed and dumb. It is the time of first experiences; but first experiences can be read either as engravings from which all further iterations are struck and decline in clarity, or as defective and insufficient premonitions of a reality that will only develop in adulthood. We know the beauty of the young, which it is traditional to admire—their unlined features, their unworn flesh—but we also can know that the beauty of children is the beauty of another, merely incipient form of life, and nothing to emulate. One view of the young body is as an ideal. The other is as an unpressed blank.

A second solution would be the trivialization of sex altogether. This is much harder, because every aspect of the culture is so much against it, counterliberators and prudes included. Aldous Huxley warned of a world in which we'd arrange sexual intercourse as we make dates for coffee, with the same politeness and obligation. That now seems like an impossibly beautiful idyll. At least coffee dates share out assets pacifically. You meet for coffee with people you don't really want to see, and people who don't want to see you agree to meet you, and yet everyone manages to get something out of it. If only sex could be like coffee! But sex has not proved adaptable to this and probably never will, despite the recent overcoming of a heretofore limiting condition—the inability to control physical arousal at will. The new pharmacopoeia of tumescence drugs will soon give way, according to reports of current clinical trials, to libido drugs that act directly on the brain rather than the vascular system—and for both men and women. I'm still not optimistic they will produce a revolution in etiquette.

The reason it seems a sex of pure politeness and equal access does not work is that the constant preparation to imagine any and every other person as a sexual object (something our culture already encourages) proves to be ruthlessly egocentric and antisocial, making every other living body a tool for self-pleasure or gain. At times I wonder if we are witnessing a sexualization of the life process itself, in which all pleasure is canalized into the sexual, and the function of warm, living flesh in any form is to allow us access to autoerotism through the circuit of an other. This is echoed at the intellectual level in the discourse of "self-discovery." The real underlying question of sexual encounter today may not be "What is he like in bed?" (heard often enough, and said without shame) but "What am I like in bed?" (never spoken). That is to say, at the deepest level, one says: "Whom do I discover myself to be in sex?"—so that sex becomes the special province of self-discovery.

Meanwhile the more traditional way of trivializing sex, by subordinating it to overwhelming romantic love, has diminished as an option as the focus on self-discovery has increasingly devitalized full romantic love. Self-discovery puts a reflecting wall between the self and attention to the other, so that all energy supposedly exerted in fascination, attraction, and love just bounces back, even when it appears to go out as love for the other. When self-discovery is combined with the notion of a continually new or renewed self, and this newness is associated with literal or metaphorical youth—well, then you simply have a segment of the affluent first world at the present moment.

This means the trivialization of sex and the denigration of youth will have to start with an act of willful revaluation. It will require preferring the values of adulthood: intellect over enthusiasm, autonomy over adventure, elegance over vitality, sophistication over innocence—and, perhaps, a pursuit of the confirmation or repetition of experience rather than experiences of novelty.

The trivialization of sex and the denigration of childhood can still be put on the agenda of a humane civilization. However, I think it's basically too late for us. Perhaps I simply mean that I know it is too late for me. If you kick at these things, you are kicking at the heart of certain systems; if you deny yourself the lure of sex, for example, or the superiority of youth, you feel you will perish from starvation. But if I can't save myself or my children, probably, I still might help my grandchildren. The only hope would be, wherever possible, to deny ourselves in our fatuousness and build a barricade, penning us inside, quarantining this epoch which we must learn to name and disparage.

Let the future, at least, know that we were fools. Make our era distinct and closed so that the future can see something to move beyond. Record our testament, that this was a juvenile phase in liberation which must give way to a spiritual adulthood! Turn back to adults; see in the wrinkles at the side of the eye that catch the cobalt, the lines of laughter in the face, the prolific flesh, those subtle clothes of adulthood, the desire-inspiring repositories of *wisdom* and *experience.* Know that what we wish to be nourished upon is age and accomplishment, not emptiness and newness. Then, in sophisticated and depraved sexuality, rather than youth's innocence and the fake blush of truth, let our remaining impulses run in the sex of the old for the old—until they run out. Make a model for a better era. Once more, my moderns—in a superior decadence, in adult darkness rather than juvenile light—rise to the occasion! One effort more if you wish to be called liberators. +

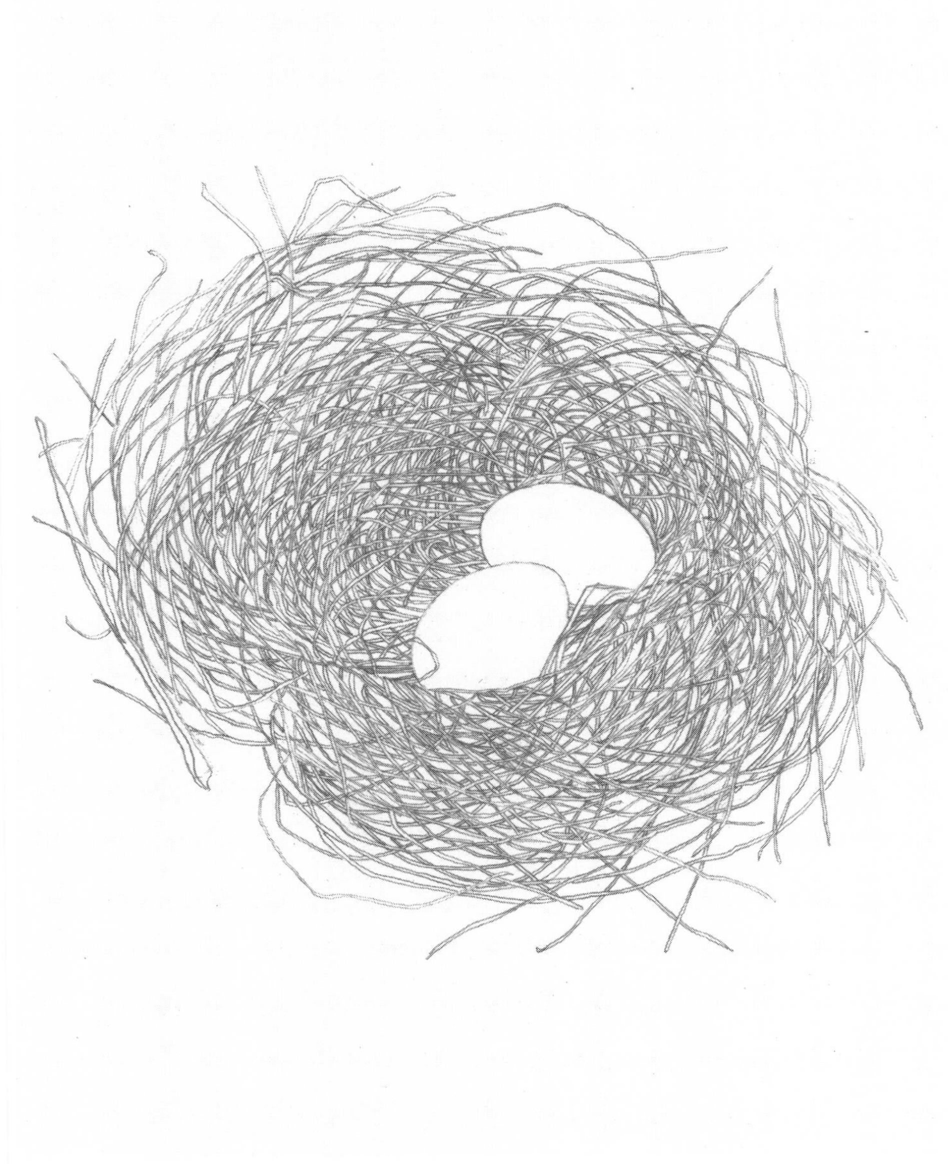

ECHO EGGBRECHT, UNTITLED, 2006,
INK ON PAPER, 16 X 23". COURTESY OF THE ARTIST AND NICOLE KLAGSBRUN GALLERY.

TWO STORIES

John Haskell

SHARK CAGE

WHAT HAPPENED TO ME—not to me, but what happened—I'm a writer of magazine articles and I was writing an article about sharks, about how they communicate with human beings. I was somewhere off the California coast with a group of scientists who were studying the human response to shark communication. They'd rigged up a fishing boat with winches and scientific instruments and a stainless steel cage, and I was inside the cage. Sensors were attached to various parts of my body, measuring my heart rate and my brain activity, and I was under the water, breathing through an air tank strapped to my back. I had my back to the boat's hull, scanning the water through the mask on my face, and even through the wet suit, I could tell the water was cold. But I didn't care because I was thinking about sharks. They'd pretty much guaranteed me a shark attack—something about an anomaly in the ocean current—and as I held the steel handrail I could hear the air as it passed from the scuba equipment into my lungs. That, plus the pressure of the water, plus the temperature of the water, plus the fact that there was going to be a shark attack, was focusing my attention.

I saw schools of little fish darting out from the darkness, I saw the speckled sunlight filtering down from the surface of the water, and I noticed pieces of meat floating down from above the cage. The scientists were chumming for sharks and I could see the blood dissolving in the water. I knew the minute I stopped expecting the shark, the minute I took my mind off the idea of shark, like a watched pot, that's when a shark would appear, and since I didn't want to miss that appearance, I kept my mind focused on the water, trying not to think about anything other than water, but I must have been thinking something, and I must have been in the middle of thinking it when a white underbelly flashed by, huge and white and slightly above me, and then suddenly the bait, which had been floating in the water, was gone.

The bait was gone and the shark was gone, but I was still there, still feeling the effect of the shark. I'm sure the scientists, looking at the data from my sensors, would have called it fear, which is a word describing a certain emotion, and it was definitely an emotion I was experiencing, and yes, my heart was pounding, and yes, my senses were acute, and I'd seen enough of the shark to feel the threat, but because I was protected by the safety of the cage, what it felt like to me was the absence of fear. I wouldn't have called it serenity because my body was full of energy. My fingertips, through the rubber gloves, seemed very alive. And although I couldn't see the shark, I was aware of it, just beyond my vision. And when I say aware I mean I was sensing some kind of signal from the shark, as if the shark was communicating. And because the most rudimentary form of communication is the expression of desire, I was feeling the shark's desire, and one of the things it was desiring was my annihilation.

So there was fear. But it wasn't overwhelming. Because the cage was protecting me I was able to communicate with the source of the fear. The human brain is capable of receiving millions of neural signals, and what I was trying to do was send signals, to the shark. I was trying to tell the shark that I understood its desire, that I accepted its desire, and I was just getting into this conversation with the shark when I felt the cage begin to rise. The scientists were bringing me back, and I tried to signal through the sensors that I wasn't ready, that I was still conducting the experiment. I tried to think those thoughts and send those thoughts, but either the sensors weren't working or my thoughts weren't working. I felt the weight of the water pushing down as the cage rose up, like an elevator, out of the water, and there I was again, in the breathable normalcy of air.

The cage was set back down on the deck and when the door was opened I remember ducking through the opening and stumbling out into the relative stability of the boat's deck. I could feel my lungs expanding in my body, and I felt light, like air, lighter than air, like a balloon. I noticed the people in front of me, and as I stepped out of the cage I embraced the first person who extended a hand—the captain probably—and more than embrace him, I locked my arms around him. I could feel his heart beating beneath my hands, and I could hear him asking if I was all right. I didn't feel my own heart but I must have been grinning at him, and it must've been an infectious grin, because he was grinning at me.

An assistant scientist, a young woman wearing overalls and rubber boots, led me to a plastic crate, where I sat, wrapped in a blue blanket. I could tell I was still feeling the lingering exhilaration of my interaction with the shark because my thoughts... I didn't have any thoughts. It was all sensation. And because thoughts maintain the idea of who we are, when my thoughts were gone, I was gone, and without the barrier between me and the world, the world looked different. I was looking at a corroded hinge on the cabin door, and instead of thinking about what kind of paint they used or imagining what I would do if I owned the boat, instead of reacting to what I saw, I just saw. Every so often I would notice a thought pop into my head. But it was easy to let it go and turn my attention to the assistant scientist. She brought me a mug of warm tea and leaned against the side of the boat, telling me that she hadn't done it yet, but that she wanted to go into the water herself. She told me that her name was Elena, that she was an intern, and we talked about U.C.L.A. and graduate school and the life of a marine biologist, and I wouldn't have called it paradise, but if paradise is a place where the need for protection falls away, then that's where I was. And the only question is: how long does it last?

And did I want that protection?

I was holding my mug of warm tea, looking at her face and the peaceful horizon behind her face, and I knew she wasn't a threat. But I was feeling something unfamiliar. Lack of thought was unfamiliar to me, and because it was unfamiliar I felt I needed to do something.

I asked for more tea. The tea was comforting. I tried to focus on this person who was saying something to me and it wasn't that I wasn't paying attention. The problem was, I didn't know I wasn't paying attention.

I could feel my butt bones on the plastic crate, my feet back in a pair of socks now, and shoes, and the sky was above me and the ocean in front of me and Elena was standing to my right. All these things were there but so were my thoughts. And while I was having them, while I was involved in the various narratives contained in those thoughts, I wasn't actually seeing the sky or the ocean or the wide blue eyes that were looking at me. What I was seeing were my thoughts. Millions of thoughts were passing through my mind, and some of them persisted, not long enough to remember them, but long enough to distract me from the world. Not that my thoughts weren't part of the world, but even as we talked I could feel those thoughts creating a barrier. I could feel my old self, the one who'd been absent when I was under the water, reconfiguring itself. Without any overt effort on my part I was going back to my habit of being, back to the safety of what I knew.

I turned to her, and I can't say I didn't feel a little relief, because who doesn't like safety? But the odd thing was, it didn't feel like safety.

There I was, having a putative conversation with her, and at the same time I was thinking about the tea, and the lack of sugar in the tea. I was oscillating between her and the tea, back and forth, neither with her nor the tea, and I obviously wasn't in a cage anymore, but I did feel confined by something, and whatever it was I wanted to escape. I wanted to reach out to this person, to enter the world and communicate with this person, to see and hear and touch the world in front of me.

Except maybe I didn't.

Maybe I wanted to be protected from the world. Maybe I wanted to keep the world at bay.

Except I didn't.

KON TIKI

SO THERE I WAS, SITTING AT A LOW TABLE in a nostalgic restaurant-bar called Kon Tiki off Wilshire Boulevard. I call it nostalgic because, although it didn't actually exist in the 1950s, it was made to seem as if, sitting at the low table, amid the bamboo walls and the Polynesian masks, you were somewhere in the middle part of the last century. It was a cultural memento, or I should say memento mori, because the past it referred to had long since disappeared and died, as everything does. The *Playboy* beach-party aesthetic that came into being after World War II, after we'd won the war in the Pacific, was part of a generalized nostalgia that included the photographs on the walls. There were publicity stills of movie stars of the past, people like Dean Martin and Tony Curtis, and because I'd been thinking of changing my own name I was aware that, for instance, Dean Martin was born Dino Crocetti, that Tony Curtis was Bernard Schwartz, that John Wayne was Marion Morrison, and that Barbara Stanwyck was originally Ruby Stevens.

Anyway, I was sitting there with Alan, my editor, and also a tall young woman, a model or swimsuit model, who wanted to become a photographer. Her name was Gabby, and although she wasn't all that garrulous, the conversation flowed. I was doing most of the talking, along with Alan, who was a friend as well as my editor, and the young woman was an acquaintance of his, someone he wanted to be an acquaintance of mine. She was transitioning, as they say, from being in front of the camera to being behind the camera, and Alan had an interest in her. Also, I'd recently come out of a fairly long-term relationship and was still slightly uncomfortable jumping into the ocean of romance. That's what it seemed like, an ocean, and Alan's way of pushing me into the water of that ocean was to introduce me to this person.

There we were, drinking our drinks and talking about photography.

"Alan told me you wanted to know about cameras."

"I think I have the camera part figured out," she said, and reached into her bag and pulled out a film camera with adjustable dials and levers.

Alan was sipping his mojito, sitting back in his chair so that the triangle formed by the three of us left him slightly removed. He'd told her I knew something about photography, which wasn't a complete lie because I did take pictures, but that was about it, and I told Gabby, "I really don't know much."

"Don't let him fool you. He's got an outstanding eye."

"That's what I want to develop," she said.

"Then he's your man."

Alan had the habit of treating people as if they were stupid, not because he thought they were stupid, but because until they told him otherwise, by assuming it was so he was able to feel safe.

My way to feel safe was different. A writer in Los Angeles is fairly far from the top of the food chain, and she would know that and naturally I wanted to do something, to seem to be a little more important than I was. I tried to stand straighter and I looked into her eyes in what I hoped was a meaningful way.

She was a beautiful actress or model whose ambition was to be something other than merely beautiful, and thinking I might be a way for her to achieve that ambition, she smiled a lot, and I could see that her teeth were perfect, and as I was looking at her teeth I was imagining going home with her and living forever in a paradise of love.

Unless Alan had hired a hooker. There was the possibility that this was a joke, on me. Either way, I wanted to seem like someone different than I was.

If she noticed, she was too polite to say anything. And I didn't say anything, and we talked like that for a while, but the talking isn't what I'm getting at. The talking was pleasant, but it was preparatory. What really happened, happened later, when we took Alan up on his suggestion and walked outside.

He suggested we stop talking about photographs and go outside and take some. So we finished our drinks, stood up, and "You two go," he said. "I have to take this call."

I don't know if there was a call, but we left Alan, walked through the lunchtime drinkers, past the bamboo walls of photographs, and when we opened the heavy wooden doors, suddenly there was light. It took a while for our eyes to adjust to the light, and when they had I asked her where she wanted me to stand. She was going to take my picture.

"Where do you think?" she said.

We were standing at the edge of the parking lot. The cars were in bright sunlight, and from what I knew about photography I knew it required light, so I suggested I stand in the sun. "I'll stand by this car," I said, staking out an area next to an expensive-looking black sedan.

She asked me to do something.

"Do what?"

"You're the model," she said. "Right? Everyone thinks it's so easy."

I didn't know how I wanted to stand, or how she wanted me to stand, and "How much are you taking," I said, meaning how much of my body.

"Act like you're walking."

I tried to do that.

"I mean really walk."

And I walked, but I walked too fast. And it would be safe to say that things, literally, weren't clicking. I made an attempt to strike a pose, and she didn't say anything but I could tell that she didn't like it, and I said, "If you were me, getting your photograph taken, how would you stand? Here," I said, and took out my little silver camera and pointed it at her.

She was standing next to a car, and still holding her camera, and she gave me a look. "I'd stand like this."

I took the picture.

And because that seemed to relax her, I took another, and then when she seemed to get more comfortable, I said, "Now me," and I stood in the same way she'd stood, and she was looking through the camera at me, and I could hear that she wasn't taking the picture. "Go ahead," I said. "Take it." I was the one in front of the camera but she was the one who was nervous. And I told her, "It doesn't have to be perfect," but she said she wasn't sure about the light. "Don't worry about light," I said. "Work with me, baby," and I did a fake fashion-model imitation.

I was joking, but she was serious, telling me about the light and the focus, and while she was talking I took another picture, of her. And when I did, she stopped concentrating on her camera and started concentrating on me.

I thought she might like to use my camera, and I held it out to her. "I think it adjusts automatically for the light," I said, and instead of saying anything she just stood there. So I took another picture. I didn't know what I was doing, but because she seemed to assume I did, I took another, and then another. She put her camera on the hood of a car and I moved so that the sun was off to the side, and she moved away from the car, and away from her camera, and she began moving her hands, not to any purpose, except the purpose of looking good. That was her mask and she was comfortable in that mask. She was creating the composition and I was behind my mask, snapping the pictures.

And sometimes you need a mask. Like the steel bars of a shark cage, sometimes you need to feel safe enough to express something that exists behind the mask. And that's fine, except in our case, instead of allowing us to reveal who we were, instead of allowing us to speak honestly from behind the safety of the masks, the masks did what masks are supposed to do, they hid who we were.

I suggested she take me while I was taking her. But she didn't seem to be listening anymore. She was lost now in what she was doing, in the role she had taken, the role of a model, which was her default role, and now she was in it, and as I kept shooting photographs of her, photograph after photograph, I could feel myself carving the rut of our relationship. And it wasn't a bad thing, this rut. It was still very shallow, but it was getting deeper and deeper, and because it was a rut, we continued to communicate in this way. She was letting me know what she wanted, and she was sensing what I wanted, and I wasn't telling her where to stand or how to stand, she was just standing there, posing, and I let her pose, and I continued taking photographs. +

MELODRAMATIC INSTALLATIONS

Ilya Kliger

INSTALLATION 2

THE TRAPEZOID ROOM IS VAST, a loft with no furniture except for a chair, standing three or four steps from the entrance with its back to it. To the convex wall opposite the entrance, at the height of seven feet from the floor (approximately at midpoint between the floor and the ceiling), a washstand is attached. Water runs constantly but unevenly from the faucet. Half the time it gushes forth, accompanied by frightful screeching that seems to rise from beneath the floor. The rest of the time, the water comes down in a soothing trickle.

A man and a woman inhabit the room. For the most part, because there is only one chair, only one of them sits. Sometimes both of them stand. Occasionally, when the man occupies the chair for too long, and the woman tires of standing, she sits down on the floor, her back against the concave wall. The man is tall, birdlike, his hair black, brushed back, shiny. He wears a dark blue suit and light glasses. The woman is large, her face round, froglike, and kindly. She wears a long, colorful skirt, white sneakers, and a loose white shirt untucked. Sometimes, a dun bandanna covers her head; when it is off, visitors can see that her cropped hair is silver with gray.

The man occupies himself with the help of a hand-held computer game. Both standing and sitting (though to those who frequent the room it becomes clear that he is mainly sitting), he is almost always pressing the buttons. Though he often presses quite frantically, his face never loses its lofty, birdlike expression. Sometimes he pauses, looks up and around him, nods to the woman, stretches and yawns. Then he reaches for the inside pocket of his jacket, takes out another game, replaces the old one in the box, and plays on.

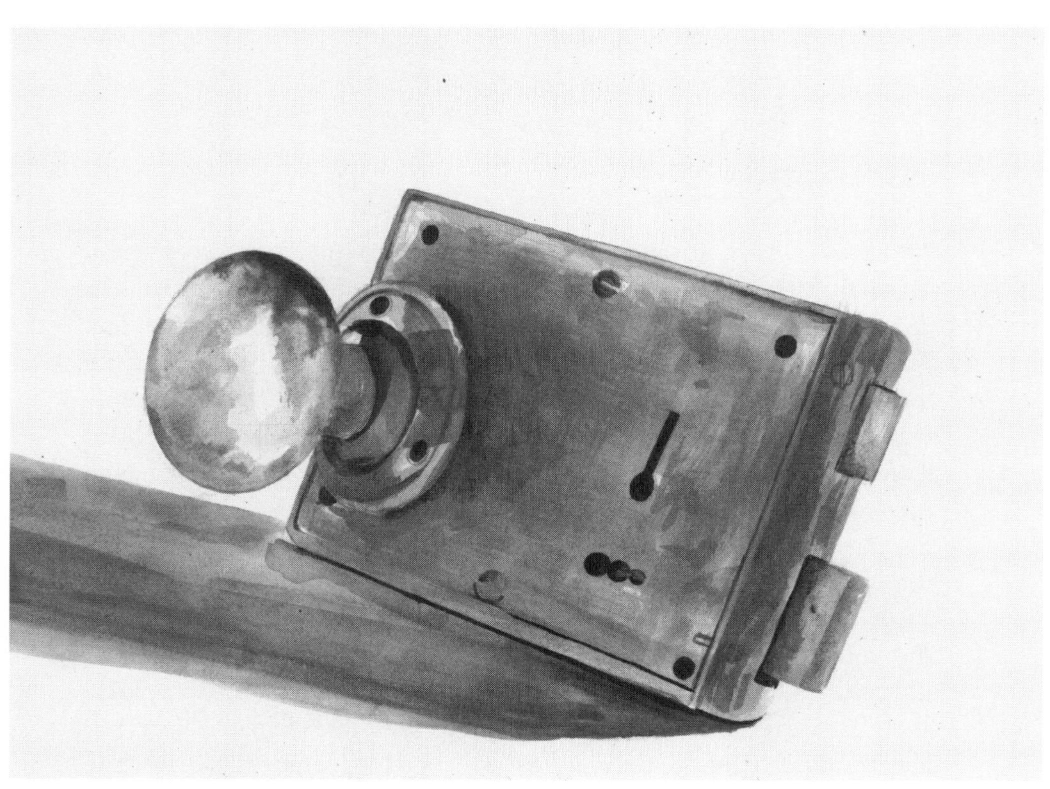

ECHO EGGBRECHT, UNTITLED, 2006,
INK ON PAPER, 16 X 23". COURTESY OF THE ARTIST AND NICOLE KLAGSBRUN GALLERY.

Perhaps because the woman has no similar means of entertaining herself, she is preoccupied with the washstand. The art critic Oliver Lieber notes that the woman's preferred place for sitting against the concave wall by the entrance is not fortuitously chosen, since it is the only place in the room from which the faucet is visible for someone of the woman's height who is sitting on the floor. Even if she is not looking, her attention is always on the washstand. When the water gushes forth, rumbling and screeching, her face reddens and her eyes widen with terror. When it quiets down, her attention relaxes without letting go. Very rarely, perhaps once every two weeks, while the water trickles, the noises that rise from under the floor are loud and terrifying. At such moments, the woman squats in the middle of the room, covers her head with her arms, buries it in her lap, and rocks back and forth. The man does not stop playing, but glances up at her now and then and occasionally, with the intention of calming her down, mumbles: "Hey, hey... don't... ."

Every day, at ten in the morning and at four in the afternoon, the man and the woman speak. During these conversations, the room becomes crowded with visitors. But for the most part, they walk out unrewarded. The conversations tend to be trivial. For example, the woman might ask the man which game he is playing. Or the man might ask the woman how she is feeling. While talking, the man doesn't look up from the game, and the woman keeps monitoring the water. They reply to each other and then stay silent for minutes, until one of them raises another question or, looking around absently, comments on the weather.

Concerning this last topic of conversation, the question has arisen as to how it might be possible for them to know what the weather is like, given that the room has no windows. The administration claims that their judgments are absolutely random. Oliver Lieber's hypothesis, supported by a number of regular visitors, is that they are based on the subtleties of water flow in the washstand.

Every Friday, sometime around noon, the room is filled to capacity. Visitors stand everywhere, whispering to each other, waiting. Soon enough, the guard closes the door from the outside and the installation appears to the viewers in its most exciting aspect. The man utters a high-pitched cry, rises from the chair and dashes about the room, stamping and shouting. He hurls the hand-held computer against the wall, kicks it, shouts and flails his arms. Often, his glasses fall off and he steps on them and breaks them. The woman hesitates for a moment, then walks up to him and gently takes him in her arms. He grows quiet, uttering soft moans now and then as she rocks him softly in her arms whispering something into his ear. Yet all along it is possible to tell that her innermost attention is still on the water. And if, while she is comforting him, the water happens to be pouring, accompanied by the usual noises, then, though she still whispers to him and pats him gently on the back, her face reddens and her eyes widen with terror.

INSTALLATION 3

THE ROOM IS FLOODED WITH BRIGHT MIST and appears to stretch out indefinitely. Visitors are not allowed to proceed past the white line painted on the floor about two feet from the entrance. In this way, no more than one person at a time can come in. Chances are that any given visitor would see very little in the mist, start squinting, and, urged on by the knowledge that others are waiting to enter, step back out. This makes it difficult to establish what exactly takes place in the room during the day.

According to the data collected by the museum administration, an average visitor spends eighteen seconds in the room. Out of approximately 1,600 daily visitors, only an average of 100 report having seen a little girl dressed in black walking toward them out of the mist or away, back into it. The girl's progress is reported to be slow. Apparently, she stops at even intervals (every five or six steps), turns to her left (i.e., to the visitor's left when she is walking away and to the visitor's right as she is approaching) and stands facing the wall. From visitor reports, it is difficult to determine exactly how long she stands in this manner, since not a single visitor has ever stayed in the room for the entire duration of her standing. One reasonable estimate, reached on the basis of reports from thirty groups of four consecutive visitors, is that she stands for about one minute.

An overwhelming majority of those who happen to enter the room at the time when the girl cannot be seen believe it to be completely empty, except of course for the mist. But most of those whose stay coincides with the girl's visible movement through the room notice also the existence of several objects positioned along the walls. It is precisely in front of them that the girl pauses every five or six steps and toward them that she turns.

Now, with regard to precisely what these objects are, the greatest confusion reigns. The data list "an oval mirror for the girl to see herself" as the highest-rated object, listed by fifty-two visitors. Next comes "a TV set playing the girl's favorite cartoon," at forty-five. Then "a note written to the girl by her mother" (thirty), "a framed photograph of the girl as a baby" (twenty-five), "an old tape recorder with the girl's favorite music" (twenty-one), and "a little bookcase, filled with shiny volumes of a children's encyclopedia" (twenty). The remaining objects—such as a window, a bucket, a milk carton, a thermos, a little boy or a wax figure thereof, and a pile of colorful wooden letters of the alphabet for children—are all listed at very low frequencies.

Lastly, with regard to what happens to the girl when she is out of sight of visitors, it is of course difficult to tell. When asked their opinion, the majority of visitors believe that she walks to the end of the room, wherever it may be, and returns. Those who have noticed objects along the walls believe them to be similarly distributed along the invisible portions of the walls (i.e., at a distance of the girl's five or six steps). The art critic Oliver Lieber famously disagrees with this view. Opinions also vary as to the size and shape of the room itself.

INSTALLATION 4

ON THE DOOR TO THE ROOM, a sign is hanging. It reads: OPEN. But the room remains locked at all times, except for about a minute once a day. No one has been able to predict when it will happen, but every day, a man comes up to the door, keys jangle, the door opens, and those who stand outside it can see a small room, trapezoid in shape, with the two parallel walls curved. The room is unfurnished and empty, except for a narrow archway at the center. The archway is plaster-white, its haunches resolving smoothly into the ceiling. For a minute, perhaps for ninety seconds, the door stays open or rather ajar.

The man who comes every day to open the door is short, sturdy. His face is the color of the room he unlocks—white, with a thick layer of dampened white powder covering little abrasions and scratches on his forehead and cheeks. The whiteness is emphasized by long, thin red hair on top and by a yellowish suit below. Having opened the door, the man turns his wide back sharply to it and strikes up a conversation with the visitors. He talks of the weather, of celebrities, of sports. He looks everyone in the eye, tries to involve as many people as possible in the conversation. He has nothing interesting to say about any of the subjects he raises, and the questions he asks have none but trivial replies. Who won last night? And hasn't it been cold for this time of year? And who left whom? And where can one get the best steak around here? Yet for as long as the door stays open, he manages to keep the audience's attention.

Throughout his stay by the door, he is visibly nervous, rocks slightly from side to side, wipes sweat off his forehead. Sweat comes off, darkening the handkerchief, but plaintive wrinkles remain, grow deeper as time passes. When the handkerchief is back in his pocket, his fingers run through a heavy bunch of keys like a rosary. Now and then he glances at his watch, slightly bends his knees, bobs. He looks like a little boy who needs to go to the bathroom, but, unable to tear himself off from an interesting game, won't admit it even to himself. When time is almost up, his keys jangle more resolutely. He averts his eyes from his interlocutors, nods, incongruously says: "I see, I see." Then, after one last glance at his watch, he turns to the door and hastily shuts and locks it.

Every time the doorman unlocks the door, the crowd starts for the entrance. But for the most part, the doorman proves to be a greater attraction than the room itself. In any case, what the visitors can glimpse of the room doesn't tempt them. The archway looks perfectly plain, with no hint of antiquity, and there is apparently nothing else inside. Occasionally, however, one of the visitors makes an attempt to enter the room.

Most recently, it was a lanky young man with a ponytail and a pimply forehead, wearing torn blue jeans and flip-flops. He attracted the doorman's attention from the very beginning with his fidgety movements and a determined gaze. Several times, with a complaisant smile on his face, the doorman tried to address him directly. But the young man pretended he didn't hear, kept his eyes fixed on the entrance, and at last started making his way through the crowd, mumbling "What kind of bullshit is this?" and heading for the door.

What happened next was no different from what always happens on such rare occasions.

The doorman utters a piercing shriek, collapses on his knees and, still shrieking, begins to strike himself on the face with the large bunch of keys. People crowd around him, murmuring, gazing, reluctantly calling out for help. The culprit (most recently, the young man) turns from person to person in panic. "What does this mean?" this one keeps asking. "What did I do?" But soon the doorman stops screaming and rises from his knees. He takes out his handkerchief and wipes blood (if there is any) off his face. Then he glances at his watch, walks up to the door, and locks it.

Whether or not things go smoothly, once the door is locked, the man is utterly transformed. "He is no longer a bungling, pathetic master of ceremonies," writes Oliver Lieber, "but a wooden idol, wearily stepping down from his high place."

INSTALLATION 5

THE ROOM IS FURNISHED LIKE A CHILD'S BEDROOM. Immediately to the right of the entrance is a little bed, its slight curvature following precisely that of the wall against which it stands. A large map of the world hangs on the wall over the bed. Those with a good eye for such things appreciate how nicely the colorful bedding harmonizes with the colors of the map. A small desk stands along the adjacent wall, cleared of everything but a well-sharpened pencil, pointing left, its trajectory blocked two to three inches beyond its tip by an oblong blue eraser. The chair does not stand at the desk, but next to it, further along the wall, facing the room. Flush against the wall opposite the entrance stands a chest. Like the bed, it is slightly curved to fit the shape of the wall. Most visitors infer that the chest holds toys from the fact that on top of it sits a teddy bear, holding between his paws a little red heart. The bear sits very still, gazing across the room at the bed. The left side of the room is oddly empty, formerly occupied by a stereo stand or some such thing.

Approximately two thirds of the visitors will know that the room is occupied by Oliver Lieber. Even they, however, not to mention those who come altogether unprepared, aren't immediately aware of his presence. Only having made a few steps into the room, having met and followed the teddy bear's blank gaze to the bed, do they find him. It is at this point that the prepared can be distinguished from the unprepared. The loud exclamations of the latter are frowned upon as tasteless and provincial by the better-informed majority, who, because they knew what to expect, manage to suppress all expressions of surprise and simply nod or fold their arms knowingly. In fact these too later tend to admit that they were shocked by what they saw. Oliver's thin face with light blue eyes and greenish skin is lost in the play between the blue of the pillow and the identical blue of the seas and oceans on the map. As for the rest of him, his body has been rendered so slight by his illness that it could be mistaken for folds in the blanket.

The room is open to visitors for only a limited time each day. The reasons for this are obscure. Perhaps the administration is unwilling to expose visitors to the frightful exhibit for too long for fear of being sued for psychological damages. But surely, also, the dying man himself must find it difficult to have too many people around at all times. Whatever the reasons may be, it remains the case that the installation is open for only a limited amount of time each day, on some days for two hours, on others for three.

The manner in which visitors use the time lends itself to the following tripartite classification. One group of visitors, after the first signs of surprise, stays as far as possible from Oliver Lieber. Though perhaps they would have liked to, they don't leave immediately, out of a vague fear of offending the dying man. They while away their time, pacing back and forth with downcast eyes, gazing at walls, stopping in front of the teddy bear—pretending, in short, that they haven't noticed Oliver Lieber at all. Yet it very well may be that, of all visitors, it is they who notice him the most profoundly. Many of them later report being shocked at the thought of a death so inhumane (for lack of medical care and religious consolation) and so demeaning (in a child's room, exposed to the gazes of strangers).

The second group of visitors is also ashamed to show too lively an interest in the sufferer. They, too, tend to stay away from the deathbed. This group can be distinguished from the first, however, by the lively interest they pretend to take in the pencil-and-eraser configuration on the desk as well as by the fact that, hoping to take as full advantage of the exhibition as possible, they again and again cast curious glances at the bed and strain to overhear a sigh or a whisper. For the most part, they see and hear very little, however, because the third group of visitors, immediately upon detecting Oliver Lieber on the bed, approaches and forms a semi-circle around him. Many of these are probably long-time admirers of the critic. They want to ask him one last question or overhear a word of his moribund wisdom.

The most faithful of these have recently set up a website, where people can post the master's dying words. Quite a list of his final utterances has been compiled, and the administration has been compelled to appoint a commission of seven curators to sort out authentic from invented and misheard statements. So far, only one has been authenticated:

". . . The notion that everything 'there, in the mist' is 'pretty much the same' as it is in the realm of the visible is of course an age-old view, supported by numberless vulgar superstitions and metaphysical assumptions. This is not of course the place to counter them in their entirety. What must be pointed out resolutely, however, is the extent to which, in our particular case, such a conjecture concerning the state of affairs in the realm of the invisible remains blind to what is surely the most important fact of all, the fact of this little girl's life. How, one might want to ask—thus reminding us how often the profound ends up on the side of common sense—how is the little girl sustained through the day? Would it not be both more humane and more insightful to suspect that 'out there in the mist' a little kitchen is hidden, and perhaps even a cook or the girl's mother, who feeds her to make sure that the child goes through the day without collapsing and cheers her up with a supportive word or a kindly smile so that the child does not break out in tears from loneliness and lack of human warmth? Would this suggestion not lead us toward what is both a more supple aesthetics and a more humanly palatable ontology? Would it not promote a view of art so much more, shall we say, nurturing, and at the same time so much more open-ended?" +

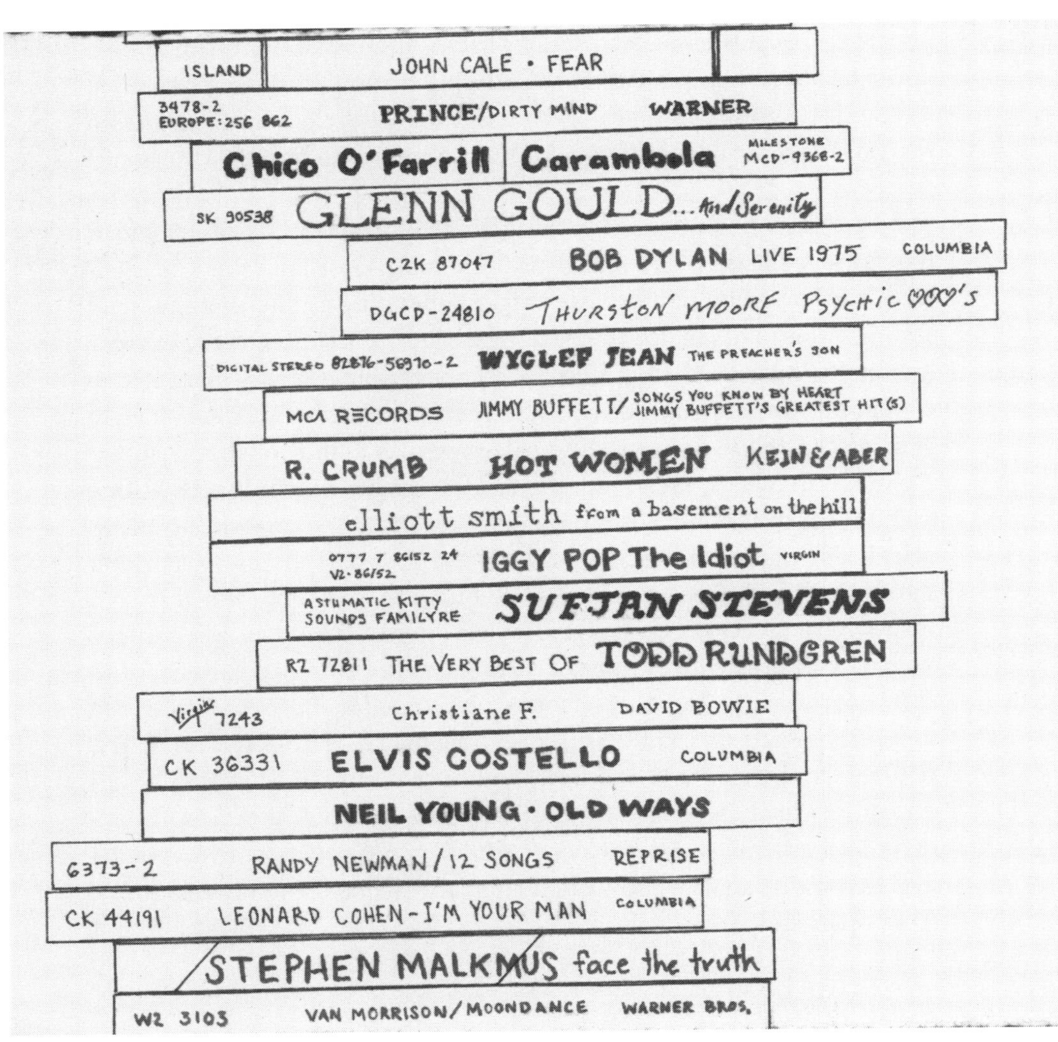

ECHO EGGBRECHT, UNTITLED, 2006,
INK ON PAPER, 16 X 23". COURTESY OF THE ARTIST AND NICOLE KLAGSBRUN GALLERY.

THREE STORIES

Rebecca Schiff

THE BED MOVED

THERE WERE FILM MAJORS IN MY BED—they talked about film. There were poets, coxswains, guys trying to grow beards.

"Kids get really scared if their dad grows a beard," I said.

Finally, I had an audience. I helped a pitcher understand the implications of his team's hazing ritual. I encouraged indecisive dancer/premeds to double major. When a guy apologized for being sweaty, I got him a small towel. I made people feel good.

Then I took a break. Then I forgot that I was taking a break. Spring was here. Jake was here. Also Josh. One dancer/premed dropped medicine, just did dance. He danced with honors.

"Mazel tov," I said.

The bed moved. Movers moved it. Movers asked what my dad did, why he wasn't moving the bed.

New guys came to the bed. New guys had been in the Gulf War, had been bisexual, had taken out teeth, had taken out ads. Musical types left CDs with their names markered on—I kept a pile. I was careful not to smudge them, scratch them. (Scratch that, I wasn't careful.)

"So many musicians in this city," I observed, topless.

Boxer shorts were like laundry even on their bodies. Guys burrowed in my sheets, popped up, smiled. Did I have something? Did I have anything? Afterwards, cell phones jingled.

"No, wait, that's mine."

Be Bop, Mariachi Medley, Chicken Dance, Die Alone.

I rang and jangled around town. Nervous, I felt nervous. It was mariachi in the trains, or else just one guy playing "La Bamba." Some days, I lost it, banged my face against the bed. Be easy, girl, I thought. Be bop. Something was definitely wrong with me—I never called myself "girl." I played CDs, but CDs by artists who had already succeeded. They had succeeded for a reason. They weren't wasting time in my bed. One did pass through the bed, to brag. He had been divorced, had met Madonna. He asked if this was what women were like now.

"What do you mean, now?"

I didn't know what women were like now. I don't know now. I'm only one. The others would be mad if I spoke for them. The others are already mad.

ON THE BUS

ON THE BUS, I WAS JEALOUS. I was jealous of the girl in front of me, and I was jealous of the girl diagonal. I was jealous of the elderly Chinese woman, sleeping by the window. It was the Chinatown bus. The bus was taking me to see a guy who had come to see me twice, a guy who held doors, a guy who told me I was cute like he was trying to ward something off. He would find all these girls cute. Any of us could step off the bus and be his girlfriend.

By the time I got off the bus, I was done with him. He was there anyway, waiting to take my bag. The problem was, it was his birthday. I had a box of Italian cookies and a card I had written on the bus.

"You are special," I had written. It was the only thing I could think of that wasn't a lie. Everyone was special.

"I hope you like cookies..." I had added. That was a lie. I knew he liked cookies. The cookies were in one of those white boxes that make baked goods seem promising.

"Some may have broken on the bus," I said.

"I can't wait," he said. He really liked cookies. What else did I know about him? He cared about real estate. His mother was dead. So was my dad. Cookies and real estate. I did not care. This was my first boyfriend since the last one.

Does it matter that we were in Boston? We had to stay at his dad's house in Newton, since my unwanted boyfriend wouldn't rent an apartment. He only wanted to own. I wanted to meet the dad, but we got in too late. We put the white box on the white countertop, an island bisecting the kitchen, just like in my mother's house. His dad had the same cheeses in the refrigerator, the same jams. The house had the same quiet.

"Welcome Lilah!"

On a bright square of printer paper, the dad had left me a note, a note that maybe needed a comma.

"I made a reservation for tomorrow," said the son. It was actually only almost his birthday.

"For all of us?" He'd mentioned father, sister, maybe grandpa.

"No, just us."

I didn't know his father, his sister, or his grandpa, but there had been a chance they'd be people I'd like to know. I wanted to watch him with people he didn't find cute. Maybe I could blend into those people. Though maybe he found his sister cute—not unfeasible.

"I'm going to have one." He opened the white box, and held up the kind with a fruit center, the dark womb of cookie.

"I wanted to meet your sister."

"You will."

I wouldn't. After the birthday ended, I was getting on a bus going the other way. Still, I liked the idea of the sister.

He tiptoed to get something from the pantry, and I watched his pants, dark gray with a little stretch in them. He shook a box of cereal. I saw that he wasn't a boy, my boyfriend, but a small, clean man. He had come straight from work. Work was law. Real estate was his area. He had a client dying of AIDS who was suing his sister over a house they'd both inherited. I liked him best when he talked about the case.

"HEY," I SAID OVER DINNER WITH JUST US, "when you turned 20, did you care about real estate then?"

We were high up on plump cushions, intimidated by our steaks.

"I guess. Sure." He started to cut a piece.

"How about when you were 16?" I looked at my knife, fork, perfect on the white cloth. I didn't want to bloody them. It occurred to me that he would pay for dinner and that the paying would matter after I dumped him. I was taking pains to wait until the birthday was over, but unless I waited a week, it would still be his birthday. And he would have paid even if I had broken up over dinner, to show that he would.

"No, then I wanted to make films, I guess—documentaries."

"What did you want to document?"

"I wasn't thinking about what I would shoot. My mother."

Documentarian—that's what everyone wants to be before they decide to be something else. It's a good imagined profession. Creative, yet factual. Lions, yet poor people. Shots through the grass, the hut, the chewing beast. Or snakes that don't chew, that just suck the bump down.

MY BAG WAS ON THE FLOOR, clothes erupting out of it, starting their sprawl across the carpet, underwear puddling in the jeans. I was at the door, pushing in the lock, but it would not catch.

"My dad's sleeping," he said. "He's not going to come in here."

"I have to go to the bathroom," I said, and went down the hall and peed, peed through the swell, then washed my hands with a gray ball of soap. I had never had a boyfriend that I hadn't liked. The one I'd had before this, I had liked him a lot. He was captain of his street hockey team. He carried his stick around, even on days when there was no practice, even though he was 33. He probably still carries it around.

Back in the guest room, I said, "Listen." I said, "I feel." He backed onto the guest bed, pulled me on with him to stop "I feel."

"OK," I said. He smiled. We were still on. It was still his birthday. The track lighting lit the wine scabbed on his lip, made his mouth look a little bloody in the corner. I sat on his mouth. That had happened every time since we'd met a month before, and made it feel like we'd known each other longer.

"Keep going," I said. It was my version of "Don't stop."

"Good!" I said.

"You're doing great," I said.

"Can you breathe?" I said.

He hummed. I decided not to come.

"Thanks," I said, climbing off his head. "You were doing great stuff, but I feel a little nauseous right now."

"From the wine?"

"A little. I'm not going to vomit."

He tried to make it up with a snuggle, a hair-stroke/whisper combination. I felt sorry for myself for all the times I had been on the other side, oblivious. It wasn't just with the hockey captain. There were others, guys who'd let me hopelessly cuddle them for months, years. How had they let me go on, me not knowing what they knew? In return, I'd agree to let them be depressed.

Nobody had ever liked anybody.

PICK A FISH

HE HAD FOUND ME ON THE INTERNET, and now I was going back to the internet. He could know me through my college newspaper quotes ("The new student center is a costly mistake"), could check to see if I had added a new favorite movie, if I was growing my hair.

I am growing it. Maybe that will make this easier on him, my hair edging out from under, unblond. I wasn't blond for very long—it doesn't take that long to be blond. Long enough to make some mistakes. I was once a real blond—tiny, enthroned on shoulders, dangling little white shoes, the kind kids have been wearing since shoes started. It was a mistake to try to get that back. It got me the wrong guy. The internet is full of them.

Pics of them at sunset somewhere. Their favorite books that meant something to them. Them just wanting someone to make them laugh, stay up all night laughing.

Me, blond in my pic, at an impromptu street fair, also wrong, but he had found me there, in between trips to the copy machine, where he was xeroxing fish, fish pics for a calendar about fish. He worked for a calendar company, and in my pic, I was clutching a fish in a baggie, jubilant in a tube top (I had won the fish), and he was thinking about fish: September's Fighter, October's Monk. He was thinking about time, xeroxing next year's October when it wasn't even this year's October—how much time since he had had a girlfriend, before he could break for lunch, the amount of time he spent online at work, was it wrong? He was thinking about fish. I was blond, tubed, a winner of fish. It was time for a girl like me. He clicked.

"Coincidence?"

I answered, volleyed back his better jokes, introduced new queries. We exchanged additional pics—me reading at an unusually flattering angle, him toasting the end of the calendar year. We exchanged birth-towns, sibling counts. We mentioned coffee, but decided on drinks. Coffee always gets mentioned. Drinks always win.

Time passed. I arrived—not tube-topped or jubilant, but cardiganned and nauseous, on time. I slurped an icy gin. I retold some of my best stories, without remembering why they were important. In "Every Foreign Country I Visit Reminds Me of Long Island," I forgot to say that's where I'm from. In "The Summer I Spent Working with Pigeons," I left out the lab assistant with the hyperactive thyroid. I left out Jen. He bit anyway. Soon we were negotiating—maybe we should go somewhere, and where should we go? Somewhere.

Jen had huge, pop-out eyes, like a fish. She had cystic acne, defeated breasts, a crush on our mentor, Dr. Walikson. She believed in comparative cognition, distrusted Freud. She taught me the milk ratio in Dr. W's coffee. She taught me that a lot.

My date and I didn't go to bed that night. We started dating instead. Then we went to bed. Bed was fine, bed was bed, except the one time he held his hand over my mouth. That was pretty good. I think it was an accident, though, because I never saw that hand again.

Xerox that hand, I should have said. Make me twenty copies. I'll tell the pigeon story with all the good parts, with the Skinner boxes and the pellets and the time I caught the bird that escaped using just a flashlight and my hand. +

THE JOY OF EDGE TOOLS

Misha Hoekstra

GUIDE TO NAVIGATION

A YOUNG BOY NAMED ADKIN narrates *The Joy of Edge Tools.* In the opening paragraph, Adkin's mother uses sundry tools and ingredients to birth from his right shoulder brother Misha, a happy-go-lucky monster whose head tapers off into a fatty, fishlike tail. Adkin conceives a vast hatred for this sireniform neonate, but his ineptitude conspires with Misha's sharp teeth to doom his murderous schemes.

Their mother sends Adkin on an errand to the root cellar, where he pockets a small silver case of frayer without knowing what it is. On his return, she grafts Misha back onto his shoulder. During this operation, Adkin experiences the aesthetic as the book's first dream, an extended metaphor for and counterpoint to his movement toward his brother, with their actual meeting a sort of catechistic amniotic communion. Coming to again, Adkin inadvertently loses his right thumb to Misha's teeth, and their mother installs a boxhook in its stead.

The two brothers now comprise a small society at war with itself, their two heads fighting for control of their single body. After a minor operation, which lets Adkin understand his brother's curious mode of vocalization, and a storytelling game, Adkin resumes his attempts on Misha's life; each time, by failing to understand the shared corporeal nature of their existence, he injures himself at least as much as he does his brother. Meanwhile, he slowly loses command of the right side to Misha. Since the boys are unable to coordinate their movements, they must now move about in a Bath chair.

Their mother then introduces them to the log and explains its use in the inscription and reading of dreams. The actual manufacture of dreams is illustrated by a tour of the root cellar. Here the mother mentions something that's only been hinted at before—the existence and disappearance of the boys' father. The lesson concludes with the

ECHO EGGBRECHT, UNTITLED, 2006,
INK ON PAPER, 16 X 23". COURTESY OF THE ARTIST AND NICOLE KLAGSBRUN GALLERY.

concoction of a simple dream, in black and white. With the addition of some stain and delay, they are also able to see how one enters and leaves a dream: a red rope swings you over the abyss to the other side.

What would happen if you were to release the rope on the way to dream? Would you become instantly extinct? fall into a new fleshly shell? survive in suspended unknowing? Their mother cannot say. In any case, it is how, she thinks, their father decamped.

Their shared interest in dreaming only halts the boys' warfare briefly. Frustrated, and hoping that some temporary experience of unity will pacify them and permit later collaboration, their mother gives them some yoke, which merges their consciousnesses and limits their body to symmetric movements. Their first united desire is to hear more about their father. So their mother channels him, and he relates a convolved and scarcely credible tale of how he obtained his third eye. The boys grow quickly impatient with his divagations and rouse their mother from her trance.

After a common dream, which naturally reflects their blended fears and desires, the boys are unyoked and restored to their separate awarenesses. Able to cooperate now, they soon discover how to pleasure themselves by toggling a certain bit on their lower fitting with Misha's boxhook. Pressed on this manifestation of their carnal nature, their mother demurs and again channels the father, this time for advice. He responds to the boys' questions with a skewy farrago of 19th-century scientific phrases concerning such things as how ice cream is made, what the corposant is, et cetera.

Despite the racy matter, the boys again tire of the recital and raise their mother, whose enthusiasm for their crackpated progenitor they refuse to share. Dispirited, she suggests as a diversion that they port their next dream—that is, use hatchways that will allow them access to a common area within dream. As the three of them concoct their mixes, Adkin slips some of the stashed frayer into his mixbowl.

In the ported dream, the two boys are about to leave the common area when they decide on a whim to try a port-and-switch, whereby they return each by the other's rope. Waking up in Misha's body, Adkin finds himself speaking his brother's truncated syntax. But something is wrong: rather than rousing, the head beside him grows cold. His mother finds the frayer and deduces that the rope raveled on Misha's way back from dream, plunging him into the void. However, she believes him to be Adkin, and she will not heed the real Adkin's protests about his actual identity. Indeed, Adkin himself becomes progressively less certain about who he now is.

Both survivors, mother and son, are disconsolate. The narrator asks if there's any way to follow his brother into the unknown. The mother won't say much, except that to follow would be almost certainly fatal. She decides that, in their grief, their best course is to seal themselves up in two deprivation pods to embrace some welcome oblivion. But as the pods begin to harden, the boy elects to bail. In a long final paragraph that mirrors the book's opening, he shows himself finally ept as he uses his mother's implementa to slough off the dead head from his shoulder and grind it up with the log and a version of the toolbox, forming in the sandbox one grand transportive jambalaya, one doomsday slumgullion that he hopes will, at the same time as it necessarily destroys the world around him, bring him to his brother. And into the soup he jumps.

THE SISTER

In which the mother reads a sample page from the log

MY SISTER AND I SWIM, our seafloor limbs harmonic. Draw water up from beneath and push it to our fore, propel ourselves backward. The same silver ring round the same right toe. We gaze below to our shadow makrs on the scrim of obscurity, think and cold; we suspend outselves as nested zeds. Wise exes double us, the steep valley in vaccuum.

A placidity we float in: warm fetal oil. Hang, drift, tugged by offshore current toward the heated flanks of some third. We shall stand on the plain. The rain fall. Our faces wet, and darkness bloom. Fingers will touch our faces and someone stand over us, her hands cup our outer cheeks so water pools, spills, rills over the ribs of her fingers. Won't take long to fill. How we shall wish to drink there slaking forever. Electric warmth in our mouths, surging touch and go. Touch will sluice the surplus juice from isle to isle, three fleshes circulant; go stir achey longing. Our small seas will brim, the fish aleap with vimmy silver flashing. The spangle of living money.

We are that currency. Reversing motion, we swim through soft coral, a brisk scrub it is, we wriggle together to a cavern well shelved, with further stock and staples heaped in steep piles on the floor. All props and disguises lie there, and the tanks with their various airs. We valve some silver soprano from one, mouth tincted mezzo from a second, and cast about before gulping at last a percussive baritone from a tap in back. From there we wriggle into a wing of the theater behind, metallic trout, undulant bass. The cave's choral pulse rakes across us in soft waves of compression, and the boards creak with the yaw as we swim over, fitting ourselves for the stage en route: adornment and arms; tendril probes; some cordial against ill. And a few hard bits we pick up from the deck as they saltate past in the current.

We find our submarine legs and stride along the boards. Sister Times and Sister Plus: The Reckoning. Axeheads, broadcore and bitted double, we carry in pocket, running thumbs over burred blades. We tattoo a gamelan in crosstime. Our deltoids sport inkedin inch rules, to the eighth on the right, the tenth on the left. Then our breasts unbulb simultaneous, unswell to bud, to itch, to flush flesh.

Applause. We run offstage in tandem, as if wasped together at the waist. To our hideaway in the wings. A kneehigh sunflower grows there from a hummock in the grass, merrily abuzz. We circle our arms and lean in to tent bangs over its nodding head, the buzz rising to conjoin us. As our brows touch, a needle of pain sutures our foreheads together, squelching the sound: a bee! Seedy evil plant. . . . With more effort than genius we push each other away and slowly, burningly, painfully, we force a gap wide enough to see what it is binds us: a bloody fibrous cord, its base rasping prickly from a bulging mound in each other's brow.

Burning? We can do burning, we can fight with fire. Hundreds of flames gossip at our calves; thick orange fire tongues gorgeous hot and huge about our loins; alcohol flames lick our skin coolly where the heat damply dews us. The sunflower arches ablaze between us, seeds bursting from its face, it goes cinder, ash, paper petaled ghost. The calefaction makes the cord come a bit easier as we pull it laboriously from our heads, backing away from each other, hand over hand. But the connection's still cored with pain. This won't do. A bedslength blade rises from the floor on cue and we kneel to meet it, bending down. The scission is instant and effortless, and we each tumble gently onto the pillowed fire at our feet. A shimmery clear wall pops up between us, webbing blade and tackle, coil and cable, up to stalactic uvula far above, a surface transparent but for the reflex of fervent fire curving from the slow spiring of combusted gas. Then the membrane films and thickens, it smudges, and the ardent flames around my sister dim. She is laughing, and with laughter contrapunto the film crepitates as it skins over, and darkens, and draws her delicately aspin into diminishment. A point. Puff nil. +

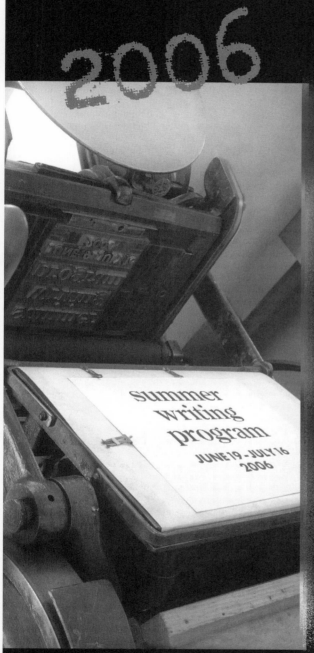

REVIEWS

ATTACK OF THE CLONES

Kazuo Ishiguro. *Never Let Me Go*. Knopf. April 2005. **Michel Houellebecq.** *La possibilité d'une île*. Fayard. August 2005. (*The Possibility of an Island*. Knopf. May 2006.)

THE NARRATOR OF *NEVER LET ME GO* HAS A SOFT plain style: "I don't know how it was where you were, but at Hailsham we used to have some form of medical every week. . . ." This is how you might talk to an equal, someone similar to you socially or economically, or, as it turns out, biologically. The strange thing about this ordinary sentence is that the narrator, Kathy H., is a clone, and when the reader discovers this, that "you" opens out beyond the mere conventional second-person to become part of the novel's drama. You, dear reader, are also supposed to be a clone among clones. And really, who'd be the wiser? Phenotypically we're the same.

Kathy H.'s Hailsham is a boarding school for the education and improvement of clones, whose fate it is to have their adult organs harvested for use by what they call "normals." Before it is their turn to be called, they act as "carers" for older clones, keeping them going from donation to donation until death. On the surface, though, Hailsham isn't so different from those other boarding schools where members of the English or American upper class go so their brains and talents can be seeded for the benefit of society and the greater good, places where they are taught to compete ruthlessly with each other for awards, honor, and affection. Hailsham has a sports pavilion, lawns, high windows looking out on a forest. The students (or inmates) get care and exercise. They study art and literature. They have teachers, called "guardians," whom they admire, dislike, fear, and fantasize about. They are encouraged to be creative above all, to cultivate collections of favorite things, but also to be selfless. It's a fine place to grow up, and leaving it is made the more terrible when the world its students enter is so manifestly cruel. Hailsham becomes consecrated in their memory as Eden crossed with Eton. It is also a bright deception the clones never manage to rebel against.

There is nothing apart from the rules of the narrative, as Ishiguro defines them, to make Kathy H.'s assumption of shared experience pitiable and horrible rather than banal. We are invited to identify with her, not as a clone, of course, because human clones don't yet exist, but as another product of families and institutions, including the venerable institution of the novel. "I don't know how it was where you were," Kathy H. says; but we were *somewhere*, that much is certain, and so we liken her experience to our own. Kathy assumes we too are clones and we assume that she's just as human we are. Neither of these assumptions is entirely valid, and yet the novel's force depends upon this useful misunderstanding.

Even though we know we're being addressed by a wholly other category of person, a sort of monster, we find it very easy to accord Ishiguro's clones the humanity his society denies them, much as though we were reading a 19th-century novel about slavery now. With his version of *Uncle Tom's Cabin*,

Ishiguro has constructed a kind of sympathy trap. The liberal ease with which we accept the premise of social injustice is really just the beginning of our entanglement. We accept that there is an injustice but we accept it too readily. As the novel goes on we find that we are treated to a spectacle of suffering humanity, not displayed to provoke us to outraged enlightenment, but for our pleasure. We like Kathy's plainness, her simple thoughtfulness, and her growing awareness of pain gives us a charge too. The sympathetic relationship of reader to character comes to mirror the sympathetic and utterly powerless relationship of the Hailsham guardians toward their charges.

In other words, *Never Let Me Go* is as much about a certain kind of education as it is about clones, specifically how the members of an entire race or class can be taught that they have a duty to lead lives devoted to misery and loss so that others will prosper (and how their counterparts in the master class make peace with these conditions even when they know what's going on). The theme is a familiar one for Ishiguro. In a sense he has rewritten his earlier tale of masters, servants, and great houses at the end of British aristocracy, *The Remains of the Day*, only setting it this time in an alternative England of the late 1990s. As in *Remains*, a love story is the engine of the plot. The earlier novel traded on the tragic paradox that the very qualities of loyalty, self-sacrifice, hard work, and dignity that make people attractive to one another can also prevent them from coming together. So the romance of butler and housekeeper is undone by the butler's devotion to his master.

In *Never Let Me Go*, Ishiguro has made the triangle more complex. Here Kathy H. occupies the role of the good servant. She recognizes that she might be one of the best carers, but she won't boast about it. And then there are her friends Tommy and Ruth. (Just to read the names Tommy, Ruth, and Kathy gives you a sense of how much Ishiguro risks being utterly banal.) Tommy is the angry misfit, the clone who senses the injustice awaiting them and yet never manages to articulate or even precisely recognize it. Ruth is the most interesting: a compulsive fantasist, the kind of person who pretends to have read everything you're reading, who makes up her own rules for chess and tries to teach others to play by them. She understands that the conditions of her life are based on deceit and yet can't make up her mind whether to acknowledge the deception or disappear into counterlies of her own. As the three leave Hailsham, Ruth guesses that Kathy and Tommy might be in love and dedicates herself to placing an Iago-esque web of obstructions between them. Her manipulations make up most of the novel, and the reader spends much of the time wanting to shout to Kathy and Tommy, "How can you stay friends with her? Can't you see Ruth means you harm?" But they remain friends with her because she arranges their denial for them. She makes it easier for them not to see their love, which, if seen, would also have to be seen as futile. Love does not undo social injustice or grant individual freedom.

Membership in the Hailsham pseudo-elite permits these characters to be lovable, because the school has encouraged them to develop temporary markers of individual distinctiveness (the very thing that no clone in Ishiguro's world can be allowed ultimately to possess). If they are denied the longevity necessary to make good on "true love," they are nevertheless permitted to have affectionate sex. The guardians teach a sort of sex ed, and the head guardian, Miss Emily, hints that the boys and girls needn't succumb to pure biological adolescence: "[I]f you can't find someone with whom you truly wish to share this experience," she warns, "then *don't*!" A kind of prudishness has long been one of Ishiguro's weak points, yet in *Never Let Me Go* his ingenuousness takes on qualities of demented genius, as when Kathy decribes her preparations for her "first time":

> Miss Emily had told us that it could be painful and a big failure if you didn't get wet enough and this was my one real worry. It wasn't being ripped apart down there, which we often joked about, and was the secret fear of quite a few girls. I kept thinking as long as I got wet quick enough, there'd be no problem, and I did it a lot on my own just to make sure.

Remember that this is the voice of the adult narrator, and yet she holds on to her schoolgirl euphemisms of "down there" and "did it." This combination of frankness and evasiveness about sex is the counterpart to the frankness and evasiveness about death. The clones know that it's their fate to "donate" until they "complete," but the language they're taught effectively obscures the horror of the situation and their knowledge of it. Kathy H. mentions that the students used to watch movies for clues about sex, but the only scene she recalls is "the moment the American jumps over the barbed wire on his bicycle" from *The Great Escape*. The students grab the remote and watch it again and again.

This is almost too much. How is it that Hailsham has never produced a Spartacus? Ishiguro's world is too neat; he takes advantage of the license granted writers of science fiction to do away with any internal opposition to it. And yet the deathly consensus of his 1990s England does concentrate our minds on the formal elements of a social problem—the construction of denial; or, what class war?—in a way that a messy dystopian science fiction with rebels hiding in the woods never quite would. In fairness to Ishiguro, his readership doesn't live in societies where open rebellion is still considered an option. Whether we harvest the organs of clones or squeeze out ever cheaper quantities of labor, we live in a world of self-blinding ideologies. No one supposes things could be otherwise, and we allow cruelties to be done to others and even ourselves because of our faith in the institutions that gratify our obsession with identity and belonging—church, state, corporation.

Who now is writing better novels about the persistence of ideology than Ishiguro? This is in part because Ishiguro suppresses any sense that ideology is what he's about, ruthlessly excluding actual political life from his novels. *The Remains of the Day* did include the Von Ribbentrop plot—when members of the British aristocracy attempted to secure an independent peace with the Nazis—but this almost baroque touch was unnecessary. The problem wasn't that some British aristocrats were Nazi sympathizers or gentlemen amateurs who believed in the kinship of the Anglo-Saxon races; the problem was that they were aristocrats, presiding over the remnants of a feudal system.

In *Never Let Me Go*, there is no rogue society for the manumission of clones, no crusading newspaper, no sense that adulthood might include becoming conscious of one's own condition and rebelling against it. And somehow this, the novel's major imaginative failing, is also its success. Only one character tries to alert the children to their scheduled deaths, and she gets dismissed early on. She exists only at the fringes of the narrator's consciousness and is almost forgotten by everybody else. Instead, Kathy and Tommy and even Ruth credit a rumor that clones who either find true love or become artistic, sensitive souls will be granted "a deferral"; and so when Tommy and Kathy finally get together they set out on a Wizard of Oz quest to find Miss Emily, the school having closed, and to be awarded a respite from the harvest. No such luck, of course.

The student of industrial efficiency may wonder why Hailsham exists at all. Why not just raise cloned human beings for their organs like so many veal calves in pens? Why educate them more expensively than most normals? The answer is that Hailsham turns out to be a contemporary meliorist institution, an attempt to improve the lives of clones but not their collective fate. Many generations of clones will be sacrificed in the attempt to persuade the world of their full humanity. And, curiously, in this futuristic novel a person's humanity is ascertained in an old-fashioned way: by exposure to a liberal arts curriculum. No tenured radicals, however: that is why Miss Lucy, the consciousness-raising guardian, had to go. Miss Emily explains it this way:

> [W]e were able to give you something, something which even now no one will ever take from you, and we were able to do that principally by sheltering you. . . . Yes in many ways we fooled you. I suppose you could even call it that. But we sheltered you during those years, and we gave you your childhoods. Lucy was well meaning enough, but if she'd had her way your happiness at Hailsham would have been shattered.

It's almost as though Ishiguro himself were apologizing to his characters, and in a sense he is. A real human organ industry might not see the benefit of a heart or spleen stuffed with Shakespeare. Ishiguro needs his characters to have had happy childhoods and to have read poetry so they can react to their world with the right degree of heartbreaking sensibility and restrained lyricism. Witness Kathy's last journey to Norfolk:

> I found I was standing before acres of ploughed earth. There was a fence keeping me from stepping into the field, with two lines of barbed wire, and I could see how this fence and the cluster of three or four trees above me were the only things breaking the wind for miles. All along the fence, especially along the lower line of wire, all sorts of rubbish had caught and tangled. It was like the debris you get on a sea shore: the wind must have carried some of it for miles and miles before finally coming up against these trees and these two lines of wire. Up in the branches of the trees, too, I could see, flapping about, torn plastic sheeting and bits of old carrier bags. That was the only time, as I stood there, looking at that strange rubbish,

> feeling the wind coming across those empty fields, that I started to imagine just a little fantasy thing . . .

And so recurs a truly annoying and truly brilliant tendency in Ishiguro: his characters' aesthetic visions are not distinguishable from their pain.

ISHIGURO IS KNOWN as a master of subtlety, but (after his first novel) he's never so subtle that we don't perceive what he's being subtle about. That first published novel, *A Pale View of Hills*, adapted the techniques of modernist fiction to obscure rather than reveal a character's emotional state. So a woman invents a double to deal with her guilt at having survived the Nagasaki bombing and her daughter's suicide; she then has the audacity to tell her story from the double's point of view. Indeed the reader can never know which of the two women the narrator happened to be. This taste for unreliability never left Ishiguro, as he followed with *Artist of the Floating World* and *The Remains of The Day*. These, however, were more conventional novels; the readers' prejudices and expectations could be counted on to keep them ahead of the self-blinded narrators.

Ishiguro might seem to have adopted different thematic genres—the war novel, the great house novel, the historical novel—but in fact he's stuck to his own invented genre or mood: each novel stages the slow horror of cognitive restraint, a traumatic refusal to recognize the awful truth until the last possible moment. Each novel displays careful authorial "craft" (a word that occurs more in discussions of Ishiguro than of most novelists), but the more he honed the craft and repeated the old reliable "unreliable" trick, the more it all began to feel like shtick.

The narrator of *Never Let Me Go* is very similar to her predecessors, and yet Ishiguro has found, in his clones, a subject that faces this very problem of conscious repetition; Kathy's story turns into both a critique and a justification of Ishiguro's own early work and of the enterprise of fiction generally. Ishiguro, the author, clones his own narrators and now writes a book about that experience. These cloned creatures are also known as characters (pieced together from real life humans), harvested and put through pain mostly for our sake. Their genteelness makes it possible to hear them screaming, in the way the out-loud scream of revolt would not. Look, a person tortured, howling—no tears for him. Look, the perfect English butler, his life ruined by his utter devotion to an evil way of life—for him, we do cry. Despite this suggestion of a novel about and against novels, like J. M. Coetzee's *Elizabeth Costello*, Ishiguro also uses the parable-like qualities of *Never Let Me Go* to affirm the rightness of his own work and an enduring humanism. By turning to science fiction, away from his earlier historical fictions, Ishiguro seems to be saying, "Even into the future our problem will remain this perennial one I've identified: people invested in the rightness and beauty of their way of life manage with great elegance and skill not to see the horror of what's right in front of their eyes."

ISHIGURO ISN'T THE ONLY midcareer novelist to make human clones the subject of his latest book. Published in France only a few months after *Never Let Me Go*, Michel Houellebecq's *The Possibility of an Island* (*La possibilité d'une île*) also asks us to leap into an alternative universe where cloning has been perfected. Houellebecq's clone novel is almost a perfect counternovel to Ishiguro's, or a sequel. His clones are the master race, not the servants. It's as though Ishiguro's normals had stopped having children and gradually become so dependent on clones that the clones took over. These clones emerge from the central facility as full adults. They have no childhoods.

Houellebecq is as explicit and gregarious as Ishiguro is restrained. Together, they'd make a literary Laurel and Hardy; alone they struggle against the burden of repeating themselves. Now the subject of parodies, a savage biography (Denis Demonpion's *Houellebecq non autorisé*), and an entire issue plus DVD of *Les Inrockuptibles* (France's more intellectual version of *Rolling Stone*), Houellebecq must cope with having become a kitschified "bad boy." He's sought the reputation of an opinionated ass, and in this novel he's cast himself as an ultra-successful, legendarily offensive stand-up comic who grows tired of his own act. (Philip Roth at least had the grace to make Mickey Sabbath an obscure puppeteer.) Then again, Houellebecq doesn't really have an act; he has theories. He writes novels *à thèse*, with the same relentlessness as Balzac, a novelist Houellebecq has said he admires for his fearless production of clichés.

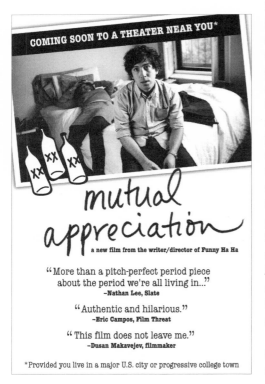

The outlines of the Houellebecquian cliché machine appeared before he'd written a novel. In an essay on H. P. Lovecraft, "Against the World, Against Life," he isolated what he called an aesthetic of disgust, and in the years since he has done his best to describe the ordinary human business of watching pornography, fucking, and going on package vacation tours in the same light as Lovecraft described multidimensional aliens and demonic cults. His novels are narrated by ranters and ancient mariners, the old horror-story trick of a man who has seen what he was not meant to see: it's spoiled his life, but he thinks less of everyone else for not having seen it too. Houellebecq's middle-aged Michels, Brunos, and Daniels uncover the inherent cruelty of human sexuality and the superadded cruelty of a supposedly liberal society that has set up pleasure and sex as its idols. Our choice of sexual partners requires selection, and this inflicts pain on those left out: the aged, the ugly, the maladjusted, the poor who can't pay for it. It also inflicts pain on those who are forced to opt in and get exploited by the ugly, maladjusted, and rich. The dominion of sex is no better and perhaps worse than the rule of religion it replaced. That most people fail to recognize this and continue to fall in love and, worse, reproduce sexually, is a catastrophic *bêtise*. In *The Possibility of an Island* this theory reaches a *reductio ad absurdum* when one of the narrators remarks that "the standards of physical love are the same as Nazism."

The traditionalists who resist this dominion of sex, however, are nothing but puritans, fanatics, and ignoramuses; Houellebecq usually calls them Muslims. The West, the most advanced society in world history, is literally fucking itself to death, while another, less advanced society endeavors to blow itself up and take the West with it. It's a story told again and again in the linked essays that make up the bulk of most Houellebecq novels. Fortunately, he also has very good novelist's instincts. The ranters get the most airtime, but they are not the only voices. The longer they go on, the more the reader begins to resist them, and Houellebecq's plots help cultivate the resistance to his voice. Remarkably, his characters are always falling head over heels in love. What does it mean that these disabused devotees of the unregulated new world order of sex can experience selflessness and care for others?

The Possibility of an Island reproduces Houellebecq's familiar theories and conflicts; what is new is that it also recounts a history in which Houellebecq's worldview has become enshrined as the dominant one. Whereas Ishiguro tries to ensure his readers' sympathetic participation by having Kathy address us directly, Houellebecq compels the reader to assent to his doctrine, slam the book shut, or decorate the margins with notes of furious opposition. His multiple cloned narrators do not try to elicit sympathy; they write as practical historians. All named Daniel, but sequential Daniels, numbered 2 through 25, these narrators supplement their genetic continuity by writing autobiographies and commentaries on the autobiographies of their predecessors, thereby ensuring some extrasomatic continuity of identity among clones—and, incidentally, a continuity between our human present and a post-human future in which clones are elite "last men" and humans have regressed evolutionarily to savagery that recalls H. G. Wells's Morlocks. The generations of Daniel write in order to leave a record for "Les Futurs," that is, their future selves. The reader is left staring backward into the past, borne ceaselessly into the future. We can't do anything about events Houellebecq calls "the first diminuition" and "the great drought."

This is a rather nifty way to revive the French Romantic genre of "confessions," or at least put it to good use. The confession, even in France, now means *Oprah* and reality TV as much as it means Augustine and Rousseau; and Houellebecq, too, by juxtaposing himself with his literary ancestors, courts extreme banality. The subjects of Daniel 1's confession are his calculatedly provocative sociopolitical comedy, projects like "Munch on My Gaza Strip (My Huge Jewish Settler)," and his sexual education beginning with a woman he refers to only as Big Ass. He also describes his unhappy marriage to the editor of a glamour rag called *Lolita* (for women who want to look 14 and the men who want to look at them): she loves him but hates sex and fears getting old; he loves sex and knows she's right to fear aging. They hate children and adopt a dog. After the inevitable breakup, he gets the same treatment in turn from a young Spanish porn actress and concert pianist (!) named after Balzac's famous courtesan, Esther. (Literary influence too can be a kind of cloning.) Esther 2, as we might call her, breaks Daniel 1's heart and puts him on the path to life as a shut-in on the Andalusian coast.

So what saves this novel from turning into a completely formulaic and unreadable extension of Houellebecq's first novel, *Extension du domaine de la lutte*? First, the writing: many of the linked essays of Daniel 1's autobiography are written in a style that's more declarative Montaigne than elliptical Proust. Consider this passage from

Montaigne's essay on the affection of fathers for their children:

> Puisqu'il a plu à Dieu nous douer de quelque capacité de discours, afin que, comme les bêtes, nous ne fussions pas servilement assujetis aux lois communes, ainsi que nous nous appliquassions par jugement et liberté volontaire, nous devons bien prêter un peu à la simple autorité de la nature, mais non pas nous laisser tyranniquement emporter à elle, la seule raison doit avoir la conduite de nos inclinations. J'ai, de ma part, le goût étrangement mousse à ces propositions qui sont produite en nous sans l'ordonnance et entremise de nôtre jugement... Je ne puis recevoir cette passion dequoi on embrasse les enfants à peine encore nés, n'ayant ni mouvement en l'âme, ni forme reconnaissable au corps, par ou ils se puissent rendre aimables. Et [je] ne les ai pas souffert volontiers nourris près de moi.*

And then Daniel on the same, with fewer subjunctives:

> Il n'y avait pas seulement ce dégout légitime qui saisit tout homme normalement constitué à la vue d'un bébé.... Il y avait aussi, plus profondément, une horreur, une authentique horreur face à ce calvaire ininterrompu qu'est l'existence des hommes. Si le nourrison humain, seul de tout le règne animal, manifeste immédiatement sa présence au monde par des hurlements, de souffrance incessants, c'est bien entendu qu'il souffre, et qu'il souffre de manière intolérable.... À tout observateur impartial en tout cas, il apparaît que l'individu humain ne peut pas être heureux, qu'il n'est en aucune manière conçu pour le bonheur, et que sa seule destinée possible est de propager le malheur autour de lui en rendant l'existence des autres aussi intolérable que l'est la sienne propre.†

Daniel labels these theories "peu humanistes," but they are rather too precisely antihumanist. It smacks of hating God because he doesn't exist. Where Montaigne insists that language, reason, and free will separate us from beasts so that we may choose to love our children and they may choose to love us, Houellebecq wants to reduce everything to the tyranny of nature, to lay bare the cruelty of life. Humanity may make us special, but only special sufferers. What

* Since it has pleased God to bestow some slight capacity for discursive reasoning on us so that we should not be slavishly subject to the laws of Nature as the beasts are but should conform to them by our freewill and judgement, we should indeed make some concessions to the simple authority of the common laws of Nature but not allow ourselves to be swept tyrannously away by her: Reason alone must govern our inclinations. For my part, those propensities which are produced in us without the command and mediation of our judgement taste strangely flat. [In the case of the subject under discussion,] I am incapable of finding a place for that emotion which leads people to cuddle new-born infants while they are still without movements of soul or recognizable features of body to make themselves lovable. And I have never willingly allowed them to be nursed in my presence. (M. A. Screech translation.)

† It wasn't only that legitimate disgust which seizes any normally constituted man at the sight of a baby.... It was also, more profoundly, horror, an authentic horror when faced with the uninterrupted Calvary that is human existence. If the human nursling, alone in the whole kingdom, immediately reveals its presence in the world by screams of unceasing suffering, it's well understood that he is suffering and suffering in an intolerable way.... To any impartial observer, it appears that the human individual cannot be happy, and is in no way conceived for happiness, and that his only possible destiny is to propagate unhappiness, making the existence of those around him as intolerable as his own. (Reviewer's translation.)

Montaigne puts down to the intercession of "judgment," Houellebecq thinks of as necessity. Daniel delights in lots of sociobiological nonsense—"Maybe human babies are so unhappy because they've lost their protective fur?"—but in fact, whether intentionally or unconsciously, Houellebecq is writing in a long Catholic tradition of original sin and *contemptus mundi*, only without hope of redemption or immortality of the soul. We are born to suffer. Daniel acknowledges this and chooses to blot out his knowledge by pressing his face between the legs of women.

This guy (recurring in each Houellebecq novel) who tries to recreate moments of perfect happiness and self-annihilation in the pursuit of pussy does get tiresome. In the earlier novels, Houellebecq would occasionally give his character an interest in abstract art or something to make us believe he was less monomaniacal than he appeared. In *Possibility*, Houellebecq introduces this tendency toward sublimation through a new character, the artist Vincent. Vincent begins the novel as a maker of abstract video installations who knows that he's retreated to his tiny basement studio to make a "facile little world where all you encounter is happiness." He compares himself to a teenager who collects stamps. *The Possibility of an Island* is as much his history as Daniel's, and this shrunken man becomes the pope of the cult of the Elohim, the cloners who take over the world.

The description of the cult is worth the whole novel. Liberally drawn from the Raëlians (the Quebec-based group that made headlines a few years ago when they announced that they'd cloned a human), the Elohimites are also a deliberate humbug combining an authoritarian free-love, partner-sharing philosophy and a 1970s aesthetic of big beds, big hair, poofy cushions, and early *Star Trek*. Later, when Vincent takes charge, they evolve toward a combination of Catholicism and Buddhism. As Daniel 1 meets the cult members and gets drawn into their inner circle, he records both the silliness of it all and its understandable attraction: lots of sex, eternal youth, immortality of the body, an end to suffering, a tendency to hold annual retreats at cool vacation spots like Lanzarote (one of the titular islands), a healthy appreciation of money. If Western consumer capitalism needed a religion, this would be it. The Elohimites are us, only self-consciously so.

Houellebecq has done his research on cults, and he's probably read *Moses and Monotheism*. So it comes as no surprise that the genesis of the new religion is an operatic farce of jealousy, ritual murder, and fraud. The first prophet hits on the wrong girl and gets hurled out a window by her jealous lover, who hasn't heard the news about free love. After some amusing hand-wringing, and the dismissal of some real ethical scruples, witnesses and perpetrators are cleaned up and Vincent is persuaded to present himself as a prophet and a clone—indeed, a prophet of cloning. Daniel may be an unfunny theoretical comedian, but Houellebecq is a camp maestro. This scherzo episode isn't just a necessary relief in this very long novel; our own political realities have accustomed us to the triumph of mediocrity, and the ways a fanatical cult of loyalists protect the secret of that mediocrity. There's little reason to imagine anymore that great events in world history will be brought about by great men. The worst thing about Houellebecq's science fiction is that it seems too probable.

Houellebecq, in person, would seem more than half a hostage to the ideas he puts into the Elohim cult and the mouths of his male narrators. (To the delight of the French press, he has admitted that a scene in which the narrator washes his Mercedes and declares himself to have finally understood what it is to be a man is straight autobiography.) And this too is a large part of Houellebecq's achievement: his confessions are satires, his satires, confessions. Houellebecq's elaborate pronouncements about the way things are come to feel like a form of critique and self-critique by exaggeration. Through the narrator's cackling, self-accusing voice, we sometimes catch glimpses of strong all-too-human emotions. For all the intelligence of Daniel's propositions—all the quotations from Schopenhauer, Kleist, Nietzsche, and Dostoyevsky to back them up, all the abstract Frenchiness and all the specific scenes of human loneliness and despair, all his silly praise of dogs and disparagement of children—Daniel fundamentally believes in the one thing neither his experiences nor his philosophy nor his newfound religion allow him to believe in: love. He is, in short, a romantic, a humanist in spite of himself.

Such, at least, is the conclusion the novel forces us to draw when Daniel 25 sets out across the changed landscape of Andalusian Spain, last home of his original namesake. After twenty-four generations of Daniels, number 25 simply decides he's had enough of living inside "the protected zone," watching subhumans on security cameras the way we watch nature shows, teleconferencing now and then with other clones (including Esther 31!), and reading books. (There really isn't much to do in Houellebecq's new world.) On his way to Lanzarote, Daniel 25 is diverted to Madrid, where "the idea came to me to look up the Calle San Isidor, where, on the top floor of number 3, Esther's birthday party took place, the party that put an end to their relationship. I remembered well enough what the city looked like on a map from Daniel's era, but some streets were entirely destroyed, others remained intact without any apparent logic. It took me almost half an hour to find the building I was looking for. It was still standing." Can you imagine a more clichéd image for "enduring love," even if the monument itself is a monument to that love's failure?

So much energy and imagination and history—and yet love cannot be eradicated, not even after the neo-humans no longer need to eat, outfitted as they are with photoelectric cells and a few other special effects, like so many pimped-out cars. Daniel 25 succumbs to the standard-issue romantic fantasies of the ancestor whose complete life story makes up his only education. Daniel 25's last journey is cheeringly familiar; he goes as a tourist in search of the ghost of an emotion that he believes has been eradicated, only to find that he's still capable of the same pain and the same love. After twenty-five incarnations (and several hundred pages of cynical theorizing and autobiography), he's still human.

BUT WHY THIS SUDDEN OBSESSION with clones? We've grown used to the leveling of distinctions between high and low, science fiction and so-called "literary fiction" in our contemporary postmodern culture of the novel, but something more than a wish to escape the boxed-in categories of publishers' marketing strategies must motivate this curious decision from two novelists whose primary interests remain the twists of human consciousness and the interactions between real people in present or historical settings. As a character in our recent literary history, the human clone appears as a remarkable synthesis of the thematic concerns of postmodern experimental writing and the enduring tradition of "realism." New novelists in France and their experimental counterparts like John Barth, Robert Coover, and others in the anglophone world had been engaged in an Ahab-like quest to strike through the mask and lay bare the fictiveness of their fictions. By extension, this quest would also reveal the fragility and fictiveness of our own self-conceptions. We were all supposed to be so many narrative functions and textual codes. To these meta-writers, the old realist novel was guilty of a fraud, of covering up the truth of a self that no longer existed. Its mechanisms must be revealed, its characters dissected and displayed like trophies or specimens in the laboratories of writers who compared themselves to scientists. Over the same period, biological science revealed our genetic codes.

Now, after all these years and so many novels dedicated to this fruitless pursuit and misleadingly praised or blamed under the heading of "experimental writing," we've reached a point where novels can once again be written in which characters and human beings are acknowledged to be both formulaic and unique. The techniques of literary realism can be harnessed to explore this paradox, not to conceal it.

Of course there's also a social element to the rise of the clones: biotechnology is now part of reality, as are our fears and fantasies about its uses. The clone is our latest version of Frankenstein's monster, though with our own displacement from physical ugliness to inner ugliness. We don't fear that clones will be physical grotesques, but, in our neo-Hobbesian age, we fear that they will at last reveal the truth of human nature in all its selfish monstrosity, a pure will to survive, reproduce, and dominate. This anxiety has heightened all the more since biology has replaced psychoanalysis in popular culture. The advantage and flaw of Freudian psychoanalysis was that it posited eros and self-preservation as opposed drives—the death instinct grew out of the organism's wish never to change, never to become other, never to be open to new experiences, new stimuli. Reversing these categories, the "selfish gene" theorists and their drones in the pseudodiscipline of evolutionary psychology posited a sort of volitional DNA that preserves itself through driving its human hosts to mantislike annihilation through reproduction. Love has become death. Everyone is afraid of death, but now we must fear love too. The promise of cloning, however, as a controlled process, would give us the illusion of the unchanging and unchangeable self that could be carried on perpetually without any need for love.

Both Houellebecq and Ishiguro have written their novels in the face of this anxiety, and they work through the anxiety mainly by emphasizing the continued importance of culture, especially in a world where scientific approaches dominate even private, nonscientific conceptions of the self. Both authors are modest about their clones. They understand that the most a clone could be is a physical copy of some primal ancestor (even if the physical goes all the way down). Now that we're closer to these things, our science is more pragmatic and less wildly ambitious than the dreams of early-20th-century eugenicists. There are no Alphas in tubes as in *Brave New World*, no human-animal hybrids as in H. G. Wells's *The Island of Dr. Moreau* or the President's bioethics panel. They assume no advances in our knowledge of what is genetically determined and what is learned, only that the techniques for cloning have been invented and put to use. The biggest problem facing the clones in these novels is that they must somehow be educated. They live through history, encounter others, read books, and all this changes them, as do their own experiences. In other words, cloning does not solve the nature-nurture problem, it displaces it again into a choice about which nature we end up nurturing.

"Though it hampers communication, PowerPoint is ubiquitous, because it renders invisible the distinction between businesspeople who can write and those who can't."

These novels are fictions, but they are no more fictions than the assumptions about human nature that govern game theory. In both novels, cloning fails to alleviate human suffering in the end, because to clone a human is to create a character who loves and therefore suffers; a society that allows human clones for the purposes imagined in their pages or as slave labor or cannon fodder would be a society that no longer believed in love, yet that society would create loving beings all the same.

Both novelists suggest that we already live in this world and these tragedies of nostalgia and belated recognition already play themselves out continually. They don't go so far as to suggest that we need a politics that recognizes and honors love and beauty as much as it honors "a culture of life." After all, they are novelists, not political theorists, and it's extremely difficult to articulate what this new politics might look like.

They are critical novelists above all, though their criticism is not without a comfort offered up to present and future readers. It's a deeply ironic form of comfort, but a comfort all the same: at whatever level of determination and despite all determination, some humans are programmed to love even if that love is futile, estranged, and promises certain death and unavoidable pain. You may be one of them. As Houellebecq's Elohimites put it, "Welcome to life eternal."

—*Marco Roth*

DEATH SENTENCES

William T. Vollmann. *Rising Up and Rising Down: Some Thoughts on Violence, Freedom and Urgent Means.* Ecco. 2004. Abridged version.

YOU ALREADY KNOW A LOT ABOUT WILLIAM T. Vollmann if you know that the abridgment of his seven-volume book about when to kill people is still 733 pages long. He missed a couple of spots. It is not enough that Death farted; instead, "Death joked and drank and vulgarly farted." It is not enough that guns have a use; instead, we read about "what Plato would call their 'virtue'—their function, their raison d'être, the thing they do best." A man "died and fell forward, his face swelling and purpling with lividity." Yes, but what color was his prose?

> My argument so far is the less than original one (most often disputed on religious or legalistic grounds—disputed, in short, according to stone-carved moral codes) that it is the right of the self to defend itself, or not defend itself, or even end itself, as it sees fit; that the self is, in short, the basic indissoluble element of autonomy; that whoever attacks another unprovoked imperils those rights, and, therefore, in the course of being repelled, may forfeit them on his own account, should circumstances require it.—"Good thing this won't be read by social insects," responds one reader. "Even so, it's possible to think, 'How American!' or whatever."

"In short" twice in the same sentence? That's funny. It is difficult to regard with solemnity the "moral calculus" of a writer who cannot subtract.

> Thank you for reading this book. My sincere intention in writing it was to be helpful. . . . I offer it to you, my unknown reader, in the hope that it may someday save a life or comfort a seeking mind. . . . I am proud of it, and I hope that it can benefit someone.

Never trust a man who insists that he is *sincere.* How does Vollmann intend to be *helpful,* to *save a life,* to *benefit someone*? "My own aim in beginning this book," he writes, "was to create a simple and practical moral calculus which would make it clear when it was acceptable to kill, how many could be killed, and so forth."

As it happens, I don't need a murder-evaluation protocol at the moment, but I'm willing to listen. Can Vollmann tell me a little about how it works?

> Should you find fault with the calculus, as you ought to (I do my best to find fault with everybody else's; and my chapter on defense of animals remains especially unsatisfactory), I respectfully ask you not to leave a vacuum, but to construct your own. The translator of two old collections of Zen koans has noted that there is no "correct" answer to a koan, and, indeed, one student's right answer may be wrong if uttered by another. Which does one put first, defense of gender, which might repudiate female

> circumcision, or defense of culture, which might demand it? . . . My moral calculus cannot tell you that. However, what it can do is to remind you that if you consider only one of those two categories of defense, your judgment will remain superficial, unfair, and therefore unrealistic. Can defense of gender meet defense of culture somewhere? I hope and believe so, provided that both sides respect each other by applying some approximation of the Golden Rule.

Behold: a simple, practical toolbox that does not open. What can the moral calculus tell us about, say, cutting off little girls' private parts? *Perhaps* the defense of gender can meet the defense of culture *somewhere*—at least we may *hope* and *believe* so—*provided* both sides respect each other by applying *some approximation* of the *Golden Rule.*

The Golden Rule!

Help us, Vollmann. Save our lives. Comfort our seeking minds.

> *How to Form a Moral Code.*
>
> 1. Follow your own inner logic and feeling in order to postulate laws of conduct which seem to you good;
>
> 2. Follow those laws if they correspond to local norms, and reconsider them if they violate those norms; but
>
> 3. Above all, choose the right regardless of local authority or custom, and then act accordingly . . .
>
> 4. Follow the Golden Rule where possible. And give it the most generous interpretation.

Go to your room and think about it first, and then *Do as thou wilt* shall be the whole of the law. Much depends on the meanings of "inner logic," "feeling," "good," "generous," and "the right."

Having an opinion is not murder. Frankness is not murder. Decision is not murder. Arriving at a conclusion is not murder. Definition is not murder. Even dogmatism is not murder. *Murder* is murder. That's a tautology, but at least it isn't a preening metaphor.

NOW IT'S TIME FOR ANOTHER exciting episode of *Press Release.*

Announcer. The acclaimed novelist William T. Vollmann was born in Los Angeles in 1959. He attended Deep Springs College and Cornell University, from which he graduated *summa cum laude* in comparative literature. He is part of the generation of David Foster Wallace (b. 1962) and Jonathan Franzen (b. 1959), and is an heir to the encyclopedic big-book tradition of Pynchon and Gaddis. Like his predecessors and contemporaries, Vollmann is self-consciously erudite—

Willis. Change the channel.

Hayden. Shut up. I'm trying to get educated in here.

Announcer. —but unlike his contemporaries, Vollmann has left the house. In 1982, he went to see the war in Afghanistan, which informed *An Afghanistan Picture Show: Or, How I Saved the World,* a book "dedicated to all who try to help others, whether they succeed or fail." That trip was the beginning of novelist Vollmann's parallel career as a scholar of war zones. "Part II: Studies in Consequences" in *Rising Up and Rising Down* ranges over Malaysia, ex-Yugoslavia, Somalia, and Jamaica; the unabridged version also visits Cambodia, Thailand, Burma, Madagascar, Iraq, Yemen, Colombia, and so on. Vollmann has sought out civil wars, poverty, and women held in sexual slavery, though he is not any kind of "realist" writer, instead applying the methods of Wallace and Pynchon to description of calamities across the world, many of which he has witnessed.

Willis. Don't make me take the clicker away from you.

Hayden. That would be horrible. [*Sticks remote down the front of his pants.*]

Willis. Come on. Let's watch *Appearance Versus Reality.*

TONIGHT ON *Appearance Versus Reality,* we'll match hyperbolic appreciations of Vollmann by Larry McCaffery (co-editor of *Expelled from Eden: A William T. Vollmann Reader*) to passages from the novels in question.

> In one of the most ambitious and original debuts since Pynchon's *V.*, Vollmann develops a dense, sprawling, novelistic "cartoon" in which bugs and electricity become motifs used to explore the revolutionary impulses that have arisen in response to the evils of industrialism. . . . [F]illed with arcane information and surrealist literalizations of sexual longings and violence, this book's wild flights of improvisational prose and intensity of vision signal the arrival of a major talent.
>
> —*Storming the Reality Studio: A Casebook of Cyberpunk and Postmodern Fiction.* Ed. McCaffery.

> The reader must now picture Earl at the end of his training, off in Kentucky selling electricity for Mr. White . . . "Hey, Drummer!" said the sturdy farmboys. "Whatcha got to sell?"—Earl knew that what they wanted were Bowie knives and Colt pistols, but he figgered it was worth a try to sell 'em what he had.—"You boys ever hear of electricity?" he said.—"Lecktrickery?" grinned the fool boys . . . "Well, how about you?" says Earl to a ragged bully.—"I wanna gun," the boy snarls. "Got any guns?"—"Wrong," says Earl.—"I sez you got any guns?"—"No, sir," says Earl . . . what I have to show you is better than guns, you'll see—"—"Better than guns!" the bully interrupts in disbelief, spitting on Earl's shoe. "No such thing as better than guns!" . . . "He don't have no guns!" says the bully. "Beat the crap outta him!"
>
> —*You Bright and Risen Angels*

The first of this novel's many epigraphs is "Only the expert will realize that your exaggerations are really true." I was born and raised in Kentucky. I lived there for twenty-seven years. Then I moved to Boston, where I learned to tolerate *Deliverance*-style jokes after realizing how many otherwise sophisticated men are afraid I'm going to knock over their canoes and rape them. The only true thing about this particular instance of "intensity of vision" is its hickface-as-blackface—the exaggerated American that Vollmann both feared and wished to become: to wit, guns, guns, and more guns, with whoring to follow hard upon.

One more, please. The back matter of *Rising Up and Rising Down* mentions "a series of novels entitled *Seven Dreams: A Book of North American Landscapes,* about the collision between the native populations of North America and their colonizers and oppressors." McCaffery writes of "projects that are virtually unprecedented in terms of their range of styles and thematic ambition: his *Seven Dreams* series and his monumental study of violence, *Rising Up and Rising Down*.... The only novel series I am aware of that may rival *Seven Dreams* in this regard are Durrell's *Alexandria Quartet* and Anthony Powell's *A Dance to Music* [sic] *of Time*."

This sounds promising until you open the books and endure that spot in *The Rifles,* Volume Six of *Seven Dreams: A Book of North American Landscapes,* where Mr. Franklin

> pushed PLAY and dialed Track 5, his favorite, "In the Court of the Crimson King," and though he could not hear it himself it didn't matter; gleefully he watched the counter go from 000 to 001 (as Jane called: John, darling, won't you ever be finished with your little Esquimau squaw? Or is squaw the proper word? Forgive me if I speak incorrectly...) and so now the song would be commencing with that delicious drumbeat and he watched Reepah's face and saw it come alive with joy and delight and he laughed to know that that majestic acidhead chord was burning her so pleasurably that she was grinning and her mouth gaped even more happily when the knowing singers went: *In the Court of the Crimson King—Ahhhhhhhhhhhhhhhhhhhhhhhhhhhhhhhhhhhhhhhhhhhhhh!* and Reepah was nodding and her lips were moving and to increase her pleasure he turned the volume knob from 2 to 3 and King Crimson went: *AHHHHHHHHHHHHHHHHHHHHHHHHHHHHHHHHHHHHHH!* and Reepah was laughing and singing aaah and now they must be singing about trampling the flowers and how the Pattern Juggler did something or other.

"Yes, if they wanted my blood, I thundered to myself, I'd give them vintage blood, and a very good vintage at that, and they would drink it in remembrance of me."

That sentence isn't over, by the way. What this sort of anti-writing has to do with unprecedented thematic ambition, colonization, or oppression—or why it deserves mention alongside Anthony Powell—eludes me. It looks like Vollmann is just fucking around.

> I believe that this book is worthy of standing in the shadow of Gibbon's *Decline and Fall of the Roman Empire*. Few people read Gibbon these days, and doubtless few will make it through *Rising Up and Rising Down*. That doesn't concern me much... it is my life's work, and if it comes remotely close to realizing its

> aims, it should be classed in the canon of great books.
>
> —"My Life's Work" in *Expelled from Eden: A William T. Vollmann Reader*. Ed. Larry McCaffery and Michael Hemmingson.

What is this abridgment? It consists of a preface; another preface; a reprint from *McSweeney's* called "Three Meditations on Death"; an introduction; a 387-page book report on Lincoln, Stalin, Marx, Trotsky, Pol Pot, Napoleon, Hitler, and others; "The Moral Calculus," Vollmann's tool for not figuring out whether violence is justified; and about 200 pages of reportage sold previously to the *Los Angeles Times, Esquire,* and so on—or, as Vollmann would have it, "a series of case studies in violence and the perception of violence."

At St. Elizabeth's Primitive Baptist Church, I once heard a hymn that went like this: "You don't know what the Lord has done for me. You don't know, you weren't there, you don't know when and you don't know where." It's true—I don't know, I wasn't there. But Vollmann *was* there, and he still can't figure it out:

> Were it possible to create a weapon which would function only in self-defense, most of us would be all for it. *But what is self-defense?*
>
> What is self-defense? Ask whom you like, and you'll get the answer you like.
>
> Above all, kill only in self-defense. (Ah, but what is self-defense?)

And then there are the guns:

> I was preparing to go on a long trip, and remembered that my pistols needed cleaning. . . . I thumbed the magazine release, swung back the slide to unchamber the last round, rotated the barrel bushing an eighth of a turn or so and took my gun apart. . . . The heaviness, the substantiality of those strange dark pieces, some cylindrical, some angular, some both—complex polygonal solids which fit inside one another in marvelous and obscure ways—and the smell of the nitro powder solvent, the rich blackness of dissolved lead on my fingers, the slickness of the six pieces after I'd oiled them; all these were overpowering sensory proofs, however delusional, that I could act; and the sureness with which I could disassemble my guns and then put them back together by memory (the Sig Sauer was the easiest; the DC Tec-9 Mini, whose fifty-shot capacity was offset by poor-quality cast and stamped parts, remained the hardest), the knowledge that when I'd finished, each barrel would be clean and every part, as far as I could tell by inspection, in working order (of course there must always be a "so far as I can tell" because certainty does not go down to the molecular level)—these facts lulled and relieved me.

What is "strange [and] dark" or "marvelous and obscure" about this nerdtacular gun-porn to a man who can reassemble his firearms from memory? Such "strange dark pieces" are not strange to him; they are familiar. Such ways are not "obscure"; they are clear.

> The simple law of might accords respect to an armed individual, who may well come to respect himself accordingly. . . . The capacity to do violence extends the self: it does not only arm it, it also "hands" it, awarding it extra fingers of choice. The weapon becomes a limb, a friend.

About those guns: There are less romantic ways to think of them. I like the .22 rifle my father gave me for my twelfth birthday. I like his old .357 Magnum: the one we used to take to the range out near Bashford Manor, the one he kept under the driver's seat. My grandfather died fifteen years ago and left me all his shotguns. When my grandmother had a couple of strokes in quick succession and started thinking that I was my father and that he was his brother Mike, we took away her .38, and that's probably mine, too—I don't know why my father would need another revolver. Those guns are in storage, mostly. I don't want to talk about them. It's not just bad manners to talk about guns: it's bad luck.

We know something about a certain kind of American artist who likes to talk about his guns, who likes to show us photographs of himself with guns—Ernest Hemingway, Kurt Cobain, Hunter S. Thompson—especially when he likes to be photographed putting a gun to his head.

If you don't buy this magazine, we'll kill this dog:

Vollmann writes:

> I wanted to find a base point below which we couldn't go—the "floor" of evil. I could then note that at least the fall would not be bottomless. I might hit it and die from the distance but at least I wouldn't fall forever. It was a way of seeking *control*. . . .
>
> One's self is one's own. The enemy of an unhappy self is that self. The self is within its rights to destroy itself. . . . The virtue of suicide is *control*. No one knows the future. If one feels *control* over one's life in the present, why, then—one has *control* in the present, no matter what happens later. I reiterate: If the self has any rights at all, those must include the basic right to continue, to constitute itself over time, to will itself—hence the corresponding right to unwill itself.

Emphases mine, of course. *Rising Up and Rising Down* turns out to be a postponement. Vollmann, who pretends not to judge, has already reached a verdict; but he defers its execution, and we are better able to comprehend his garrulous sentimentality once we've understood what the penalty is to be. This is the sad secret of *Rising Up and Rising Down*: the death wish hidden in plain sight, the suicide he yammers to forestall. You can hardly blame him. Why are his books so short?

THANK YOU FOR CALLING The Historical Novel. Press *one* for the Holocaust. Press *two* for the Bolshevik revolution. Press *three* for September 11th. (Please hold. Due to unexpected call volume, et cetera.)

From *Europe Central*, winner of the 2005 National Book Award:

> Between exploit and recompense lay only four days, which in most histories would comprise but an ellipsis between words, a quartet of periods, thus: . . . . —but which, if through close reading we magnify them into spheres, prove to contain in each case a huddle of twenty-four grey subterranean hours like orphaned mice; and in the flesh of every hour a swarm of useless moments like ants whose queen has perished; and within each moment an uncountable multitude of instants resembling starpointed syllables shaken out of words—which [*sic*] at the close of this interval, Fanya Kaplan was carried beyond *Tau*, final letter of the magic alphabet.

Uncountable multitudes and magic alphabets—pink hearts, orange stars, yellow moons, green clovers, blue diamonds, and purple horseshoes. The nightmare of history is over. Now you can eat your breakfast cereal.

All the disaster novelist has to do is run his mouth. Disaster itself does the heavy lifting. Hitch your wagon to the Holocaust, then cue the strings; and who dares to mention, in that hallowed context, that your instruments are not in tune?

This is Vollmann's game. He hitches his wagon to violence. He brings the news. The news is bad. The gory background is the gaudy plywood cutout standing on the beach: the ready-made circus strongman's body waiting to bear Vollmann's face on its thick neck.

BUT VOLLMANN'S BAD NEWS isn't so bad. Violence is just another chance for him to write poetry about angels and blue light—especially when people are putting guns to their heads.

> An acquaintance of mine who was very high-strung and often talked about his enemies suffered politico-academic reverses and blew his head off. . . . So the lightning went off inside his skull, charging that darkness with slate-blue light for an instant until everything became dark again; then again that surge, shocking and horrible light between darknesses, like the gaze of the Gorgon's head—what color was it really? Not slate blue, not dead white, not blinding grey; it was always the same color but it was indescribable . . . and so one of those flashes, the last one, was the flash when the bullet breached the cranial vault and for that one quarter-second his dying brain lay exposed to the light of the world as it had never done from womb-time to skull-time to now, and never would after now from tomb-time to dust-time; that was the light of the terrible answer he'd learned, or taught himself.

Here's Adolf Hitler in the same predicament:

> He raised the Walther to his head, then hesitated, lowered it a trifle, and peered into the barrel to see what he might see within the mountain. First it was dark, then dark, and then far inside shone a pale blue light which must have come all the way from Russia; he thought he could spy the Grand Salles de Fêtes of the Empress Elizabeth Petrovna at Tsarkoie-Sélo, the carpet as vast and multiply monogrammed as a collective farm's sugar-beet field, cartouches of angels dimly hovering on the ceiling, then a casement window opened onto vistas of other castles.
>
> —*Europe Central*

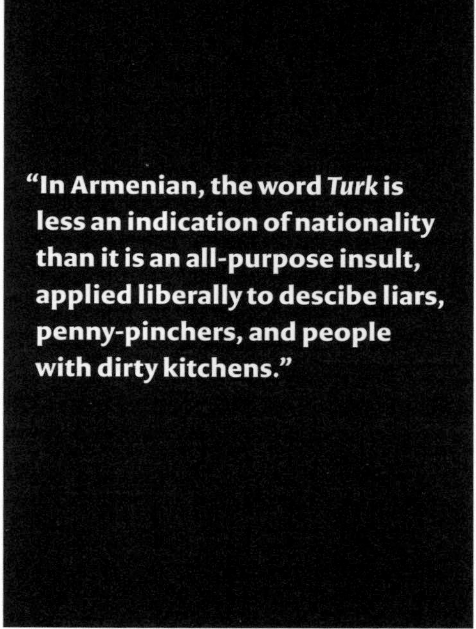

"In Armenian, the word *Turk* is less an indication of nationality than it is an all-purpose insult, applied liberally to descibe liars, penny-pinchers, and people with dirty kitchens."

Only Vollmann could write this way about what it's like to kill yourself—a chicken in every pot, blue light down the barrel of every gun.

WHEN I LEFT HOME, my mother collapsed on the porch and sobbed and shook. I listened for half an hour. Then I got into the truck and drove away. She was still curled up, screaming. I think I was supposed to interpret this behavior as a sign of her devotion—her *sincerity*—but I felt crowded out of my own leave-taking. I wanted to say goodbye to my father: no dice. Maybe I wanted to do a little crying myself. Who cares? Her *sincerity*, all seven volumes of it, had expanded until there was no room for anyone else to exist.

One reason criticism stings is that, after a certain level of basic technique has been established, we criticize the man and not the thing he made: not only his execution but his plan, and the character, values, and habits that gave rise to it. The gibbering McCaffery calls Vollmann's corpus "deeply intellectual and analytical and... frequently rendered in sentences of delicate refinement and exquisite aesthetic control." All right, bring me his letters; let me see his *style*. Style and substance are not separable. If writing has anything to do with precision, judgment, or selection, these books are not written. It's no surprise that Vollmann's big flowchart about deciding who can be eliminated doesn't work. I wouldn't let him run the office photocopier, much less hold the keys of hell and death.

Don't forget the Golden Rule when you read the last lines of Vollmann's first novel: "This book was written in urine... I piss on you all. This is my gift, you angels; love me."

It would be easier to love you if you would stop urinating on me, Vollmann. I am not a fire hydrant.

—*J. D. Daniels*

OUR CONTRIBUTORS

Daniel Alarcón is the author of *War by Candlelight*, a book of short stories.

Elif Batuman is a Senior Writer at *n+1*.

Grégoire Bouillier's *The Mystery Guest* will be published by Farrar, Straus and Giroux this fall.

Stephen Burt is a professor of English at Macalester College and author most recently of *Parallel Play*, a book of poems, and *Randall Jarrell and His Age*.

Philip Connors is a fire lookout in New Mexico.

Caleb Crain, a critic and scholar, is author of *American Sympathy: Men, Friendship, and Literature in the New Nation* and is at work on a history of the divorce of Edwin and Catharine Forrest.

J. D. Daniels's essay on wifebeaters and trucker hats appeared in *n+1* Number Three.

Echo Eggbrecht is an artist living in New York. She is represented by Nicole Klagsbrun Gallery.

Andrew Ellner is a medical resident in Boston.

Rodrigo Fresán is the author of *Kensington Gardens*, forthcoming in English translation in June.

Vivian Gornick is a critic and memoirist, author most recently of *The Solitude of Self: Thinking About Elizabeth Cady Stanton*.

John Haskell is the author of *I Am Not Jackson Pollock*, a collection of short stories, and *American Purgatorio*, a novel.

Misha Hoekstra is a writer living in Denmark.

Gerald Howard is an editor at Doubleday.

Ilya Kliger is a writer living in New Haven.

Mark Sackmann is an elementary school music teacher and an artist in New York.

Rebecca Schiff is a writer living in New York.

Pauline Shapiro is a photographer living in New York.

Lorin Stein is an editor at Farrar, Straus and Giroux.

Meline Toumani has written about Armenia, Turkey, and classical music for the *Nation* and the *New York Times*.

Johannes Türk teaches at the Freie Universität Berlin.

n+1 *would also like to thank our production team: Jon Baskin, Joshua Brau, Alex Carnevale, Anne Diebel, Alexandra Heifetz, Gregory Jackson, and Nikil Saval.*

YOSHIO ITAGAKI, *NATIVE AMERICAN RESERVATION ON THE MOON #1*, 2001,
C-PRINT ON FUJI-FLEX, 30 X 40". COURTESY OF JACK THE PELICAN PRESENTS, NEW YORK.

LETTERS

IN MEMORIAM: PATRICK GILES, 1957–2005

Dear Editors,

I read Keith Gessen's lovely remembrance of our friend Patrick Giles [www.nplusonemag.com/giles.html]. I was late in getting the news since Patrick and I had a falling out a few years back and I assumed we would have more time to put things right. You mention at the end of the article "I wonder what he wrote for *Homo Xtra*?" A question which is only too funny to answer.

He and I often shared bylines on the "Summer Reading List" and short book reviews. I remember him double-talking "Joe," the then editor of *HX*, into believing that Tina-tweaking gay party boys would LOVE to know more about the hardcover box set of Robert Musil's *The Man Without Qualities*, Susan Sontag's *The Volcano Lover*, and whatever opera compendium came out that spring. We would then rip apart a few gay genre novels and hand it in with a straight face. This is the stuff we got away with when Patrick did the talking. The odd part was, since we both worked at A Different Light bookstore in Chelsea, we would actually see customers coming in to buy Sontag or Musil while clutching our article. Patrick knew what he was talking about. His knowledge was infectious. I'm glad he passed it on to me. I will miss him so much.

—*Otto Coca*

SMALL THINGS OF US FORGOT

Dear Editors,

I read with great interest your new magazine *n+1*. It is perfectly crafted to the times. Many of the best pieces in the magazine appear to be watched over by the angel of Walter Benjamin, of whom Hannah Arendt once said (and I am paraphrasing here since I don't have a copy of *Illuminations* to hand): For Benjamin the value and importance of a thing was in inverse relation to its size.

Where the magazine occasionally falters is in its earnest desire to take in the whole big sweep at once. Perhaps the most egregious example of this is "Death Is Not The End" ["The Intellectual Situation," Issue Two]. A certain wistfulness hovers over that essay, especially when the writer laments the literal death of so many giants of theory. It is a wistfulness, I fear, that has very nearly paralyzed the writer's critical capacity.

For what were two of the major themes of theory (especially French theory) during this period if not the death of the author and a thoroughgoing suspicion of the "universal intellectual"? Nowhere is the writer's longing for the lost great theorists of the past more apparent than in his sad résumé of what remains post-Derrida. After reminding us that Althusser is no longer alive, the writer follows with a brief catalog of those who remain—Žižek, Badiou, Ferry, Virillio, Agamben, Negri, Vattimo, Sloterdijk, Luhmann, Kittler—only to conclude that compared with giants like Foucault and Derrida they "seem somehow, well, small by comparison." First there is the undisguised nostalgia for the very thing (i.e., the great man of theory) that at least one of these figures sharply opposed. Second, there is a rather facile dismissal—no doubt due to a lack of real acquaintance—of a very diverse body of interesting work. To regard Niklas Luhmann's work on social systems and systems theory as "small" betrays a rather profound ignorance of both the ambitiousness of Luhmann's project and the extent of his influence. He was influential enough for Habermas to devote a whole section of *The Philosophical Discourse of Modernity* to a critique of systems theory. Finally, as Luhmann died in 1998, he really ought to be accounted among those who have moved beyond the pale rather than as someone who remains in the wake of Derrida's absence.

—Eric Johnson-DeBaufre

THE PERILS OF "DATING"

Dear Editors,

The dating piece ["The Intellectual Situation," Issue Three] is certainly a hit. Though I would like to call it timely, I think it is way overdue—such an attack on the absurd culture of American dating should have happened some years ago.

I lived in the United States for a good part of my life (18 to 25), and during that time had three boyfriends (two of whom I was with for more than a year), but I never went on a date. (One time, when I was 18, I had a potential date for Valentine's, but I refused it.) So it comes as a bit of a surprise to me that the culture at large is reacting to a prevalent phenomenon to which I am almost a complete stranger. Of course I knew that dating existed, and had even heard of distant relations who went on dates (and more recently I have been privy to old episodes of *Sex and the City* dubbed into German). But the concept always remained vague and a bit old-fashioned.

But what would an American alternative to dating look like? The answer to this question can be found, I believe, in the American understanding of the place (and significance) of marriage in romantic relations. For Americans, the end-goal of dating is the almighty ring. American-style dating is, indeed, nothing other than the outcome of a uniquely American concoction: rebellion (sexual freedom) and tradition (marriage). Americans cannot seem to let go of one or the other, and as such, dating seems to be the failed means by which these two contradictory stances have been combined. Dating allows sexual freedom, even anonymity, but always has the goal of marriage somewhere in mind. Its ground rules (independence, freedom, et cetera) undermine its end (marriage, tradition, et cetera) and vice versa. The alternative to dating will have to take into account these two American vows to rebellion and tradition.

—Dalia Nassar
Tübingen, Germany

Dear Editors,

We (in Europe!) don't have this kind of formal distinction between dating someone and having a boyfriend. You just meet people, usually because you have friends in common, and then see what happens. And as soon as you get along well with somebody (with whom you sleep), you can say he is your boyfriend, even if you're not sure you'll marry him... you don't need a conversation to decide if you're "allowed" to date different people at the same time. If you sleep with the same person, let's say, twice a week, well, it's considered unfair to sleep with two other people in the same week. Except if you sleep with them all at the same time, but then it has nothing to do with dating, does it?

Just in case you go to Europe.

—*Jeanne Aptekman*
Paris, France

Dear Editors,

You forgot to add Mary McCarthy to your list of writers and their sexual sums. The following is from her *Intellectual Memoirs*:

> I realised one day that in twenty-four hours I had slept with three different men. And one morning I was in bed with somebody while over his head I talked on the telephone with somebody else. . . . I did not feel promiscuous. Maybe no-one does. And maybe more girls sleep with more men than you would ever think to look at them.

She is said to have slept with more than 100 men. But, and maybe this is the real difference between our sex-filled age and hers, she gave up counting.

—*Miriam Bale*

PHALLOGOCENTRISM?

Dear Editors,

I've been pleased to see more pieces by women in your second and third issues than in the first one: we shouldn't have to count, but of course we do count (and that "we," unlike the editorial "we" of "The Intellectual Situation," is certainly female). But I was nonetheless disheartened by the experience—or rather, by my specifically female experience, though it's not a phrase I usually invoke—of reading the third issue. Despite excellent essays by and about women (Emily Votruba's piece on women's boxing comes to mind) as well as by men on topics that are obviously of interest to both sexes (the inspired pairing, for instance, of Walter Benn Michaels on the scholarship novel with J. D. Daniels on wifebeaters and trucker hats), something about the issue still struck me as deeply inhospitable, inhospitable to me personally: it wouldn't be too strong to say that I felt actively unwelcome on the basis of something awfully like sexual difference.

This feeling coalesced around "Dating," which certainly seemed to me the most infuriating piece in the last issue. Take a look back at it and think about how you'd feel if you were reading *n+1* and you weren't male, or you didn't have an Ivy League degree, or you weren't white and well-off or "broke" in the way of the privately schooled bohemian, or if you were a man who didn't sleep with women or perhaps just a woman dismayed to realize that the Brooklyn hipster-intellectuals who made up her obvious sex-partner demographic had taken to amortizing the time they spent with her ("Two hours at $40 an hour when we could have been doing our freelance copyediting. Then dinner, another $100. Drinks, $30. The cab ride over the bridge to our little room, $15. Coffee the next morning, $8. That's $233 and on a Tuesday. For Saturday dates add the price of brunch and $3 for the Sunday *Times*"). I enjoy the energy and intellectual ambition of *n+1*, but the "we" of "The Intellectual Situation" needs to start talking a different game before *n+1* can make a persuasive claim to be the voice of what Intellectual Situation Man calls "our generation."

At the time, I wrote in my blog that the magazine had alienated me with what I can still only call "the feeling of guy-ness," and I went on to rant about not wanting to read "high-falutin philosophizing about pop music and reality TV; it seems to me that the ideal of crashing together the academic and the journalistic should take you altogether the other way, with a more accessible and down-to-earth prose style but a high level of intellectual acuity about important things." This is another way of phrasing something I say periodically to some of my brightest students at Columbia; I ask them to take an essay or chapter they have written, undoubtedly brilliant but brilliant in a way that calls attention to its own cerebral force rather than actually bothering to invite the reader in (so to speak), and to revise it with the goal of turning it into something that can be read and enjoyed by a conjectural figure I call "someone's well-educated mother," a reader—a female reader—who might be a lawyer or a high school principal or a financial journalist, who would look at the first page of the piece as it currently stands and say to herself, "This is smart but it is not for me." And who will therefore put it aside, though it may be full of insights and observations that would have enriched her had she only been made to feel welcome.

Now, I'm not saying you shouldn't ever write grand expansive sentences full of latinate abstractions like the parenthetical aside on the sublime in Mark Greif's essay on Radiohead: "(By compassing the unencompassable power in inner representation, it was even suggested, you could be reminded of the interior power of the moral faculty, the human source of a comparable strength.)" Sometimes you have to use words like "de-enunciation" or "counterslogan" to say what you mean, or adopt a certain elevated diction that harks back to the sublime pronouncements of Adorno and company. Maybe the most brilliant among us will do those things a lot. But how smart can you be if you want to write something about which someone's (perhaps even your own) well-educated mother is going to say, "It's brilliant—I didn't read it, I was sure

I wouldn't understand a word of it"? It's a deeply inhospitable writing gesture, one made too often by people whose humanity and hospitality seem to desert them when they sit down to put words on paper.

Maybe the thing here is less about talking and more about listening; the strain that disturbs me—OK, that pisses me off—in *n+1* is akin to what Keats objected to in Wordsworth, "the wordsworthian or egotistical sublime." Keats laid out in contrast the "poetical Character" in which he chose membership: "it is not itself—it has no self—it is every thing and nothing.... A Poet is the most unpoetical of any thing in existence; because he has no Identity—he is continually in for—and filling some other Body." You guys could use less of the egotistical sublime and more of "the camelion Poet"—it would make things more fun for everyone concerned, readers and writers alike.

—Jenny Davidson

POP PHILOSOPHY

Dear Editors,

I think it's super that Mark Greif digs late '90s alterna rock. I like Radiohead, too. A thought experiment: use your word processor's search-and-replace function to replace the search string "Radiohead" with "Pink Floyd," and see whether the essay changes at all.

No one would, of course, take "The Philosophy of Pop: Pink Floyd" seriously. And yet, it's probably true that some part of the *n+1* readership won't laugh at the idea of "Radiohead, or the Philosophy of Pop." We should be asking ourselves why, and not be surprised if the answer is something other than the one offered in the piece. Greif acknowledges up front that it's a foolish enterprise. He then proceeds to write beautifully about Radiohead. Radiohead sounds like the way I feel, he tells us. Isn't that what rock bands do? But he's taken something at face value that he shouldn't.

Rock 'n' roll began as the music of malevolent hicks like Jerry Lee Lewis and screaming black fairies like Little Richard and truck-driving mama's boys like Elvis Presley. It quickly became, in the 1960s, the music of middle-class baby boomers. They turned rock 'n' roll into the basis of a new kind of cultural hegemony. Acts of conformity began to present themselves as nonconformity. Greif doesn't claim that Radiohead gets out of that system. But then he doesn't acknowledge that that's how the system is working here now too. It's a curious omission. Greif rightly observes that when the children of the middle class started to tattoo the gap between the bottoms of their cropped T-shirts and the tops of their low-slung jeans, they were conforming to rather than rebelling against something. Yet he sees listening to his favorite rock band differently—which shows that, just like the rest of us, even very stringent thinkers can be sentimental about their favorite things.

Greif tells us that one of the things Radiohead does is remind us that we ought to resist those voices that tell us to seek happiness by turning to doctors and corporations and purchases to find fulfillment. But he also tells us that this is inevitably futile—"one person's shaken fist." He's right about this, but this should give him a clue about what Radiohead and bands like them really do in the culture of broadcast. Affecting to hold at bay the anxieties and blandishments of middle-class life has now become a reliable way for a certain kind of person already poised to benefit from middle-class life to bid up his own price. The idea of a more serious, less easily indulged revolt strikes all

The Kitchen Club
open 7 days a week
for lunch and dinner
30 Prince Street 212-274-0025

of us as hopelessly misconceived, crazy, impossible.

The perception reinforces the fact. If we're going to be, as Greif puts it, "fool enough to attempt" something, we should do more than write an essay reminding us that a shaken fist is the best we can do. What could be more readily permitted by the powers that be? A certain kind of person is intent on living a lush life but wants credit for being a conscientious person. Such people are fascinated by this commonplace ambivalence, which they think is their own personal cross. A whole class did it through the 1990s—that's Clintonism, those are the boomers. They enriched themselves at the expense of others while basking in a fantasy of their own virtue and uselessness that let them dissemble away their will to power. They're still at it, even in these dark times. If we are to survive, the politics of the new age will begin by rejecting this kind of pseudo-politics.

—*Wesley Yang*

Dear Editors,

I was very impressed with the critical insights in "Radiohead, or the Philosophy of Pop," and the lucidity of their presentation. But I disagree.

I consider Radiohead a marginal, not a representative, case. Mark Greif takes his fundamental question to be whether a pop act can represent some aspect of exterior history. (He says "represent," but also means "influence" as the essay goes on.) Radiohead is selected as the "case study" precisely because Radiohead was best able to "pose the question: How should it really ever be possible for pop music to incarnate a particular historical situation?" He's selected the band most likely to answer his own question; but then, logically, every other band, and there are a lot of them that go into the whole of pop, is less likely than Radiohead to represent some aspect of exterior history (even if some subset of them can and do).

"Pop"—and here I really mean "rock"—is rooted in a set of ideas labeled "counterculture": an aura of personal freedom, youth, sexual license. Its birth coincides with the odd demographic moment when the first baby boomer became a teen. Any analysis must determine whether rock started out as "counterculture" for its own internal reasons or was transformed into counterculture by the dominant culture. It has, for sure, maintained its (cynical?) denial of itself as part of the mainstream. (As late as 1995, the best-selling music was "alternative"!)

Someone cooler than you inevitably tells you about new music. This person knows because he is, in a sense, less of-the-culture than you. With each new discovery, which you then pass on, you too become less of-the-culture. You, the fan, enact this constant dialectic of not-being-in-the-culture/being-in-the-know. (All this ends at some ever later "adult moment" when you keep listening to whatever you liked between 18 and 21, or trade it all for Schubert.) Rock's standing as counterculture (as freedom) is vital to its reception and pleasures. But pop music is mercilessly and permanently wedded to the idea of cool, which requires the idea of the uncool mainstream to maintain its distinctiveness. If there were no squares, they would have to be invented. And so pop cannot seed true revolution.

Anyone who tries to take culture seriously must face the fundamental question of whether the rebellious elements of culture are genuine (as Mark Greif defines it, likely to produce revolution) or mere illusions into which people can pour their anger and dislocation. For any artifact of our culture, it's now possible to argue both sides persuasively—that it is a seedbed of revolt or steam-valve for social control. There is no possible means to prove it either way, save perhaps some tally of results.

Let's pause to tally those results. Since the coming of rock counterculture (say 1960), there has been no successful political revolution in the West save a conservative "Reagan" version. Was that the one? Rock has coincided with a revolution in sexual mores, drug use, and personal mobility, the dismantling of many restrictions on economic life and consequent fraying of the social functions of the state. I suggest it has done some work, but its work is ambiguous. While we—I mean here you and I—probably consider the personal freedom to use and abuse ourselves a "good," we are probably dismayed at the "anything goes" political and social life which opens the field to predatory action by anyone with a modicum of power. The violence in rock may have fit very well with the emerging symbolic and actual violence of American life.

The achievement of Radiohead may be the discrediting of rock's possibilities as rebellion, as validation of feelings in a mass arena. I don't think, as art, Radiohead's songs have the closed space the essay ascribes to them; we wish to grant them special knowledge (which they could tell us if they stopped singing and were just plain) because they display the absence of those levels of privacy we understand, regret, and cling to in ourselves. They are, we sense, where we are headed, when the last fortress falls.

—Joshua Poertner

FRAMED?

Dear Editors,

As James Wood knows perfectly well—but seems at pains to pretend not to know—I have nowhere in any of my essays espoused a "thin aestheticism" of the sentence. His original claim was based on a brief parenthetical passage, near the middle of a 14,000-word essay, in which I described my gratitude at finding refuge in a Janet Frame novel after being subjected to a couple of hours of airplane television. Here are the sentences of Frame that I quoted:

> Poor Noeline, who was waiting for Dr. Howell to propose to her although the only words he had ever spoken to her were How are you? Do you know where you are? Do you know why you are here?—phrases which ordinarily would be hard to interpret as evidence of affection. But when you are sick you find yourself in a new field of perception where you make a harvest of interpretations which then provides you

> with your daily bread, your only food. So that when Dr. Howell finally married the occupational therapist, Noeline was taken to the disturbed ward.

The beauty of these sentences is unmistakably a beauty of humaneness, sympathy, and fully realized tone. This is the kind of beauty that Wood champions in his own criticism. But how curiously difficult it is for him to see this beauty championed by anybody else! And, though he does charitably "doubt" that "Franzen himself" subscribes to a thin aestheticism, what an odd sort of charity this is! Given that he invented the notion to begin with!

I want to admire Wood. But if he won't tell the truth here—if he insists on repeating a misrepresentation that is unique to him and is plainly contradicted by everything I've ever written—why should I trust him anywhere else?

—Jonathan Franzen

James Wood replies:

Jonathan Franzen wants to admire me, and I want to admire him, so perhaps, like two amorous crabs, we can haltingly make a path to each other.

He is right, of course, that no "thin aestheticism" hovers around Janet Frame's strong sentences, and he and I would doubtless agree on the kind of prose that might constitute such aestheticism (say, Updike during a bad decade or so). But within the context of his entire *Harper's* essay, I think that his plucking of three sentences of Frame, and his mournful rhetorical question—"To write sentences of such authority that refuge can be taken in them: Isn't this enough? Isn't it a lot?"—does sound, to my ears, both a bit too thin and a bit too aestheticizing.

The problem is that in his *Harper's* essay, Franzen, as readers will recall, combines a serious discussion of the fate of the novel with a discussion of his own depression and isolation. The essay offers a very American arc, whereby young Franzen battles with himself and with the culture, and finally cures his sense of isolation—by talking to a professor who has been doing research into readers and audiences and social isolation, and by "doing some journalism and even hitting a few parties." The cured Franzen emerges from his depression ready to renew the American novel, and to resume work on his third book: he has found a way to take refuge in sentences of authenticity. Look, I have come through!

But does the refuge he can now take in such sentences have to do with the power of the sentences, or with the fact that Franzen just now feels better about himself? Franzen undermines his optimism in two other moments in the essay. Ten pages before his quoting of Janet Frame, Franzen had delivered himself of these convictions: "I can't stomach any kind of notion that serious fiction is good for us, because I don't believe that everything that's wrong with the world has a cure, and even if I did, what business would I, who feel like the sick one, have in offering it?" This, perhaps, is Franzen's characterization of himself as a former depressive. But the present tense gives one pause, as does the next assertion: "I resist, finally, the notion of literature as a noble higher calling, because elitism doesn't sit well with my American nature, and because even if my belief in mystery didn't incline me to distrust feelings of superiority, my belief in manners would make it difficult for me to explain to my brother, who is a fan of Michael Crichton, that the work I'm doing is simply better than Crichton's."

Now, a criticism that simply refuses to account for the ethical power of literature (except by recourse to the findings of an academic audience researcher), and can't or won't argue for the aesthetic superiority of one text over another; yet which, at the same time, simply makes a religious leap into the "refuge" of authentic sentences (again, without any explanation)—what can this be, really, but a "thin aestheticism"? And even if Franzen insists that this is how he used to feel, not how he currently feels, the difficulty remains that the terms of his personal recovery from his "bubble of despair" remain so vague ("hitting a few parties"), that their entanglement with the "refuge" of authentic sentences only softens the absoluteness of that refuge.

I wrote that Franzen seems not himself to believe in the conclusions of his *Harper's* essay partly because it is very hard to determine from that essay what indeed he believes in, but also—on a much more positive note—because *The Corrections* is neither thin nor an example of aestheticism. At its frequent best, as I wrote in the original review which spurred this discussion, his novel is "clear, direct, humane, and sensitively intelligent." On this, he and I, mutual almost-admirers, surely agree.

THE WILD WORLD OF THE WEB

Dear Sir or Madam,

Just to say how sad it is that your web link on Google has to contain the f-word.

> This is the fucking tambourine player. We share the absurd humor of his better moments: when he signs the TVT record contract for the Jonestown he announces . . .
> www.nplusonemag.com/dig.html

The reference that I searched was "tambourine playing," which could as easily have been put in by my wife or a child. Despite society today being as it is, some of us still do find such words quite offensive.

—[--]
United Kingdom

Marco Roth replies:

Dear [--],

We're very sorry you were offended by the appearance of the f-word in that particular piece. You may not be aware that we have absolutely no control over what Google links to, nor can we suggest links to them. Once an article is on the web, Google searches its contents and shows you a link to it even if it has nothing to do with your original search. So we're as surprised as you are that we turned up under the heading of "tambourine playing." Short of imposing a rigorous standard of censorship on web publishing or inventing a better search engine, there's no way you or your family can be protected from an encounter with the obscene or the offensive while using the web. For all I know, "tambourine playing" might be a code word for some strange sexual practice. There's no telling what people will think up when they're denied the ordinary obscenities. Still, I'd like to think that if you or your wife and child read *n+1*, you'll find that it contains a whole range of language and thought on a fair array of topics from global politics to wrestling and film. You may not always be safe from rough language when reading it, or when walking down the street, but we like to think we know when it's called for. +